Comments from people who have read the book:

**Surpriseingly amazing book.**
This is a surpriseingly interesting book. Highly recommended.

**The best insight into the holy Granth!**
It tells us about the deeper meaning of many of the verses. **A must read**.
Dr. Raminder Bir Singh, Ophthalmologist
Birmingham, United Kingdom

The message in the book is timeless. Addresses the human predicament and error in perception of "Reality". **A must read for even the busy reader**.
Dr. Harjinder Singh, DVM
Cincinnati, Ohio USA

**I enjoyed reading this great work.** Very interesting concept of understanding who I am. **Gurbani quotes and their English translation are superb.**

Dr. Amarjit Singh, Surgery Specialist
Buffalo, New York USA

D1737938

# INSIGHTS FROM THE SIKH SCRIPTURE SRI GURU GRANTH SAHIB

Pritam Singh Bathla

ISBN: 9798804072088
ASIN: BOB28KR3R9

For questions and comments contact
"InsightsfromGurbani@gmail.com"

Printed in the United States of America

For

My Parents

Who brought me up in a spiritual atmosphere in the home. Being the youngest in the family, I probably got more attention than my siblings. When I was about eleven, I remember, my dad would take me to his farm to give him company. While working in the farm, he would relate to me short stories from the lives of the Gurus. He encouraged me to write books on their message, when I grew up. He would even name some of the book titles which I forget now, but they all had to with Love of the Truth.

I am thankful to Dr. Gurkiran Kaur Singh and Simarjeet Singh, for helping me with the computer work such as using Punjabi fonts, editing and formating the manuscript, and uploading it for publication.

I am also thankful to Suneet Kaur Singh and Sayva Kaur Bathla, for proof reading an initial copy of the book, and making valuable suggestions in streamlining the English grammar.

# CONTENTS

# INTRODUCTION

If someone said:

-that there is only One Reality, that has become all,
-that we are not body minds, that we think we are,
-that we do not have a free will of our own,
-that the world we live in, is a grand illusion,
-that everything in our life, is happening inside US,
-that almost all of us are going through life, fast asleep,

It may sound a little strange but these statements are not untrue. Additionally, if we are told that we ourselves are responsible for our life's circumstances, no matter how dire they may be, we may not believe it, but that is true too. In fact, all our circumstances are created by none other than our own Self. The Sikh Scripture Sri Guru Granth Sahib gives us insights into these kinds of mysteries, and does so repeatedly in very plain language, if only we would ever pay attention. Gurbani (Hymns from the Sikh Scripture) is a storehouse of such knowledge. In fact, Guru Ji says that precious jewels, gems and diamonds lay burried in It, implying that the knowledge contained in Gurbani is invaluable and beyond compare. We are asked to do a deep search in Gurbani's message and find these precious jewels and diamonds. At times, Gurbani scolds us that we have gotten this human birth after going through 8.4 million incarnations, but we are letting it go to waste.

This book takes a look into the statements made above and brings out the insights from the Sikh Scripture. It also gives glimpses of understanding into some other topics of spiritual interest and our daily life experience. It brings out invaluable wisdom on everyday topics like who we are, what our Real

Home is, do we have free will, what is this world all about, etc. Also there are discussions on meditation, self realization, and the science behind doing the practice of Nitnem (daily recital and listening of specified Hymns). There are quotations from Gurbani along with open minded discussion on these topics. This book is especially suited for the younger generation who may not be familiar with the Gurmukhi script, in which Sri Guru Granth Sahib is transcribed. The youth, not being familiar with Gurmukhi, may not be able to fully explore the treasures embedded in Sri Guru Granth Sahib. Of course, I will like to state here that this effort merely scratches the surface as far as understanding of Gurbani is concerned, and no effort, however large, can reveal the deeper depths of Gurbani.

One thing else the author wants to mention here is that there may be some repetition in discussions from one topic to the other. The repetition is more noticeable where an effort has been made to focus on our false identification with the body and mind. Our identification with body and the mind is the root cause of all our major problems in life. It generates ego in us which leads to hate, arrogance and many other problems. Ego is responsible for our separation from our Real Self or God. So the repeated focus on our belief in false identity is somewhat intentional. If this repetition can drive home this one point into the reader's mind that we are not body and mind but we are something beyond, the purpose of this book will be well served. This something beyond that we are is the One Reality, named Ek Onkar in Sri Guru Granth Sahib. Moreover, an effort has been made here that each topic of discussion is a "stand alone" reading and does not depend upon reading the other essays in the book. One other reason of repetition is that, in the final analysis, all these topics end up talking about the One Reality (ੴ), which is the cause of everything in the universe. This One Reality is not only the cause of everything, but It is the only Entity that exists and has become everything that is experienced. So all discussions concerning human spiritual life lead to the One Reality.

The author has been blessed to have interest in these issues right from the young age. Born in Punjab, India, the author moved to the United States of America in the mid sixties to persue higher education, and then proceeded to work in corporate America for over 35 years, after attending an American Engineering University. In the late sixties, the author had the gracious company of Dr. Raghbir Singh Sandhu of Xenia Ohio, a lovingly spiritual and a blessed soul, which left a spiritually rich and positive influence on the author.

The author hopes that the reader will benefit from the reading of this book. it will help him align his daily living in accordance with the insights offered in this book. Incorporating this new understanding in one's daily life will enhance peace and happiness in every sphere of his or her life.

For those who are not familiar with the Sikh Scripture, Sri Guru Granth Sahib, it is the Holy Book of the Sikh religion, which is the fifth largest religion in the world. The Sikh Scripture, composed in early 1600, is the newest religious Scriputre, and is probably, the only holy book, which begins with its first hymn that defines the One Reality. It is defined as, "There is only One Reality pervading endlessly, Real (not a concept), the Creator, Fearless, without enmity, never dies, never born and is Self Luminous." After defining the One Reality in the first hymn, the Scripture then goes on to expound on It with over five thousand devoional hymns, on 1430 pages. The poetic hymns were composed by the six Sikh Masters called Gurus, and fifteen non-Sikh Indian Saints, including Hindus and Muslims.

The Sikh Scripture offers various approaches to unite with One Reality, the Lord. Remeberance of the Lord with love and devotion, is given the top preference. Other approaches presented are, doing the right karma, serving the humanity regardless of religion, caste or creed, and following the path of knowldge (Gyan) for understanding the Truth. **In this book, greater emphasis is given to exploring the path of knowledge for the Truth,** even though other approaches have been discussed, wherever appropriate. The Sikh Scripture talks about the importance of exploring the path of knowledge to understand the Truth. It says that when the jewel of spiritual knowledge fires up in oneself, the heart is enlightened and the ignorance is eradicated.

ਗਿਆਨ ਰਤਨੁ ਬਲਿਆ ਘਟਿ ਚਾਨਣੁ ਅਗਿਆਨੁ ਅੰਧੇਰਾ ਜਾਇ ॥ (Ang 368)

(*When the jewel of Divine Wisdom lights up, the heart is illumined, and ignorance is dispelled.*)

# THERE IS ONLY ONE REALITY

ੴ ਸਤਿਨਾਮੁ ਕਰਤਾ ਪੁਰਖੁ ਨਿਰਭਉ ਨਿਰਵੈਰੁ
ਅਕਾਲ ਮੂਰਤਿ ਅਜੂਨੀ ਸੈਭੰ ਗੁਰਪ੍ਰਸਾਦਿ॥ *(Ang 1)*

*(There is only One Reality, Endlessly
pervading, True, Creator, Without
Fear, Without Enmity, Beyond Death,
Beyond Birth, Self Luminous)*

This hymn is the beginning of the Sikh Holy Scripture Sri Guru Granth Sahib (SGGS) and describes the One Reality (ੴ) that is pervading the universe. This is called Mool Mantar and is sung with utmost devotion by the sikhs around the world. Guru Ji names this One Reality as "ੴ" and then lists some of the attributes of this Reality in the words that follow. Although it is impossible to describe the Reality in words, Guru Ji is giving us a few pointers for our understanding. Guru ji describes some other characteristics of this Reality through Shabads (Hymns) recorded in the Sri Guru Granth Sahib. There are many shabads in Sri Guru Granth Sahib stating that the One Reality (ੴ) is unknowable (ਅਲਖ), infinite (ਅਪਾਰ), unapproachable (ਅਗੰਮ) and imperceptible (ਅਗੋਚਰ). This Reality is unknowable but It knows everything. It is infinite but It exists in everybody and everything. It is unapproachable but is closer than close. It is imperceptible but It perceives everything. It is made of no things but everything is made out of it. It is made of no things means there are no objective qualities of One Reality like those of the things. That is why the Reality is imperceptible.

This One Reality has three parts to it, Ek Ong Kar (ੴ). Ek means One, Ong is a Sanskrit word and it means Braham or God; and Kar means pervading endlessly. So Ek Onkar (ੴ) means there is only One Reality that pervades endlessly everywhere throughout the cosmos and beyond. This One Reality is further named by many many names in Sri Guru Granth Sahib. Some of the religious names stated for this reality are Guru, Satguru, Raam, Hari, Gopal, Gobind and Atman etc. There are many more names mentioned in Sri Guru Granth Sahib. Additionally, Guru Gobind Singh Ji has described this One Reality by many more names in Jaap Sahib, one of the five Nitnem Banis. The entire Bani of Jaap Sahib consists of names for this Reality, full of love and devotion. Guru ji says in the first hymn of Jaap Sahib, "O lord, who can describe all your names. Only the names based on your actions are mentioned here with utmost respect".

ਤ੍ਰ ਸਰਬ ਨਾਮ ਕਥੈ ਕਵਨ ਕਰਮ ਨਾਮ ਬਰਨਤ ਸੁਮਤਿ ॥ (Jaap Sahib)
(*Who can say all Thy Names? I mention Thy Action-Names only, with great respect*)

Guru ji then recites Jaap Sahib with estimated one thousand names based on the activities of One Reality. It is such a devotional and loving Bani. It recites name after name in every line and bestows praises on that One Reality. If one could recite Jaap Sahib with heartfelt loving feeling, it is bound to bring peace and tranquility to his or her mind. The most common religious name for this One Reality is God, which is used all over the world. Then, there are philosophical names like Infinite Being, Knowing Presence, Consciousness or Awareness etc. Here we will address this Reality as Atman and Awareness most of the time. Other appropriate names will also be used in context with the topic of discussion. All these religious and philosophical names are used synonymously in this book.

We normally state that there is only One God implying God has no competition. That is very much true, but there is more to this statement than just that. The statement really means that nothing else exists other than God. This statement has a great significance, so it needs to be repeated. When we make the statement that there is One God or One Reality, we generally imply that God, us and the rest of the creation exist simultaneously. The fact of the matter is that there is only God there. Nothing else exists. God has become everything, you, me and everything else in the universe. That is why Reality is labeled as "One"? This is being done to make us understand that this One Reality is the only reality there. There is nothing else that exists. Gurbani states that this One Reality is pervading the cosmos. This statement is being made in simple words so we can grasp what us being said here. Actually the cosmos does not exist in its own right independent of this Reality. There is no universe separate from Ek Onkar. Everything that we see including our body, minds and all the objects around us are none other than this One Reality. When we were children, we used to look at the clouds in the sky and would play fun games, imagining various figures like a horse or an elephant, out of the clouds. These figures were just that and of course, not real. World and its objects are figures like the cloud figures, the only difference is that these are made out of the One Reality, Ek Onkar or God.

ਏਕੰਕਾਰੁ ਅਵਰੁ ਨਹੀ ਦੂਜਾ ਨਾਨਕ ਏਕ ਸਮਾਈ ॥ (Ang 930)
(*Only one Reality bar none is pervading the cosmos.*)

Why don't we see the Reality? It is because of the play of Maya. Maya is a sort of a veil that covers up Reality. Maya is a very complicated phenomenon and is almost beyond explanation. We won't discuss Maya here but will just quote a Gurbani shabad that defines Maya. Maya is something that creates an illusion in the mind. This illusion then makes us forget the One Reality, which causes attachment with the other.

ਏਹ ਮਾਇਆ ਜਿਤੁ ਹਰਿ ਵਿਸਰੈ ਮੋਹੁ ਉਪਜੈ ਭਾਉ ਦੂਜਾ ਲਾਇਆ ॥  (Ang 921)
(*This is Maya, by which one forgets the Lord,
And attachment wells up; and love for the other develops.*)

So the number "One" with Onkar implies that there is only
One Reality that has real existence. Anything else, living, non-
living and the cosmos, have no existence of their own. Why
do we see people, animals, birds and all kinds of objects? It
is because of the illusion caused by maya. There is no other
existence whatsoever, other than the One Reality, Ek Onkar or
God. As someone said, the world is an illusion, only God exists,
and God has become the world.

ਓਅੰਕਾਰਿ ਏਕੋ ਰਵਿ ਰਹਿਆ ਸਭੁ ਏਕਸ ਮਾਹਿ ਸਮਾਵੈਗੋ ॥
ਏਕੋ ਰੂਪ ਏਕੋ ਬਹੁ ਰੰਗੀ ਸਭੁ ਏਕਤੁ ਬਚਨਿ ਚਲਾਵੈਗੋ ॥   (Ang 1310)
(*One and only One Reality is All-pervading everywhere. All shall
merge into the One. His one Form has one and many colors; He leads
all according to His Command*)

ਪ੍ਰਿਥਮ ਕਾਲ ਜਬ ਕਰਾ ਪਸਾਰਾ ॥ ਓਅੰਕਾਰ ਤੇ ਸ੍ਰਿਸਟਿ ਉਪਾਰਾ ॥  (Ang 114)
(*In the beginning, when the world was created, it was brought into
being by One Reality, Ek Onkar*)

There are many shabads in Sri Guru Granth Sahib which
describe the essence of the universe we live in. At times it is
described similar to a dream at night. We all know that there is
no reality in the dream. Gurbani says this world is like a dream
and has no reality of its own. There is nothing in it that is
real, other than God Itself. Gurbani says that this world is God's
image, so we should see it that way only. It further states that
everything is made out of the One Light. The One light referred
to is the Light of One Reality, the Ek Onkar.

ਜਿਉ ਸੁਪਨਾ ਅਰੁ ਪੇਖਨਾ ਐਸੇ ਜਗ ਕਉ ਜਾਨਿ ॥
ਇਨ ਮੈ ਕਛੁ ਸਾਚੋ ਨਹੀ ਨਾਨਕ ਬਿਨੁ ਭਗਵਾਨ ॥   (Ang 1427)
(*As we see a dream at night, know that, so is this world. None of this
is true except God, O Nanak*)

9

ਇਹੁ ਵਿਸੁ ਸੰਸਾਰੁ ਤੁਮ ਦੇਖਦੇ ਇਹ ਹਰਿ ਕਾ ਰੂਪੁ ਹੈ ਹਰਿ ਰੂਪ ਨਦਰੀ ਆਇਆ ॥
(Ang 922)
(*This whole world that you see is the image of the Lord, only the image of the Lord is seen*)

ਏਕੁ ਨੂਰ ਤੇ ਸਭੁ ਜਗੁ ਉਪਜਿਆ ਕਉਨ ਭਲੇ ਕੋ ਮੰਦੇ ॥ (Ang 1349)
(*From one Light, the entire universe welled up. So who is good and who is bad?*)

A heartfelt realization that whatever we are seeing, is in fact the Lord Himself or Herself, can change our lives. Everyone of us longs to see the Lord, but we are unaware that we are seeing the Lord all the time. Only we do not recognize Him. It looks like we are under a kind of hypnosis not to recognize Him or Her, even though we see Him or Her all the time. If we adopt this one understanding that everything around us is God and God alone, wholeheartedly, it can do wonders in our life. Our behavior to everyone in the world will change for the good. Hate will be replaced by love, enmity will change into friendship and there will be no fear of the other, because there is no other. Our attitude to the world will be more like the one depicted by the following shabad:

ਨ ਕੋ ਬੈਰੀ ਨਹੀ ਬਿਗਾਨਾ ਸਗਲ ਸੰਗਿ ਹਮ ਕਉ ਬਨਿ ਆਈ ॥ (Ang 1299)
(*No one is my enemy and no one is a stranger to me, I get along with everyone.*)

Guru Ji further describes the characteristics of this reality in the mool mantar. Mool mantar consists of seven attributes enclosed by ੴ in the beginning and ਗੁਰਪ੍ਰਸਾਦਿ at the end. We have already talked about ੴ, while ਗੁਰਪ੍ਰਸਾਦਿ means that this Reality is attainable only through the grace of the Guru. We will briefly discuss each of the attributes of this One Reality. For the sake of clarity, each attribute is separated by a comma in the Mool Mantar listed here.

ੴ, ਸਤਿਨਾਮੁ, ਕਰਤਾ ਪੁਰਖੁ, ਨਿਰਭਉ, ਨਿਰਵੈਰੁ, ਅਕਾਲ ਮੂਰਤਿ, ਅਜੂਨੀ, ਸੈਭੰ, ਗੁਰ ਪ੍ਰਸਾਦਿ ॥

## Satnam (ਸਤਿਨਾਮ):

The reality is Truth, meaning God is not a concept or an imagination, He or She is Real. There is no doubt about His Being. At times a person faced with problems and adverse circumstances loses faith in God's existence. Guru Ji says that one should not lose faith in God. He has been there right from the beginning, is there now and will be there forever.

ਆਦਿ ਸਚੁ ਜੁਗਾਦਿ ਸਚੁ ॥ ਹੈ ਭੀ ਸਚੁ ਨਾਨਕ ਹੋਸੀ ਭੀ ਸਚੁ ॥  (Ang 1)
(*God is True from the beginning, has been True throughout ages, is True now, O Nanak He will be True for ever and ever.*)

ਸਤਿ ਸਤਿ ਸਦਾ ਸਤਿ ॥  (Ang 1201)
(*God is True, True, forever True*)

## Karta Purakh (ਕਰਤਾ ਪੁਰਖ):
He is the creator of everything. There is nothing there that is not made by Him or more precisely not made out of Him. It is not that God created the creation but He has become the creation. There are three important aspects of God's creation. First, everything is made out of Him, second, everything is made in Him and third, everything is made by Him, just like the waves in the ocean are made out of water, are made in water and are made by water. So the whole creation is made out of Him, made in Him and made by Him.

ਆਪੇ ਕਾਰਣੁ ਕਰਤਾ ਕਰੇ ਸ੍ਰਿਸਟਿ ਦੇਖੈ ਆਪਿ ਉਪਾਇ ॥
ਸਭ ਏਕੋ ਇਕੁ ਵਰਤਦਾ ਅਲਖੁ ਨ ਲਖਿਆ ਜਾਇ ॥  (Ang 37)
(*The Creator Himself created the Creation, He produced the universe and He Himself watches over it. The One and Only One Lord is pervading and permeating all. He is indescribable and cannot be described.*)

ਆਪੀਨੈ ਆਪੁ ਸਾਜਿਓ ਆਪੀਨੈ ਰਚਿਓ ਨਾਉ ॥

ਦੂਜੀ ਕੁਦਰਤਿ ਸਾਜੀਐ ਕਰਿ ਆਸਣੁ ਡਿਠੋ ਚਾਉ ॥ (Ang 463)

(*He Himself created Himself, and He Himself assumed His Name. After creating the other world, He Himself seated within the Creation, and beholds it with delight.*)

**Nirbhau (ਨਿਰਭਉ):**

He has no fear. How can One Reality be afraid when there is no one there other than Him? Guru ji is saying that the nature of this Reality is fearlessness.

ਤੈ ਵਿਚਿ ਸਭੁ ਆਕਾਰ ਹੈ ਨਿਰਭਉ ਹਰਿ ਜੀਉ ਸੋਇ ॥ (Ang 586)

(*The entire universe is in fear, but the Lord is without fear.*)

ਸਗਲਿਆ ਤਉ ਲਿਖਿਆ ਸਿਰਿ ਲੇਖੁ ॥
ਨਾਨਕ ਨਿਰਭਉ ਨਿਰੰਕਾਰ ਸਚੁ ਏਕੁ ॥ (Ang 464)

(*Everyone is subject to fear as written in their fate, but O Nanak, only One True Lord, who is without form, is without fear.*)

Not only He is without fear, the people who remember Him also become fearless.

ਸਿਮਰਿ ਸਿਮਰਿ ਪ੍ਰਭੁ ਨਿਰਭਉ ਹੋਇ ॥ (Ang 184)

(*Meditate, meditate on the Lord, and become fearless*)

**Nirvair (ਨਿਰਵੈਰ):**

One Reality has no enmity with anyone. Again it can be said that if there is no one else out there how can there be enmity. But Guru ji is speaking about the real nature of this One Reality, that it is really full of love and compassion. One Reality is like the space of a room. The space of the room does not care what happens in the room. It accepts anything in the room without any likes and dislikes. Space of the room does not object to anybody walking in, or any furniture in the room or even being without anything in it. It does not care if the people in the room are dancing or fighting with each other. It accepts anything and everything. One Reality is like that space, accepting everything without any resistance at all.

ਹਰਿ ਸਤਿ ਨਿਰੰਜਨ ਅਮਰ ਹੈ ਨਿਰਭਉ ਨਿਰਵੈਰ ਨਿਰੰਕਾਰ ॥ (Ang 302)
(*The Lord is Truth, Pristine, Eternal, without fear, without enmity and without form*)

ਨਿਰਾਹਾਰ ਨਿਰਵੈਰ ਸੁਖਦਾਈ ॥ ਤਾ ਕੀ ਕੀਮਤਿ ਕਿਨੈ ਨ ਪਾਈ ॥ (Ang 287)
(*One Reality is not sustained by food, She has no enmity or vengeance; She is Giver of peace. No one can estimate Her worth.*)

### Akal Murat (ਅਕਾਲ ਮੂਰਤ):

One Reality is beyond death and as such, is eternal. It is timeless. Everything in the universe is subject to death. No one is going to live forever, but the One Reality or God is eternal and is beyond death.

ਸਫਲ ਦਰਸਨੁ ਅਕਾਲ ਮੂਰਤਿ ਪ੍ਰਭੁ ਹੈ ਭਿ ਹੋਵਨਹਾਰਾ ॥ (Ang 609)
(*Blessed Vision of Reality is fruitful, Reality is deathless. It is and always will be*)

ਤੂੰ ਅਕਾਲ ਪੁਰਖੁ ਨਾਹੀ ਸਿਰਿ ਕਾਲਾ ॥ ( Ang 1038)
(*The Reality is deathless Primal Being, death does not hover over its head*)

### Ajuni (ਅਜੂਨੀ):

This Reality does not take birth like all other creatures. It is beyond the cycle of birth and death. In fact One Reality controls the birth and death of all other creatures, but Itself is beyond all that.

ਅਕਾਲ ਮੂਰਤਿ ਅਜੂਨੀ ਸੰਭਉ ਕਲਿ ਅੰਧਕਾਰ ਦੀਪਾਈ ॥ (Ang 916)
(*Reality is Immortal, without birth. She is Self luminous and She brings Light in the dark times.*)

### Sabhang (ਸੰਭੰ)

Sabhang means self-luminous, self existent and self conscious. Just like the sun is self illuminated and does not need any light from outside to light itself, One Reality is self luminous and knows everything by itself. Sometimes It is called "the Knowing", the One who knows everything by itself. Additionally, the One Reality exists by itself and has no primal cause. All the characteristics of the Realty are self manifest.

**Our Relation With The One Reality:**

One may be thinking about how this One Reality relates to me. How does this affect me? Guru ji points out that this Reality is not in the clouds, but it is closer than close to us. It is really not even close to us, it is us. There is no difference between this Reality and us.

The simple statement, "there is One Reality" makes it very clear that this One Reality has become everything. This includes us too. This is a point that we mostly miss. We think we are outside this One Reality. We believe we can view the One Reality from outside, considering ourselves to be separate from It. That is not true because we are not different from this Reality. Just like the eyes cannot see themselves, similarly we can't see the One Reality because we are one with it.

ਤੋਹੀ ਮੋਹੀ ਮੋਹੀ ਤੋਹੀ ਅੰਤਰ ਕੈਸਾ ॥
ਕਨਕ ਕਟਿਕ ਜਲ ਤਰੰਗ ਜੈਸਾ ॥ (Ang 93)
(*O God, what is difference between you and me, it like the difference between gold and bangle, or water and the water wave*)

ਬ੍ਰਹਮ ਮਹਿ ਜਨੁ ਜਨ ਮਹਿ ਪਾਰਬ੍ਰਹਮੁ ॥
ਏਕਹਿ ਆਪਿ ਨਹੀ ਕਛੁ ਭਰਮੁ ॥ (Ang 287)
(*Human is in God, and God is in the human. He alone is, there is no doubt about this*)

From these shabads it is clear that there is no difference between us and the One Reality. Only difference between the One Reality and us is, that Reality is pure Reality, while we are the same One Reality but call ourselves body and mind. The only thing is that we have forgotten our true identity. As pointed out in the first shabad above the difference between the One Reality and us is similar to the difference between gold and a bangle made out of gold. While the gold by itself is called gold, an ornament made out of gold, is given a different name. The jeweler names these ornaments as bracelets, earrings or rings even though they are all made out of gold. Our story is not different from that. When the One Reality localizes itself as the body and mind, it becomes man, woman, animals, birds etc. One Reality takes the form of every creature in the universe. This localized Reality as our body and mind starts calling itself human beings and gives itself different names to differentiate one localization from another. Keep in mind that the One Reality is capable of assuming multiple localizations. There are almost seven billion localizations as human beings right now and there are billions more in other forms of creatures in the universe. These localizations are somewhat similar to our dream at night. Almost every night our mind adopts innumerable localizations of various characters and things in the dream.

In the next line of the same shabad Guru ji says that the difference between the Reality and us is like water and its waves. Even though the waves can be recognized distinct from the main body of water, and from other waves, they still are water and made only of water. We are like those waves in water. Just as waves are made of water only, we are made out of the One Realty (ੴ) even though we have assumed different names and a forms like the waves. We have become objectified and distinct and have become recognizable from one another, just like the waves.

ਸਭੁ ਗੋਬਿੰਦੁ ਹੈ ਸਭੁ ਗੋਬਿੰਦੁ ਹੈ ਗੋਬਿੰਦੁ ਬਿਨੁ ਨਹੀ ਕੋਈ ॥  (Ang 485)
(God is everything, God is everything, there is nothing else without God.)

ਆਪੇ ਪਟੀ ਕਲਮ ਆਪਿ ਉਪਰਿ ਲੇਖੁ ਭਿ ਤੂੰ ॥
ਏਕੋ ਕਹੀਐ ਨਾਨਕਾ ਦੂਜਾ ਕਾਹੇ ਕੂ ॥  (Ang 1291)
(O God, You Yourself are the writing tablet, and You are the writing pen, You are writing on it too.

*Speak of only One Lord, O Nanak, how could there be any other?)*

There is an old Indian story about a king who ruled for a long time. He was sitting on his throne one day and dozed off. In his sleep he had a dream. He dreamt that he got attacked by the neighboring king, and lost the battle. The defeated king was spared his life but he was expelled from his own kingdom and ordered never to return. He was taken to the border and let out on his own without any relative or friend to accompany him. The king started walking trying to find some shelter in the jungle. The king was feeling tired and hungry. Eventually, he got to a village where they were distributing food to the poor and the hungry. He stood in line and got some food to eat. As he sat down to eat the food, a bird scooped down and snatched food from his hand and flew off. The king felt so miserable that it woke him up from his sleep. His heart was pounding but he was thankful to see that he was still the king and everything was fine.

One thing started bothering him though. He started wondering if his kingdom is real, or the dream he just had was real. He asked many wise people in his kingdom if this kingdom was real or his dream was real, but did not get a satisfactory answer. Then a saint came along and gave him a satisfactory answer. The saint said, O king, do you really want to know which is real, this kingdom or your dream. The king replied I will be very thankful to you for knowing that. The saint said, listen king, neither the kingdom you see is real, nor the dream you had was real. Then the king asked, What is real?" The Saint replied, only that is real, who knows both the kingdom and the dream. The Saint said, O king you are the one who knows both the kingdom and the dream. So only you are real, everything else is just a dream. This kingdom that you think is real, is also a dream like the dream you had when you dozed off. Waking state is a dream, and dreaming state is, of course, a dream. The Saint tells the king that only he is real. The saint is not talking about the king as a body mind. What the Saint is talking about is the king as his Real Self. The Saint is talking about the One Reality that is the king's real Essence.

What is meant from this story is that nothing in this world is real. It is just like a dream, only the dreamer is real. The dreamer is the One Reality. This One Reality is dreaming the world and everything in it. We are all subjects of this dream. We think ourselves to be real and independent entities, but that is not true. In our night dream, the subject in the dream also feels that he or she is real and independent but when we wake up we find that there was nothing real about the dream subject. Similarly, when the One Reality will fold up its dream we will find there was nothing real about our existence. We will find that the only entity that was real, was the One Reality. One point that needs to be made here is that when we say we will find out, it really means the One Reality Itself will find out, because there is no one else there except the One Reality.

The One Reality has become all of us. As the process of manifestation proceeds, the One Reality assumes the limitations of the body and mind and becomes human beings, animals and all the living and nonliving things. After assuming these limitations It forgets the fact that It is the One Reality. That is why Guru Ji emphasizes the importance of us recognizing ourselves. We listen to the message but don't follow it. We still think that God is separate and far away from us. Guru Ji calls us for not recognizing ourselves, and then thinking that God is far from us. This is such a direct message to anyone who would listen that God is not away from us rather He is one with us, better yet He is us.

ਅਪਨਾ ਆਪੁ ਨ ਪਛਾਣਈ ਹਰਿ ਪ੍ਰਭੁ ਜਾਤਾ ਦੂਰਿ ॥   (Ang 854)
(*One does not recognize himself and he thinks that the Lord is far away from him*)

Let us use analogy to make our relationship with the One Reality clearer. This analogy has been used by Rupert Spira, an English non-dual teacher. It is to think of the One Reality (ੴ) like an unlimited open space. Make two simple assumptions about this space. One, assume the space to be completely empty of any objects and second, assume it to be conscious. The space now has two qualities: it is unlimited and it is conscious. Now start populating this unlimited conscious space with innumerable houses of different shapes and sizes like we see in the world. Each house and in fact, each room in every house has enclosed a small portion of the unlimited conscious space. The enclosed space in each room has been limited by the walls and ceiling of the rooms. In other words, the conscious space in each room thinks itself to be limited by the walls and the size of the room. In summary, unlimited conscious space has been divided into multiple limited small conscious spaces.

Exactly, in the same way, the Unlimited and Conscious One Reality has divided itself into innumerable bodies and minds and has assumed the limitations of each respective body and mind. What are these limitations of the body and mind? These limitations are made of thoughts which grow into beliefs. Once One Reality assumes the limitations of the body and mind, It starts to believe that it has become an independent entity. It adopts the identity of being limited body and mind and forgets that it is the unlimited Reality. This is the beginning of an ego in everybody. One Reality not only takes the form of men, women, animals, birds and other living organisms, it also takes the form of non living things and the whole universe and beyond.

In summary, we can say that we all come out of that One Reality, and as such our original nature is Divine. In other words, we are all Divine, but the Divinity in us has assumed the limitations of bodies and minds and has forgotten Its Essence. This is what is called ignorance or doubt (ਭਰਮ) in Gurbani. We are Divine but we think ourselves to be limited bodyminds.

ਮਾਧਵੇ ਕਿਆ ਕਹੀਐ ਭ੍ਰਮੁ ਐਸਾ ॥ ਜੈਸਾ ਮਾਨੀਐ ਹੋਇ ਨ ਤੈਸਾ ॥ (Ang 657)

*(O Lord, what can I say about the illusion? Things are not as they seem to be.)*

ਓਹੁ ਜੁ ਭਰਮੁ ਭੁਲਾਵਾ ਕਹੀਅਤ ਤਿਨ ਮਹਿ ਉਰਝਿਓ ਸਗਲ ਸੰਸਾਰਾ ॥ (Ang 611)
*(The whole world is entangled in what is called the delusion.)*

That is why the world is called a big drama of the One Almighty. The One Reality has hid Itself in every one of us and is playing world drama through the use of our bodies and minds. Following shabad explains in detail that this world is a big show of the One Reality or God.

ਵਾਹੁ ਵਾਹੁ ਕਾ ਬਡਾ ਤਮਾਸਾ ॥
ਆਪੇ ਹਸੈ ਆਪਿ ਹੀ ਚਿਤਵੈ ਆਪੇ ਚੰਦੁ ਸੂਰੁ ਪਰਗਾਸਾ ॥
ਆਪੇ ਜਲੁ ਆਪੇ ਥਲੁ ਥੰਮ੍ਨੁ ਆਪੇ ਕੀਆ ਘਟਿ ਘਟਿ ਬਾਸਾ ॥
ਆਪੇ ਨਰੁ ਆਪੇ ਫੁਨਿ ਨਾਰੀ ਆਪੇ ਸਾਰਿ ਆਪ ਹੀ ਪਾਸਾ ॥
ਗੁਰਮੁਖਿ ਸੰਗਤਿ ਸਭੈ ਬਿਚਾਰਹੁ ਵਾਹੁ ਵਾਹੁ ਕਾ ਬਡਾ ਤਮਾਸਾ ॥ (Ang 1403)

*(Great is the Play of God,*
*He Himself laughs, and He Himself thinks,*
*He Himself illumines the sun and the moon,*
*He Himself is the water,*
*He himself is the earth and its support,*
*He Himself abides in each and every heart,*
*He Himself is male, He Himself is female,*
*He Himself is the chessman and He Himself is the board,*
*As Gurmukh, join the Sangat, and all think about this,*
*Great is the play of God.)*

## Getting Feel Of One Reality:

It is good to talk about the one Reality to understand intellectually but experiential understanding goes much further. One thing to mention here is that one cannot experience this Reality while our mind is running out of control. One has to control the mind to get a feel of it. Gurbani says that the mind has to die, or the mind has to be conquered to be able to get a feel of this Reality.

ਮਨ ਮਾਰੇ ਧਾਤੁ ਮਰਿ ਜਾਇ ॥ ਬਿਨੁ ਮਨ ਮੂਏ ਕੈਸੇ ਹਰਿ ਪਾਇ ॥ (Ang 665)
(*When the mind is controlled to the point of its death, it's wandering comes to an end. Without conquering the mind, how can one meet the Lord.*)

Even though the realization of the Reality is an enormous accomplishment, there are some pointers that can give the reader a feel of the Reality. We will look into some of those pointers now and try to get a feel of the One Reality. It would be very important to pay attention to these pointers because they are kind of subtle in nature.

**Changeless vs Changing:**
We see the things around us are ever changing. There are three different types of changes that are happening all the time. Our perceptions of the world are changing, our bodies are changing and our minds are changing. We see the world changing right before our eyes. Day changes to night and then to day again. Weather is changing all the time. There are hundreds and thousands of other changes happening in the world all the time. One thing that is not changing, which, normally, goes unnoticed, is the one which notices all these changes. That is our Real Self, the One Reality.

Our body is constantly changing. It starts as a baby, changes into toddler, teenager, adult, middle aged and ends up as an old man or woman etc. But our Real Self watches this body grow from childhood to old age. It itself does not change at all. In old age, our Real Self can look back at all the stages in its life like watching a long movie, not two hours long but eighty, ninety years long, even longer at times. Anyway, if we look back at our life, no matter what stage in life we are, we can see that our life has run like a movie or a dream. And our Real Self, the watcher, has been watching it all along. That watcher is the One Reality or God.

Our mind is changing too all the time. Mind is made out of

thoughts and feelings. We feel happy, sad, angry, loving at different times depending on the mood of our mind. Sometimes we have good generous thoughts, other times mean and nasty thoughts. But in the background something is aware of all the moods of the mind and its thoughts. This is our Real Self, in the background, watching the mind and its activities.

This real Self, the unchanging Watcher in the background is the One Reality (ੴ). It Is watching all the changes going in our life, but It Itself never changes.

**Centering Yourself For A Moment:**

This technique is so simple that it is easy to miss it. It involves instantly freezing everything that is going on in one's body and mind.
It is something like the freeze game where you freeze in place like a statue. In this centering process the body has to be still, but more importantly the mind has to be still too. Try being thoughtless even for a moment. Don't think you are a man or a woman. Don't think you are a teacher or a doctor or an engineer or anything else. Don't think about where you live, the country, or the house. Just forget everything about yourself. Forget your past and your future. Just freeze completely, no activity at all in both body and mind. Once you do that, what is left of you is the One Reality. Gurbani talks about this technique in the following shabad.

ਟੂਕ ਦਮੁ ਕਰਾਰੀ ਜਉ ਕਰਹੁ ਹਾਜਰਿ ਹਜੂਰਿ ਖਦਾਇ ॥ (Ang 727)
(*If you will only become still for one breath, then you shall find the Presence of God, right where you are.*)

In this shabad, Bhagat Kabir says that if one can hold one's mind still for a time span that is even as short as needed to take one breath, one can feel the Presence of God right then and there. No other effort is needed.

**Seer And The Seen:**

This is another way of getting a feel of that One Reality. When we see an object we are essentially focusing our attention on the object. Now instead of focusing our attention on the object, if we turn our attention around 180 degrees and look for the one who is looking at the object, what do we find? If we look closely we will notice that it is not the body or the mind which is doing the looking. The body is just clay according to Gurbani and is insentient. So it cannot be doing the looking. The mind is a bundle of thoughts, sensations and perceptions. The thoughts, sensations and perceptions have no awareness of their own. So the mind is not doing the looking either. This shows that there is something beyond the body and mind that is really seeing the object. This something beyond body and mind is the One Reality or Ek Onkar that Guru Ji is talking about. There is a more detailed discussion on this techniqe in the article "Know Yourself and Meet the Lord" in this book. This One Reality resides in the innermost recesses of our heart beyond all thoughts, feelings and sensations. Gurbani in the following shabad points to this Reality and tells us to recognize it.

ਦਾਸੀ ਰਬੁ ਹਿਆਲੀਐ ਜੰਗਲੁ ਕਿਆ ਢੂਢੇਹਿ ॥   (Ang 1378)
*(The Lord abides in the heart, why are you looking for him in the jungle)*

**Our Words Point To Truth:**

We make statements all day long that I am so and so, I am an engineer, I am a doctor, I am a man, I am a woman etc. These statements are not made by one person but by every one of us. All of us address ourselves by the letter "I". These statements made by us are very simple but hide a great truth behind them. Looking at the statements closely we can see that there are two parts to each statement, the subject "I" and the object that the subject has become. Subject in all the statements is one, called

"I". This one "I" has become many. It has become a man, a woman, a doctor, an engineer etc. Why do all of us call ourselves by one name "I"? That is because One Reality has become all of us and we are naming the One Reality as "I". That is the great truth being revealed by our simple statements. So this word "I" that we use every day, represents the One Reality. I hope that next time we call ourselves "I" we pause a little and remember that we talking as One Realty (ੴ); and try to get a first hand feel of it.

Guru Gobind Singh Ji states in the shabad in Jaap Sahib:
ਏਕ ਮੂਰਤਿ ਅਨੇਕ ਦਰਸਨ ਕੀਨ ਰੂਪ ਅਨੇਕ ॥
ਖੇਲ ਖੇਲ ਅਖੇਲ ਖੇਲਨ ਅੰਤ ਕੋ ਫਿਰ ਏਕ ॥   (Jaap Sahib)
(*One Reality, apparent as many, creates innumerable forms. After playing the world drama, when She stops the play, they all become One again*)

I, sometimes wonder if the children when they are young are taught about this One Reality (ੴ), we would probably be living in a different world. The children should be taught that this Reality is not anything different from them, that they are not this body and mind, but are this one infinite Reality. That there is no difference between us all, even though we look different and dress or speak differently. One thing would come out of it, if the children were made to understand this fact, and then as children carried this understanding into the world as they grew up, the hatred, jealousy and enmity etc. would almost disappear from our life and the world would become a much better place to live in. It would be better if the children were taught this first before teaching them about the material world. Right now there is no education in schools about what we really are and what this world is all about. There should be at least some basic courses in the education system to enlighten the new soul with the truth about life. Our education system prepares the children for dealing with the outside world but not the inside world. It does not teach them about themselves

◆ ◆ ◆

# KNOW YOURSELF AND MEET THE LORD

ਸੋ ਬਊਰਾ ਜੋ ਆਪੁ ਨ ਪਛਾਨੈ ॥ ਆਪੁ ਪਛਾਨੈ
ਤ ਏਕੈ ਜਾਨੈ ॥ *(Ang 855)*

*(Those who do not recognize
themselves, are insane. When they
recognize themselves, only then
they know the One Reality)*

uru Ji is a bit harsh in this Shabad when He is saying that those who do not recognize themselves, are insane. Even though Guru Ji's message is harsh, his message applies to us, all the same. If one knew his or her real nature, then he would not be called insane. It is only due to this ignorance that one lives an unworthy way of life. If one had real knowledge about himself, he would save himself.

ਅਨਜਾਨਤ ਬਿਖਿਆ ਮਹਿ ਰਚੈ ॥
ਜੇ ਜਾਨਤ ਆਪਨ ਆਪ ਬਚੈ ॥   (Ang 277)
*(Because of ignorance people are engrossed in bad behavior,
if they knew better, they would save themselves.)*

Gurbani says that it is necessary to know oneself. The reason is that, unless we recognize ourselves we cannot know the One Reality or God. Most of us never think about our true identity because of our conditioning and our upbringing. We have never been taught about this by our parents or school teachers or our culture. We have been convinced because of our conditioning that we are this body and mind. We never question the validity of this statement and defend it vehemently if questioned. Let us explore this topic in detail and investigate what Gurbani teaches us about it.

The current life model that we live in, is that we are bodies with minds and we have individual parcels of consciousness. It is further believed that these body mind combinations are independent entities in their own right and have control over their activities. Then there is a world out there which is different from us, that we interact with. There are certain things in the outside world that we can control but there are many other things that happen in the world that are beyond our control. We do believe that there must be some power which must control the world. As a result, we believe that there is a supreme controller of the world called God. Whenever we can't control certain things we blame it on others or the controller. This is essentially our current life model and it has been passed on from generation to generation for a  long time. However, when we examine our everyday experience, this life model does not prove out to be true. We will try to discuss and understand from our everyday experience why this life model is not true.

If we ask a stranger on a street corner a simple question, who are you, what kind of answer will we get? Initially, he or she would probably be confused about the question. Eventually after a little thinking and understanding the question, he may say his or her name. When reminded that it is the name of the body, he or she will start talking about his profession such as I am a school teacher, engineer or a doctor. People with a little deeper understanding may say I am my mind, my thoughts and feelings. We may get some other vague answers but it would be rare to get answers that would be specific and to the point. Few people really do this kind of introspection, and have any firm conviction about who they really are. However, they do have a vague idea in their mind that they are a body-mind combination. Here is a simple questionnaire that the reader can try for herself or himself to ponder this question. The real answer will automatically emerge as the reader continues to read the article.

Question: "Who are you, really?". Identify the correct answer.

    A. Body
    B. Mind
    C. Thoughts
    D. Feelings
    E. Sensations
    F. Perceptions
    G. Some combination of A through F
    H. Something beyond all of the above
    I.  None of the above.

Gurbani asks the same question in the shabad below: "who are you and where have you come from. You don't even know how long you will stay here, you have no hint of when you shall depart"

ਸੁਨਹੁ ਰੇ ਤੂ ਕਉਨੁ ਕਹਾ ਤੇ ਆਇਓ ॥
ਏਤੀ ਨ ਜਾਨਉ ਕੇਤੀਕ ਮੁਦਤਿ ਚਲਤੇ ਖਬਰਿ ਨ ਪਾਇਓ ॥ (Ang 999)
(*Listen; who are you and where did you come from?*
*You don't even know how long you will stay here, you have no idea when you will leave*)

We will try to get an answer to the question "who are you" from our own daily experience. In Vedantic literature this is called self inquiry. After general discussion we will explore it from Gurbani's viewpoint. Let us explore our daily experience of perception. Perception consists of seeing, hearing, touching, tasting and smelling. Let us pick one aspect of perception "seeing", which is probably the most common experience in our life. In our daily life we see all kinds of objects around us. Imagine a situation where you are seated in some place and looking at various objects around you such as a chair, a computer, a table. If we take a broader view of the process of you seeing those objects, it can be said that the process of seeing consists of objects seen on one side and you as the seer on the other side. Now rather than attending to those objects, just reverse your attention 180 degrees, from the objects inwards, towards the seer who is doing the seeing. When you do that, what do you find? Who do you think is doing the seeing? Do you think seer is the body or is it the mind or something else. Rarely such a question arises in our mind. For most of us our whole life goes by without ever thinking about who is the "seer". Our attention is always going outwards towards the objects and wanders from object to object but never comes back towards the seer. This is the way we have been brought up. We have never been taught about this, neither by our parents nor by our teachers or our culture. For that reason this question may sound a little strange to some people. It may sound confusing to others. However, we call this seer by the name "I", without having a clear idea about what the seer really is. We normally say "I" see the chair, "I" see the computer, "I" see the table etc. It is vaguely thought to be a mixture of body and mind. We seldom pay attention to this seer or the knower "I" to understand what it really is. Is it the body, the mind or something else. Here we will make an effort in the next paragraphs to figure out what this seer really is, which we call "I".

We notice here that the basic quality of the "seer" is knowing or awareness. It is due to knowing or awareness that the seer "I" sees the objects in the room. Knowing and awareness are used synonymously here. Without being aware, "I" won't be able to see anything and recognize anything. Awareness is the quality with which we get cognition of things. To find out the seer "I" in us, we need to establish what in us has the basic quality of being aware or knowing. We will examine body and mind and whatever else that we believe has the quality of awareness. Once we establish the aware entity in us then we will be able to say who the "seer" is.

We will start our exploration with the body. Science tells us that the body is made of mostly food and water. Food grows out of soil and water. So we can say that the body is made of soil and water. According to Sri Guru Granth Sahib, the body is said to be made out of clay. In fact, the body is depicted as a puppet made out of clay.

ਮਾਟੀ ਕੋ ਪੁਤਰਾ ਕੈਸੇ ਨਚਤੁ ਹੈ ॥
ਦੇਖੈ ਦੇਖੈ ਸੁਨੈ ਬੋਲੈ ਦਉਰਿਓ ਫਿਰਤੁ ਹੈ ॥   (Ang 487)
(*How does the puppet of clay dance?*
*It looks, hears and speaks, and is running round and round*)

ਦੇਹੀ ਮਾਟੀ ਬੋਲੈ ਪਉਣੁ ॥   (Ang 152)
(*The body is clay, the wind speaks through it*)

So we can say that the body is made out of clay. Clay is insentient matter and as such cannot be aware. If we watch our daily experience closely, we can also get confirmation of the fact that the body is not aware. When our body is in pain, we make statements like my body is in pain. This statement implies that I am different from the body and the body is like an object that I perceive. It further implies that I am aware of the body and not the other way around. We never say my body is aware of me. We always make statements like I know when the body is in pain, sick, healthy, hungry or thirsty etc. So we can safely conclude that our body is not aware, hence it cannot be called the seer "I".

Now we will explore if the mind meets the condition of being aware. Exploration of the mind is a bit more complicated than exploring the body. Basic components or functions of the mind are thinking and imagining, sensing and feeling; and perceiving. Perceiving can be further broken down into seeing, hearing, touching, tasting and smelling. We will abbreviate the functions of the mind into three main categories of thinking, sensing and perceiving. This can be done because thinking and imagining is one family, sensing and feeling is another and so on. So for the mind to be aware, thoughts, sensations and perceptions have to be aware.

Let us take a look at the thought first. Think of any thought in your mind. Now observe that thought closely and objectively, you will find that the thought by itself cannot see, it cannot hear and cannot know anything as the seer can. Since thought cannot see, listen or know, it cannot be said to be aware. On the contrary, the seer "I" is aware of the thought or the thoughts. The seer sees a thought appear, stay there for a few seconds and then disappear. This shows that the seer "I" is different from the thought. It is aware of the thought rather than the thought being aware of the seer. Since the thought is not aware it cannot be said to represent the seer "I".

We can apply the same test to the other faculties of the mind, sensations and perceptions and prove that they also do not meet the condition of being aware. Just to make sure the reader gets full understanding, the argument will be repeated. The sensations and perceptions are not aware because they cannot see, hear or know on their own. All these are dependent on something else behind them to be able to perform their respective functions. Sensing, perceiving and all other functions are made possible only by the seer acting in the background. For example, we have noticed at times, if we are listening to someone talking and our attention wanders away, we ask the person to repeat what he or she said. What really happened is that the seer or the knower "I" that was doing the listening in the background got disconnected from the sense of hearing or the listening. So the listening got interrupted. So it is not the sense of hearing that is doing the listening but it is the seer behind it. In conclusion, we can say that thoughts, feelings, sensations, and perceptions are not aware. Hence the mind which comprises all of these functions, is not aware. So the mind also cannot be called a seer "I". Gurbani says that this mind is enticed by Maya as such cannot see or hear.

ਇਹ ਮਨੁ ਮਾਇਆ ਮੋਹਿਆ ਵੇਖਣੁ ਸੁਨਣੁ ਨ ਹੋਇ ॥ (Ang 83)
(*This mind is enticed by Maya, it cannot see or hear.*)

There is another, maybe simpler way to get a feel of this experientially. Just analyze your current experience. Let us say you are looking at a tree outside your room, in the open. It can be said that you are aware of the tree. Being that you are aware of the tree it can be said that you are separate from the tree. You are the subject and the tree is the object. Now let's move to an object closer to you like a table or a chair in the room. Same thing can be said regarding the table that you are aware of and hence separate from it. Now move to something that is even closer than the table. Let us say your own body. Even though the body is closer to you, you still are aware of the body. If the body is in pain you feel it's pain. Note the body is not feeling it's pain. It is you, the seer or the knower who is feeling the pain of the body. That means you are different from the body. Some readers may say that they think they are the body. But that is a false belief which we are trying to get rid of. When you say, this is my hand or leg or any other part of the body you don't mean that you are the hand or leg etc. You say that this is your hand and not that the hand is you. Similarly, you are not the body but something beyond the body that is aware of the body.

Next look at your thoughts, feelings and sensations, which are even closer to the seer than the body. In fact they are inside the body. When you get a thought you know the thought. The thought stays there for a few seconds and then it disappears. You see the thought disappearing but you stay put and watch the next thought arising. Since you can be aware of the thought, you cannot be the thought. You are something beyond the thought that is aware of the thought. Similar logic can be applied to feeling and sensations and proven that you are something beyond all these. Thoughts, feelings and sensations add to make up the mind. So you are something beyond both body and mind.

So we have discovered that the seer "I" is neither body nor mind but something beyond. This has been established from our daily experience. Body and mind are not aware but on the contrary the seer "I" is aware of body and mind. As such, the seer "I" is something higher than the body and mind. Seer "I" being higher than body and mind means that the seer "I" is the subject. The body, mind and the world are the objects. Normally, we think that body-mind combination is the subject and the world is the object. We have believed this all our life. Now we find that is not true. Body and mind combination is not the subject because it is not aware. It is an object like other objects in the world. The seer "I" that is aware is the real subject. We still have to define what the seer "I" is, but one thing we have proven is that our life's beliefs have been misguided about who we are. **Our conditioned belief has been that we are body and mind or a combination thereof. Additionally, we believe that body and mind is the seer "I" or the knower of events. This belief has been proven completely false. The seer "I" has no relationship with body and mind. It is separate from the body and mind and is an entirely independent entity, higher than, and inaccessible to body and mind.**

We have established that the seer "I" is an aware entity and as such we can call it Awareness. **Awareness is defined as "the Presence that is aware".** Now we will call the seer "I" as Awareness and will try to see what is its nature. Since the Awareness is beyond body and mind, it would be safe to say that it does not contain any thoughts, feelings, sensations and perceptions. In other words the Awareness is an emptiness but an aware emptiness without any objective qualities. This is a very subtle point and is worth repeating. The Awareness, which is beyond or higher than body and mind, does not contain any thoughts, sensations, or perceptions and hence is transparent and completely empty. It does not have any objective qualities. It can be compared to an empty space which does not have any objective qualities. The Seer or Awareness, like the empty space, having no objective qualities, cannot be grasped. That is the reason that when we turn our attention inwards and make an effort to locate this Awareness we cannot find it. If we try to think about it, the thought draws a blank. There are no physical qualities in the Awareness which the mind can grab onto and locate it.

One thing else to be pointed out here is that it is not that each one of us has independent individual Awareness. That is to say that you have your own awareness and I have my own Awareness. There is only one Awareness and that one Awareness is shared by all. If we had individual separate Awarenesses then everyone would see a boundary to their Awareness. But that is not what our experience reveals. If we observe our Awareness we don't see any limit to it. We don't experience that our awareness stops beyond a particular distance. In fact, it can stretch far into the universe and even beyond. Awareness does not have any objective qualities, hence it is without any shape or form. Since It is formless it is unlimited and infinite. Only a form can have limits. Infinite Awareness also means there is only one awareness. That proves we all share one Awareness. In other words the seer "I" in all of us, is one and the same. This Awareness is a common everyday awareness we all have, with which we know our thoughts, feelings, sensations, perceptions and interact with the world. On the flip side, this is the same Awareness that in traditional religious terms is called Atman, Soul, or God. In Sikh religion it is called by names like Ek Onkar, Guru, Satguru, Raam, Prabhu, and many more names. Other names that have been used in philosophical literature are Awareness, Consciousness, Knowing, Source etc.

Gurbani refers to Awareness as bibek. Bhagat Kabir Ji talks about Awareness and says that he has found the Guru whose name is Awareness.

ਕਹੁ ਕਬੀਰ ਮੈ ਸੋ ਗੁਰੁ ਪਾਇਆ ਜਾ ਕਾ ਨਾਉ ਬਿਬੇਕੋ ॥ (Ang 793)

*(Says Kabir I have found the Guru, whose name is Awareness.)*

Guru Ram Dass Ji says that the Guru is Awareness; and He looks upon all alike.

ਬਿਬੇਕ ਗੁਰੂ ਗੁਰੂ ਸਮਦਰਸੀ ਤਿਸੁ ਮਿਲੀਐ ਸੰਕ ਉਤਾਰੇ ॥ (Ang 981)
*(The Guru is Awareness, the Guru looks upon all alike.*
*Meeting with him, doubt and skepticism are removed.)*

Bibek (ਵਿਵੇਕ) is a Sanskrit word which means Awareness.

Guru Ji further describes that the Guru or Awareness is always with us. If we examine our everyday experience we will discover that we are never not aware. The contents of our Awareness may change from time to time but Awareness never changes or is always aware. That is why Guru ji says that our Guru or Awareness is always with me. Not only is he always with me but helps me and keeps me out of trouble everywhere. When Guru Ji talks of "me" he is speaking for "us".

ਗੁਰੁ ਮੇਰੈ ਸੰਗਿ ਸਦਾ ਹੈ ਨਾਲੇ ॥ (Ang 394)
*(My guru is always with me, near at hand.)*

ਸੋ ਸਤਿਗੁਰੁ ਪਿਆਰਾ ਮੇਰੈ ਨਾਲਿ ਹੈ ਜਿਥੈ ਕਿਥੈ ਮੈਨੋ ਲਏ ਛਡਾਈ ॥ (Ang 588)
*(That Beloved True Guru is always with me. He saves me everywhere)*

The understanding that we are all one Awareness, one Seer, is of huge significance. We are not a combination of a little body and an ever changing mind, but we are the one Awareness which is aware of body and mind and the world. We have been mistaken all our life by thinking ourselves to be body and mind. The multiplicity of living beings, animals and even inanimate things that we see are simply many forms of precipitation of this one Awareness or the seer "I". This theme is echoed in Siri Guru Granth Sahib at many many places:

ਏਕ ਨੂਰ ਤੇ ਸਭੁ ਜਗੁ ਉਪਜਿਆ ਕਉਨ ਭਲੇ ਕੋ ਮੰਦੇ ॥ (Ang 1349)
*(Whole humanity has manifested from One Divine Light,*
*How can anyone be good or bad?)*

33

ਸਤ ਮਹਿ ਜੋਤਿ ਜੋਤਿ ਹੈ ਸੋਇ ਤਿਸ ਦੇ ਚਾਨਣਿ ਸਭ ਮਹਿ ਚਾਨਣੁ ਹੋਇ || (Ang 13)
(*That Divine Light is permeating through everyone,*
*they are all conscious because of that Light.*)

ਆਪੇ ਪਟੀ ਕਲਮ ਆਪਿ ਉਪਰਿ ਲੇਖੁ ਭੀ ਤੂੰ ||
ਏਕੋ ਕਹੀਐ ਨਾਨਕਾ ਦੂਜਾ ਕਾਹੇ ਕੁ ||          (Ang 1291)
(*He Himself is the writing board, He Himself is the pen and the*
*writing on the board too,*
*Speak of only One Lord, O Nanak, how can there be any other?*)

## Implications Of This Understanding:

### God Is Not Far But Closer Than Close:

First and foremost implication of this understanding is that it
brings God close to us. Our normal understanding about God has
been that He is some place unknown to us and unapproachable
to us. Many people think that God lives up in the clouds, some
place far away from them. Bhagat Kabir says in the shabad
below, something that was talked about in his times. He says
Hindus think that their God lives in the south and Muslims
think that their God lives in the west. But Bhagat Ji points out
that look deep into your heart  That is where God lives.

ਦਖਨ ਦੇਸਿ ਹਰੀ ਕਾ ਬਾਸਾ ਪਛਿਮਿ ਅਲਹ ਮੁਕਾਮਾ ||
ਦਿਲ ਮਹਿ ਖੋਜਿ ਦਿਲੈ ਦਿਲਿ ਖੋਜਹੁ ਏਹੀ ਠਉਰ ਮੁਕਾਮਾ ||  (Ang 1349)
(*God of the Hindus lives in southern lands,*
*And the God of Muslims lives in the west.*
*Search in your heart, look deep into your heart,*
*This is Home and the Place where God lives.*)

With this understanding we discover that God resides in us. He
is the Seer in us. He is the Awareness in us. God is closer to us
than anything. He is our own Real Self. In fact, we are not two
separate entities. We are not, only He is. We have realized that we
are not a body and mind combination and hence we don't have

any independent existence of our own. Gurbani says:

ਹਮ ਕਿਛੁ ਨਾਹੀ ਏਕੈ ਓਹੀ ॥ ਆਗੈ ਪਾਛੈ ਏਕੋ ਸੋਈ ॥
ਨਾਨਕ ਗੁਰਿ ਖੋਏ ਭ੍ਰਮ ਭੰਗਾ ॥ ਹਮ ਓਇ ਮਿਲਿ ਹੋਏ ਇਕ ਰੰਗਾ ॥   (Ang 391)
(*I am not, only He is,*
*Everywhere He alone is,*
*O Nanak, the Guru has dispelled my doubts,*
*He and I have merged together and become one.*)

We have discovered that if we try to know ourselves, we find that we don't even exist. What we believe ourseives to be is really, God himself or herself. It may feel unnerving to think that we do not have our independent existence. But, what it really means is that we do not exist as body minds but we exist as the Divine Beings. In fact, it is a sort of promotion for us from being "human beings" to being "Divine Beings". We should keep this new identity in mind all the time and operate in life from this new platform.

**Not recognizing our true identity is the single biggest obstacle in our spiritual progress. As long as we are stuck in body and mind, there is no way we can find the Lord.** Guru Ji says that unless we go beyond our mind we cannot get rid of Maya and as such cannot find the Lord.

ਮਨੁ ਮਰੈ ਧਾਤੁ ਮਰਿ ਜਾਇ ॥ ਬਿਨੁ ਮਨ ਮੂਏ ਕੈਸੇ ਹਰਿ ਪਾਇ ॥  (Ang 665)
(*When the mind dies or is transcended, the objective world of maya is eradicated.*
*Without going beyond the mind, how can the Lord be found?*)

So it is imperative for us to focus on our true identity. Do we want to stay stuck to our old and false identity of being body minds or do we want to adopt our new and true identity of being Divine. Gurbani tells us over and over to be a Gurmukh rather than a manmukh. Being a Gurmukh means connecting with the Guru's or the Divine presence in us. And, of course, manmukh means thinking ourselves to be body minds. Guru Ji has echoed the theme many times in Sri Guru Granth Sahib, that we should try to be a Gurmukh. There are over two thousand Shabads in Sri Guru Granth Sahib, singing praises of a Gurmukh. In the following shabad Guru Ji is saying that if one raises himself to the level of a Gurmukh, he will have lived a spiritually profitable life while the manmukh will leave after wasting his life.

ਗੁਰਮੁਖਿ ਲਾਹਾ ਲੈ ਗਏ ਮਨਮੁਖ ਚਲੇ ਮੂਲੁ ਗਵਾਇ ਜੀਉ ॥ (Ang 74)
(*The Gurmukhs have had a profitable life while the self willed manmukhs leave the world after losing even their principal.*)

**Our Ego Is A False Entity:**

Another implication of this understanding is that it reveals that the individual ego is a false entity. What is ego? It is mistaking ourselves to be little bodies and minds instead of Divine Presence or Awareness. We have established that we are not body and minds. If we are neither body nor mind, then where is the ego? We are that which is beyond body and mind, and hence beyond the possibility of being an ego. It is unfortunate that most of us are mistaken and believe ourselves to be body and minds. It is just a false belief that is the root cause of our ego. Without this false belief the ego has no existence, whatsoever. That is why ego is said to be a false phenomenon. It is strange that the whole world suffers from something that does not even exist. We will discuss this in detail in a separate article. Gurbani tells us that we have to recognize our real identity. That is the only way we can get rid of our ego.

ਆਪੁ ਪਛਾਣੈ ਘਰਿ ਵਸੈ ਹਉਮੈ ਤ੍ਰਿਸਨਾ ਜਾਇ ॥ (Ang 57)
(*Those who recognize themselves, their ego and craving are eradicated.*)

ਸਤਿਗੁਰੁ ਮਿਲੈ ਤ ਹਉਮੈ ਤੂਟੈ ਤਾਂ ਕੋ ਲੇਖੈ ਪਾਈ ॥ (Ang 353)
(*When One meets the True Guru then his ego drops,
Then that person is accepted in the Court of the Lord.*)

The irony of the situation is that even though Gurbani teaches us to recognize ourselves, we rarely pay attention to it. We do listen to shabads, enjoy the kirtan and as we walk out of the Satsang, we forget all about it. So the ego does not leave us and as such, we don't make any spiritual progress.

## We Are All One:

With this understanding we come to realize that we are all one. This understanding alone can change our world by eliminating hatred and jealousy, replacing it with friendship and love. We have discovered that we are all one Divine Presence or Awareness. This is true for not only human beings but animals and even inanimate things. One God has become everyone and everything in the universe. If we can adopt this understanding and apply it in our life, it would be hard for us not to embrace everyone with love. We will stop hating anyone and blaming others for our problems. With this understanding we see that it is not our body and mind that sees, speaks or listens, it is Awareness (God) that is speaking and seeing through us. It is not we the bodies and minds, who are the doers, but it is God who is doing everything through our bodies and minds. Following shabads make it clear.

ਸਤੈ ਘਟ ਰਾਮੁ ਬੋਲੈ ਰਾਮਾ ਬੋਲੈ ॥ ਰਾਮ ਬਿਨਾ ਕੋ ਬੋਲੈ ਰੇ ॥ (Ang 988)
(*Within all the Lord speaks, who else speaks other than the Lord?*)

ਆਖਹਿ ਤ ਵੇਖਹਿ ਸਭੁ ਤੂਹੈ ਜਿਨਿ ਜਗਤ ਉਪਾਇਆ ॥ (Ang 918)
(*O Lord, You are the only one doing the speaking and looking, who has created the universe.*)

ਸਭ ਕਿਛੁ ਕੀਤਾ ਤੇਰਾ ਹੋਵੈ ਨਾਹੀ ਕਿਛੁ ਅਸਾੜਾ ਜੀਉ ॥ (Ang 103)
(*All things are your doing, nothing is done by us.*)

## Peace And Happiness Grows In Life:

The other significance of this new understanding is that when we embrace it, we will see peace and happiness grow in our everyday life. There is a natural law that our life is a reflection of the state of our mind. Whatever we think ourselves to be, life presents itself to us in conformance with our thinking. Guru Ji says that as people think, so they carve their way in life. Based on their actions they come and go.

ਜੇਹੀ ਸੁਰਤਿ ਤੇਹਾ ਤਿਨ ਰਾਹੁ ॥ ਲੇਖਾ ਇਕੋ ਆਵਹੁ ਜਾਹੁ ॥  (Ang 25)
(*As is their Awareness, so is their way.*
*That is the one rule, we come and go.*)

So it is extremely important that we pay attention to what we think and believe. Life will present itself to us according to our thinking. If we think ourselves to be the body-minds, the world will appear to us fleeting, perishable and impermanent, but if we think we are the Divine Presence or Awareness, life will appear to us full of love, peace and happiness. Gurbani uses specific words for the two viewpoints. Those who consider themselves to be body minds, Gurbani calls them manmukh (ਮਨਮੁਖ). Those, who consider themselves to be Divine, one with the Guru, Gurbani calls them Gurmukh (ਗੁਰਮੁਖ). Guru Ji says that manmukh finds no peace while Gurmukh is wonderfully joyful.

ਮਨਮੁਖਿ ਸੁਖੁ ਨ ਪਾਈਐ ਗੁਰਮੁਖਿ ਸੁਖੁ ਸੁਭਾਨੁ ॥  (Ang 21)
(*The Self-willed manmukhs find no peace, while the Gurmukhs are wonderfully joyful.*)

Not only the Gurmukh is joyful, Guru Ji says that True Ambrosial Nectar rains on the Gurmukh and he tastes it in his mouth. His mind is rejuvenated as he sings the praises of the Lord.

ਅੰਮ੍ਰਿਤੁ ਸਚਾ ਵਰਸਦਾ ਗੁਰਮੁਖਾ ਮੁਖਿ ਪਾਇ ॥
ਮਨੁ ਸਦਾ ਹਰੀਆਵਲਾ ਸਹਜੇ ਹਰਿ ਗੁਣ ਗਾਇ ॥  (Ang 428)
(*The True Ambrosial Nectar rains down, and trickles down Gurmukh's mouths,*
*Their minds are forever rejuvenated, and they intuitively sing the Praises of the Lord.*)

**We Rise Above The Karma:**

This new understanding makes inroads into other aspects of our life. It not only eliminates ego from our life, but we find out that the Lord is the only Doer. He is the Seer, Listener and Speaker in us. One of the most significant implications of this new understanding is that by living with this new identity we do not get entangled in karmas, so we stop burdening our life with new karmas day after day. This is what Gurbani says about it.

ਸੋ ਹੰ ਸੋ ਜਾ ਕਉ ਹੈ ਜਾਪ ॥
ਜਾ ਕਉ ਲਿਪਤ ਨ ਹੋਇ ਪੁੰਨ ਅਰੁ ਪਾਪ ॥ (Ang 1162)
(*Those who chant "That I Am That",*
*Virtue or vice do not stick to them.*)

This is due to the fact that we bind karmas only when we think we are the doer or have an ego. As long as we believe ourselves to be the doer of deeds we will have to suffer the consequences of our deeds. Gurbani says in Jap Ji Sahib that whatever we do, is written in our account and when we go we take this account with us. Whatever we sow, so shall we reap.

ਪੁੰਨੀ ਪਾਪੀ ਆਖਣੁ ਨਾਹਿ ॥ ਕਰਿ ਕਰਿ ਕਰਣਾ ਲਿਖਿ ਲੈ ਜਾਹੁ ॥

ਆਪੇ ਬੀਜਿ ਆਪੇ ਹੀ ਖਾਹੁ ॥ ਨਾਨਕ ਹੁਕਮੀ ਆਵਹੁ ਜਾਹੁ ॥ (Ang 4)
(*Virtue and vice are not mere talk,*
*Actions repeated, over and over again, are engraved on us,*
*We shall harvest, what we sow,*
*O Nanak, by God's Command, we come and go in reincarnation.*)

Sant Maskeen Ji says that Guru Ji mentions the word "do" (ਕਰਿ) twice in the shabad. He says that the first mention of the word "do" is for the body's action and the second is for the mind's action. According to him Guru Ji is telling us that when a person's body and mind both are involved in the action, then that action is recorded. Sant Ji further says that mostly we work at the body level without the mind getting involved in the action. He says that when we do Naam Simran, we do it with the body only, our mind mostly stays absent during Naam Simran. It is wandering around in useless thinking. So the good act of doing Naam Simran is not recorded in our account. But when we do something bad like telling a lie or cheating someone, then the mind gets fully involved too and that action gets recorded. So no wonder, our life is drifting downhill. We are regressing rather than progressing.

When we rise above the body and mind level and believe ourselves to be Divine Presence or Awareness, then we stop contracting the effects of karma, no matter good or bad. In fact, one who has risen to Awareness level, he has really become a non-doer of deeds and no action is good or bad for him. He has surrendered all his actions to the Almighty.

I want to state here that this understanding that we have discovered, is not an intellectual understanding. It is an experiential understanding even though it is arrived at through intellectual discussion. Experiential understanding is based on the personal experience. If any doubts still exist in the reader's mind, I would implore the reader to try to find the seer in him or her and check for himself or herself. In other words, try to locate, who is the seer in you. I assure you, you will not be able to find it. We call this seer in us as "I". The reason we cannot locate it, is that the Seer does not have any objective qualities like those of the body and mind. This Seer, which we call "I" is an eternal infinite Aware Being or Aware Presence that cannot be grasped. How can a finite being, that we think we are, grasp an infinite One. Logically, a finite being and an infinite Being cannot even coexist because the whole space will be occupied by the infinite Being. There would be no room left for the finite being to exist. So we really don't even exist as separate entities. All there is God Himself or Herself. **We are not, only God is.** As Gurbani says

ਹਉ ਕਿਛੁ ਨਾਹੀ ਏਕੋ ਤੂੰ ਹੈ ਆਪੇ ਆਪੁ ਸੁਜਾਨਾ ॥ (Ang 779)
(*I am not, You are the One and Only,*
*You Yourself are all knowing.*)

His abode is in our heart. In fact, He is the only One there. There is no me, no you, or no third party in there. That is why there is so much emphasis on self realization. We just have to dive down in our own hearts and find Him or in other words, find ourselves.

ਵਸੀ ਰਬ ਹਿਆਲੀਐ ਜੰਗਲੁ ਕਿਆ ਢੂਢੇਹਿ ॥ (Ang 1378)
(*God lives in the heart, why search outside in the woods?*)

Seeker is the Sought. There are no two. When we go inside and pay attention to ourselves we will meet the Seer "I". By meeting "I" we will find peace and happiness. As Baba Farid Ji says:

ਆਪੁ ਸਵਾਰਹਿ ਮੈ ਮਿਲਹਿ ਮੈ ਮਿਲਿਆ ਸੁਖੁ ਹੋਇ ॥ (Ang 1382)
(As we *search into ourselves we will meet the Seer "I",*
*meeting Whom we shall attain peace and happiness.*)

Living with this understanding does not mean that we stop doing anything and become a recluse. On the contrary, Guru Ji instructs us to go ahead and lead our normal life with our new identity of being the Seer or the Awareness. With our new identity we have met our Guru and have become one with Him. Guru Ji says that this is the perfect way to live one's life.

ਨਾਨਕ ਸਤਿਗੁਰਿ ਭੇਟਿਐ ਪੂਰੀ ਹੋਵੈ ਜੁਗਤਿ ॥
ਹਸੰਦਿਆ ਖੇਲੰਦਿਆ ਪੈਨੰਦਿਆ ਖਾਵੰਦਿਆ ਵਿਚੇ ਹੋਵੈ ਮੁਕਤਿ ॥ (Ang 522)
(*O Nanak, meeting the true Guru, perfects the technique of living.*
*One attains salvation while living this way laughing, playing,*
*dressing and eating.*)

◆ ◆ ◆

# WORLD IS A GRAND ILLUSION

ਮਾਧਵੇ ਕਿਆ ਕਹੀਐ ਭ੍ਰਮੁ ਐਸਾ ॥ ਜੈਸਾ
ਮਾਨੀਐ ਹੋਇ ਨ ਤੈਸਾ ॥   *(Ang 657)*

*(O Lord, what can be said about
the illusion, things are not
what they seem to be)*

This world we live in is a grand illusion. As the shabad above states, this illusion cannot be described. Only thing that can be said is that the things are not what they appear to be. It should be pointed out here that the statement, "world is illusion" does not mean that the world does not exist. It means that it is not what it appears to be. For example, when we see a rainbow in the sky, it appears to exist, but it is not what it appears to be. It is only a play of light and rain drops. There is no rainbow there, but a pattern of light. Another example would be of our dream at night. It feels very real when we are dreaming. All the people, objects and buildings etc. seem to be very real but when we wake up find out it was just an illusion. The world is somewhat like that. It is not what it appears to be. It is not made out of brick and mortar. It appears to be made out of solid materials but as we investigate closely we will find that is not the case. We will try to investigate this illusion from the Gurbani point of view and also from our experiential point of view.

There are two worlds we live in, the inner world and the outer world. We believe ourselves to be bodies possessing an instrument called mind. The mind has three different faculties, thinking and imagining, feeling and sensing and perceiving. Thinking and imagining is our inner world, feeling and sensing is our body, and perceiving is the outer world. Perceiving further consists of seeing, hearing, touching, tasting, and smelling. There would be no outer world without these five faculties. Similarly there would be no inner world without thinking and imagining. We as a body believe ourselves to be in the middle of the two worlds. In this article, we will explore the reality of the inner and the outer worlds and also our body. Do these worlds and our body really exist or is it our imagination? Gurbani says that all of us are simply caught up in a misleading illusion .

ਓਹੁ ਜੁ ਭਰਮੁ ਭੁਲਾਵਾ ਕਹੀਅਤ ਤਿੰਨ ਮਹਿ ਉਰਝਿਓ ਸਗਲ ਸੰਸਾਰਾ ॥  (Ang 611)
(*The whole world is entangled in what is called misleading illusion.*)

Bhagat Kabir goes even further by holding God responsible for this illusion. He says that God has tricked the whole world by drugging the people.

ਹਰਿ ਠਗ ਜਗ ਕਉ ਠਗਉਰੀ ਲਾਈ ॥  (Ang 331)
(*The Lord is the thug, who has drugged and robbed the whole world.*)

**Illusion Of The Outer World:**

In our normal everyday experience we see objects, people and the world around us, but we never give any thought to the reality of our experience. We have been conditioned from day one to see the world as we do. We see various objects like trees, cars, houses etc. We also see people, animals, birds etc. Additionally, we see myriads of other things and phenomenons that we never think about as to what they really are. We take these experiences at their face value and think that they have an independent reality of their own. But when we look closely, we find these objects, trees, animals and people are not what they appear to be. **In**

**reality, there are no objects, no people and no real world out there**. It is just like a dream that we have every night. When we wake up from the dream we find there was nothing real in the dream. Everything in the dream was made out of imagination and thinking. Gurbani says that we are living in a dream now, even though we are awake. When we really wake up from this life dream, we will find that there was nothing real in this life. Gurbani says that this world we see outside us has no reality and is like a dream at night.

ਜਗ ਰਚਨਾ ਸਭ ਝੂਠ ਹੈ ਜਾਨਿ ਲੇਹੁ ਰੇ ਮੀਤ ॥ (Ang 1429)
(*The creation of the world is all false, know this well my friend*)

ਨਾਨਕ ਕਹਤ ਜਗਤ ਸਭ ਮਿਥਿਆ ਜਿਉ ਸੁਪਨਾ ਰੈਨਾਈ ॥ (Ang 1231)
(*Says Nanak, the whole world is totally false; it is like a dream at night.*)

Guru ji compares the existence of the world to a mountain made of smoke. It can be blown away easily and destroyed anytime. He questions our judgment asking us; "What makes you think that this world is real?"

ਇਹ ਜਗੁ ਧੂਏ ਕਾ ਪਹਾਰ ॥
ਤੈ ਸਾਚਾ ਮਾਨਿਆ ਕਿਹ ਬਿਚਾਰਿ ॥ (Ang 1186)
(*This world is just a mountain of smoke, what makes you think that it is real?*)

In the following shabad Guru ji goes into much more detail about what we see or deal with in everyday life. Guru Ji says all these things are false, they are just an illusion. They are not what they seem to be. Guru Ji says all the buildings are false, all the people who live in them are false. They look real but when you look closely they are found to be false or an illusion. Guru Ji says at the end that O God, You are the only Reality, everything else is false.

ਕੂੜੁ ਰਾਜਾ ਕੂੜੁ ਪਰਜਾ ਕੂੜੁ ਸਭੁ ਸੰਸਾਰੁ ॥
ਕੂੜੁ ਮੰਡਪ ਕੂੜੁ ਮਾੜੀ ਕੂੜੁ ਬੈਸਣਹਾਰੁ ॥

ਕੂੜੁ ਸੁਇਨਾ ਕੂੜੁ ਰੁਪਾ ਕੂੜੁ ਪੈਨਣ ਹਾਰੁ ॥
ਕੂੜੁ ਕਾਇਆ ਕੂੜੁ ਕਪੜੁ ਕੂੜੁ ਰੂਪੁ ਅਪਾਰੁ ॥
ਕੂੜੁ ਮੀਆ ਕੂੜੁ ਬੀਬੀ ਖਪਿ ਹੋਏ ਖਾਰੁ ॥
ਕੂੜਿ ਕੂੜੈ ਨੇਹੁ ਲਗਾ ਵਿਸਰਿਆ ਕਰਤਾਰੁ ॥
ਕਿਸੁ ਨਾਲਿ ਕੀਚੈ ਦੋਸਤੀ ਸਭੁ ਜਗੁ ਚਲਣਹਾਰੁ ॥
ਕੂੜੁ ਮਿਠਾ ਕੂੜੁ ਮਾਖਿਓ ਕੂੜੁ ਡੋਬੇ ਪੂਰੁ ॥
ਨਾਨਕੁ ਵਖਾਣੈ ਬੇਨਤੀ ਤੁਧੁ ਬਾਝੁ ਕੂੜੋ ਕੂੜੁ ॥   (Ang 468)

*(False is the king, false are the subjects, false is the whole world.*
*False are the mansions, false are the skyscrapers, false are those who*
*live in them.*
*False is gold, false is silver, false are those who wear them. False is the*
*body, false are the clothes, false are the beauties of the world.*
*False is the man, false is the woman, and they are defamed in false*
*relationships among them.*
*The false ones love falsehood, and they forget their Creator. With*
*whom should I become friends if all the world shall pass away.*
*False is sweet, false is honey, through falsehood, boat loads of people*
*have drowned.*
*Nanak respectfully states, without You Lord, everything is totally*
*false.)*

There are many more shabads in Sri Guru Granth Sahib
emphasizing the illusory nature of this world. One thing else
that Gurbani emphasizes is that God Himself has become this
world. There is nothing real in the world other than God. As the
quote goes "World is an illusion, only God is real and God has
become the world". Gurbani emphasizes the fact that the only
Reality of the world is Bhagwan, God, Paramatma or the One
Reality, Ek Onkar (ੴ). There is nothing else.

ਜਿਉ ਸੁਪਨਾ ਅਰੁ ਪੇਖਨਾ ਐਸੇ ਜਗ ਕਉ ਜਾਨਿ ॥
ਇਨ ਮੈ ਕਛੁ ਸਾਚੋ ਨਹੀ ਨਾਨਕ ਬਿਨੁ ਭਗਵਾਨ ॥ (Ang 1427)
*(Know that this world is like a night dream, Nanak says none of this*
*is true, but God)*

ਏਹੁ ਵਿਸੁ ਸੰਸਾਰੁ ਤੁਮ ਦੇਖਦੇ ਏਹੁ ਹਰਿ ਕਾ ਰੂਪੁ ਹੈ ਹਰਿ ਰੂਪੁ ਨਦਰੀ ਆਇਆ ॥   (Ang
922)

*(This whole world which you see is the image of the Lord, only the image of the Lord is seen.)*

ਸਭੁ ਗੋਬਿੰਦੁ ਹੈ ਸਭੁ ਗੋਬਿੰਦੁ ਹੈ ਗੋਬਿੰਦ ਬਿਨੁ ਨਹੀ ਕੋਈ ॥ (Ang 485)

(God is everything, God is everything, without God there is nothing at all.)

We will now try to understand the reality of the world from our experience. If we look at our experience closely we will see that every experience we have, is made out of a combination of thoughts, sensations and perceptions. Thoughts and sensations happen inside us. In other words, the inside world is experienced by thoughts and sensations. The outside world is experienced by perceptions, the five senses of seeing, hearing, touching, tasting and smelling. The five senses pick up the Information from the environment and then the mind analyzes it to classify the nature of experience being presented to us.

Let us take one of these examples. When we are looking at an object, what are we really looking at? We call this process a "process of perception". Perception is defined as a three part process: receipt of the sensory information, organization of the information and then interpretation of the information by our mind. When we look at an object our retina is receiving sensory information, then the Information is transmitted to our brain through the nerves, where it is organized. This information is then compared with the database in our memory to interpret the information and thus we recognize the object. **One thing that is very important to mention here is that the information received by our senses from the object is not exactly as we perceive the object. The sensory information that falls on our retina does not contain the qualities of the object like the shape, size and the color of the object. These qualities are deposited by our mind after the signal has been received and analyzed.** This is a very important point and needs to be understood properly. Let us look at color, for example. If we are looking at an apple, the color of the apple is not part of the initial information that falls on the retina. Science tells us that the objects do not have color of their own. It is really the color of light that is reflected from the object that we see. In fact, we do not even see the color of the reflected light, we just see a set of reflected light frequencies from the object. Based on these frequencies, our mind decides the color of the object. So it can be said that the color of the object is deposited by our mind and it is not transmitted with the signal coming from the object. Similarly the other qualities of the object like the shape, size are not part of the sensory information that is transmitted from the object to our retina. **These qualities make their appearance only after the mind has organized and interpreted the sensory information.** Once the sensory information is processed by the mind, then and only then, the qualities of the object make their appearance and not before. The process of seeing happens extremely fast giving the impression the qualities of the object are transmitted alongside the sensory information.

Looking at this process another way would make this point clearer. Imagine, the person who is looking at the apple, was hypnotized and was asked to believe that the apple was an onion. The hypnotized person will see the apple as an onion. If the hypnotized person is made to eat the apple it will taste like an onion to him and his eyes will shed tears which is typical when eating a raw onion. Why does the apple appear to be an onion to the hypnotized person? It is because he is depositing the qualities on the object based upon his own belief. The hypnotized person has been asked to believe it to be an onion, so he is depositing qualities of an onion on the object which is really an apple. Even though the nature of the sensory signal coming from the object is the same, the hypnotized person deposits different qualities on the object than a non- hypnotized person. This proves that the qualities of the object are deposited by the subject based on his or her own belief.

The question arises, what does the object, apple or onion look like before it's qualities are deposited by the mind. The object's media that is being perceived cannot be defined because it has no objective qualities. It is interesting to know that when we initially see the object, we do see the unqualified object, which is made out of undefinable media, but immediately the thought takes over and covers it with its own interpretation. Maybe someday a camera would be developed that would record the original image of the object in the undefinable media before the mind's interpretation takes over. Anyway, whenever we look at anything, we are looking at this undefinable media around us. After the information is organized and analyzed by our minds then we deposit the qualities on this media. The same process is carried over and over again for other senses like hearing, touching, tasting, and smelling. For example, when we taste something, the signal from the tasting process is received, it is interpreted and, then the taste is declared. Taste is not coming from outside, it is being deposited from inside. So our perception of the whole world depends upon our interpretation of the signals received from this undefinable media. This is the way we create the world around us.

An Indian saint uses an analogy to explain this process. Imagine if there is a little stump of a tree on a street corner and it is a little dark in the evening. When a policeman looks at the stump he may think it to be a thief that he has been looking for. If a thief looks at the same stump he may think it to be a policeman. A man may look at it and think it to be his sweetheart or a friend. It is the same stump of a tree that is being seen in various ways. The stump is the reality and different visions of the stump are the projections of various minds. Different persons are depositing different qualities on the same stump according to the states of their own mind. Similarly there is the undefinable media, and different persons are depositing different qualities on this media according to their state of mind. By projecting our minds and depositing qualities on the undefinable media we are creating the world around us. This understanding that when we see an object, our mind deposits the qualities on the object, leads us to a very radical conclusion. **That is, that we do not think about an object because we see it first, rather we see the object because we think about it.** There is no object out there until our mind has analyzed the incoming signal and deposited the qualities. That means the mind does not see the object in the beginning. The mind receives the signal first, decides it's qualities and then decides what the object is. So the mind sees the object only after thinking about it, and hence the statement that we see an object because we think about it. That proves that there is no material world, the way we believe, made out of brick and mortar but rather an interpretation of our mind, of the signal received. Swami Rama Tiratha, a Punjabi Saint answers a question in his book "In Woods of God Realization" Volume lll "Why does the world appear?" His answer "Because you see it. Do not see, and where is the world?". He further says that close your eyes, a fifth of the world is gone, close your ears and another fifth is gone. Do not use any of your senses and the whole world is gone. **In fact, that is what happens every night when we go to sleep. All our senses stop working and our waking world comes to an end.**

So there is no outside world. Our minds create the world out of the undefinable medium. Now we have to determine what is this outside medium, from where the signal is coming from? As discussed earlier this medium does not have any qualities, so it cannot be defined. In other words, the medium has no shape or size. If there is no shape or size, it is without boundaries and hence it is **infinite**. There are no qualities so it is **unknowable**. There is only one infinite unknowable entity that is Ek Onkar (ੴ), the Infinite Being or God. It is also called by other names like Atman, Awareness, or Consciousness. Gurbani says that Ek Onkar, the Infinite Being or God is unknowable and infinite.

ਅਗਮ ਅਗੋਚਰੁ ਅਲਖ ਅਪਾਰਾ ॥
ਕੋਇ ਨ ਜਾਣੈ ਤੇਰਾ ਪਰਵਾਰਾ ॥  (Ang 1060)

*(You are inaccessible, unfathomable, unknowable and infinite, nobody knows the extent of your creation.)*

So the Source of the signal consists of the One Reality, Ek Onkar, that pervades the whole cosmos and beyond. As stated earlier, this One Reality is called by many other names like God, Parmatama, Brahman etc. So whenever we see anything around us, as a matter of fact, we are looking at the One Reality (ੴ) or God and nothing else. Anything else is pure conjecturing or conceptualization by the mind.

ਜਹ ਜਹ ਦੇਖਾਂ ਤਹ ਤਹ ਸੁਆਮੀ ॥
ਤੂ ਘਟਿ ਘਟਿ ਰਵਿਆ ਅੰਤਰਜਾਮੀ ॥ (Ang 96)
*(Wherever I look, there I see my Lord and Master. You, the inner-Knower, are permeating each and everything.)*

ਜਹ ਜਹ ਦੇਖਉ ਤਹ ਤਹ ਸਾਚਾ ॥
ਬਿਨੁ ਬੂਝੇ ਝਗਰਤ ਜਗੁ ਕਾਚਾ ॥ (Ang 224)
*(Wherever I look, there I find the True Lord. Without proper understanding, the world argues in falsehood)*

So whatever our current experience, we are in fact, seeing the one Lord, and not the objects, animals, or people. The objects, animals, or people are just projections or conceptualization of our mind on the One Reality that is being perceived.

When we are watching a movie on a TV screen, we think we are watching objects, animals and people etc. in the movie. These objects, animals and people in the movie are of course not real. They are only a play of light. Light is modulating to make itself appear like these objects. In other words, light has become the objects, animals and people. Similarly the one Reality has become everything. There is nothing else out there other than the One Reality, Ek Onkar. One Reality is morphing itself into various shapes and forms of its own Will. This is how our world is created. It is called a play of the Lord.

ਆਪੇ ਖੇਲ ਕਰੈ ਸਭਿ ਕਰਤਾ ਐਸਾ ਬੂਝੈ ਕੋਈ ॥ (Ang 993)

*(The Creator Himself stages all the plays; rare are those who realize this)*

ਤੁਝ ਬਿਨੁ ਦੂਜਾ ਅਵਰੁ ਨ ਕੋਈ ਸਭੁ ਤੇਰਾ ਖੇਲੁ ਅਖਾੜਾ ਜੀਉ ॥ (Ang 97)
*(Without you there is no other, the entire universe is the arena of your play.)*

ਖੇਲ ਖੇਲ ਅਖੇਲ ਖੇਲਨ ਅੰਤ ਕੋ ਫਿਰ ਏਕ ॥ (Jaap Sahib)
*(After playing the world drama, when He stops the play, He becomes the One Reality again.)*

There is an example used in spiritual literature of a rope, being mistaken for a snake in the dark, instilling fear in the observer's mind. This is the type of illusion we are in, when we see the world. We are actually seeing a rope but interpreting it to be a snake. In other words, we are seeing God and interpreting It to be the world. Bhagat Ravidass Ji says that, "now I have understood this illusion where rope is mistaken for a snake. Because I have understood it now, I do not get fooled by this anymore".

ਰਾਜ ਭੁਇਅੰਗ ਪ੍ਰਸੰਗ ਜੈਸੇ ਹਹਿ ਅਬ ਕਛੁ ਮਰਮੁ ਜਨਾਇਆ ॥
ਅਨਿਕ ਕਟਕ ਜੈਸੇ ਭੂਲਿ ਪਰੇ ਅਬ ਕਹਤੇ ਕਹਨੁ ਨ ਆਇਆ ॥ (Ang 658)
*(Like the story of the rope mistaken for a snake, the mystery has now been explained to me, Like the many bracelets, which I mistakenly thought were different from gold, now I do not say that.)*

Bhagat Ji explains the illusion of the world in his own words. He makes two points in this shabad. First point is mistaking a rope for a snake, in the dark. Similarly, we mistake the One Reality for the world. There is no snake there, only a rope. The same way we are not seeing the world but the One Reality. The second point made by Bhagat Ji is that, like we see various bracelets and think they have their own independent existence, but, in reality, they are all made out of gold. Similarly, we believe that all the things in the world, animate or inanimate, have their independent existence, but in reality, are all made out of the One Reality. In summation, it can be said that everything is made out of God and nothing else. There are hundreds of shabads in Sri Guru Granth Sahib that state that He Himself has become everything. The operative word used in Gurbani is "aape" (ਆਪੇ) which means He Himself or She Herself. There is a great emphasis on the fact that He Himself or She Herself has become all the aspects of every situation. For example, if there is a fisherman doing fishing, Gurbani says that God Himself is the fisherman, the fish, the water, the net, the sinker, and the bait.

ਆਪੇ ਮਾਛੀ ਮਛੁਲੀ ਆਪੇ ਪਾਣੀ ਜਾਲੁ ॥
ਆਪੇ ਜਾਲ ਮਣਕੜਾ ਆਪੇ ਅੰਦਰਿ ਲਾਲੁ ॥ (Ang 23)
*(He Himself is the fisherman and the fish, He Himself is the water and the net, He Himself is the sinker, and He Himself is the bait.)*

Bhai Gurdas Ji describes how the Lord Himself or Herself is playing various roles in the drama of life.

ਆਪੇ ਰਸੀਆ ਆਪ ਰਸੁ ਰਸੁ ਰਸਨਾ ਭੋਈ ॥
ਆਪੇ ਭੁਖਾ ਹੋਇਕੈ ਵਿਚਿ ਜਾਇ ਰਸੋਈ ॥
ਭੋਜਨ ਆਪਿ ਬਣਾਇਦਾ ਰਸ ਵਿਚਿ ਰਸ ਗੋਈ ॥
ਆਪੇ ਖਾਇ ਸਲਾਹਿਕੈ ਹੋਇ ਤ੍ਰਿਪਤਿ ਸਮੋਈ ॥
ਦਾਤਾ ਭੁਗਤਾ ਆਪਿ ਹੈ ਸਰਬੰਗ ਸਮੋਈ ॥
ਆਪੇ ਆਪਿ ਵਰਤਦਾ ਗੁਰਮੁਖਿ ਸੁਖ ਹੋਈ (Bhai Gurdas Ji Vaar:2)
*(He Himself is the Enjoyer, He Himself is the Juice. He Himself is the tongue which relishes its taste. He Himself is posing to be hungry,* goes to the kitchen, He Himself cooks food putting in it all sorts tastes,
*He Himself eats the food, praises it and gets satisfied. He Himself is the Giver as well as the Receiver, and permeating through all, Knowing that He permeates among all, the Gurmukh feels immense pleasure.)*

*What is being said in this shabad is that God himself is playing all the roles. He himslf is the enjoyer, the tongue, the hunger, the food, the cook etc.etc.*

**Illusion Of The Inner World:**

The inner world consists of the body and the mind. Body is the outer appearance, while the mind is housed inside like a driver of the body. Mind is very complicated and is believed to be represented by the brain. The mind's main functions or faculties are, thinking, feelings, sensing, and perceiving. We believe the mind is the instrument with which we deal with internal and external world. We have talked about the outer world, and have concluded that the outer world is not what it appears to be. We have also proven that the outer world is none other than God Himself or Herself. Now we will explore the reality of our inner world like body, mind, and its components such as thoughts, feelings, and sensations.

## Illusion Of The Body:

While our mind is creating the outside world made of objects, animals and people based on the sensory signals coming from outside, the mind is also creating our body. Our body is just a concept from the sensory signals. We have two types of signals coming from our body, one by perception and the other by sensation. We can see our body and we can sense our body. Based on the combination of these sensory inputs, our mind conceptualizes and deposits qualities of the body on whatever it sees and senses. Like any other object in the world, our body is just the mind's interpretation of perception and sensation. Through its interpretation the mind gives the body a shape and size and believes it to be real. But Gurbani says that the body is false and we have mistakenly believed the false body to be real. By doing so, we are creating bondage for ourselves.

ਮਿਥਿਆ ਤਨੁ ਸਾਚੋ ਕਰਿ ਮਾਨਿਓ ਇਹ ਬਿਧਿ ਆਪੁ ਬੰਧਾਵੈ ॥ (Ang 1231)
(*We believe this false body to be real, in this way, we create bondage for ourselves.*)

ਮਿਥਿਆ ਤਨੁ ਧਨੁ ਕੁਟੰਬੁ ਸਬਾਇਆ ॥ ( Ang 268)
(*False are the body, wealth and all relations.*)

When we dream at night, the person in the dream is just a figment of our mind's imagination. Even though in the dream our body and other bodies appear to be very real, there is no real physical body in the dream whatsoever. When we wake up we see that nothing in the dream was real. Gurbani says that as the body in our dream is not real, the body in our waking state is not real either. In the dream, it is not that the body is not real, it does not even physically exist. Similarly, in our waking state the body does not have a physical existence. We have been hypnotized by our conditioning to believe that the body in the waking state is real. So we have to see through this hypnosis and understand that the body is unreal and is just a mind's imagination.

ਝੂਠਾ ਤਨੁ ਸਾਚਾ ਕਰਿ ਮਾਨਿਓ ਜਿਉ ਸੁਪਨਾ ਰੈਨਾਈ ॥ (Ang 218)
(*The body is false but they believe it to be real; it is like a dream at night.*)

Gurbani also says that the body is made out of clay and has no intelligence. In fact, Gurbani makes fun of the body being a doll of clay, and how tactfully it dances and runs around. Bhagat Kabir ji says that we are puppets of clay, but we call ourselves human beings.

ਮਾਟੀ ਕੋ ਪੁਤਰਾ ਕੈਸੇ ਨਚਤੁ ਹੈ ॥
ਦੇਖੈ ਦੇਖੈ ਸੁਨੈ ਬੋਲੈ ਦਉਰਿਓ ਫਿਰਤੁ ਹੈ ॥ (Ang 487)
(*How does the puppet of clay dance?*
*He looks and looks, listens and speaks, and keeps running around.*)

ਕਬੀਰ ਮਾਟੀ ਕੇ ਹਮ ਪੂਤਰੇ ਮਾਨਸੁ ਰਾਖਿਓ ਨਾਉ ॥ (Ang 1367)
(*Kabir, we are puppets of clay but we have named ourselves human beings.*)

We can conclude from this discussion that our bodies are not real even though they feel solid. Why do they feel solid is because of our lifetime of conditioning resulting in a kind of hypnosis. If we look at the body from a scientific point of view, we find it is really not as solid as it feels. Science tells us that it is made of tiny particles called protons, neutrons, and electrons, or atoms. The most interesting thing is that the atoms are nearly empty. The spacing between the protons-neutrons nucleus and the electrons is so vast that the body is almost 100% empty space (99.9999999% to be exact). How can the empty space be solid? Science says that if a 70 kg person was compressed and all the empty space was squeezed out of him, the person would fit into a particle of dust, and the whole human race would fit into a sugar cube. These numbers make one wonder why we are carrying such a big ego. Gurbani talks about the body being very unreliable and vulnerable. Gurbani says that any small hit can knock the body out.

ਕਹਾ ਬਿਸਾਸਾ ਇਸ ਭਾਂਡੇ ਕਾ ਇਤਨਕੁ ਲਾਗੈ ਠਨਕਾ ॥  (Ang 1253)
(*There is no reliability of this body, it breaks down with the slightest hit.*)

## Illusion Of The Mind:

Let us look at the mind to see if it is real. A close look reveals that the mind is made of thoughts, feelings, sensations, and perceptions. We have talked about the perceptions already in the illusion of the outer world. Here we will discuss the other components of the mind such as thoughts, feelings, and sensations. They all pertain to the inner world. When we think of something, feel something, or sense something it is called an inner experience. We also know from our direct experience that thoughts, feelings and sensations happen inside of us. We will investigate each one of these components of mind to see if they have any reality of their own, or if they are illusory. The test of their reality would be to see if they have an independent existence of their own and if they are conscious by themselves.

We will look at the situation from our personal experience. Look at the thoughts to begin with. Looking at any thought closely we find that the thought cannot hear, it cannot see or speak. So we can say that the thoughts are not a conscious entity.

The thoughts can be compared to water waves. It can be said that the waves are formed by the modulations of the body of water. The waves have their own form but in the final analysis they are made out of water. Thoughts are somewhat similar. They have their objective qualities, but in the final analysis they are made out of One Reality or Awareness. In fact, when Awareness modulates or vibrates it generates thought waves. So it can be concluded that the thoughts do not have independent existence of their own but are just modulations of Awareness like the waves are modulations of water. That means when Awareness wants to manifest something, it modulates in the form of a thought as a first step. It is similar to what happens in our daily life. When we want to do something we start the process by thinking about what we want to do. So thinking or thought is just an instrument to achieve the intended goal. It does not have an independent existence of its own. As said earlier, It is modulation of Awareness. When the modulation ends, the thought ends too. We can apply the same logic to other components of mind such as feelings and sensations, because they are also the modulations of Awareness. So we can say that thoughts, feelings and sensations do not have an independent existence of their own. They can be classified as modulations of One Reality or Awareness.

So we have found that the One Reality or Awareness is not only pervading the outer world, but the inner world too. Gurbani says in the following shabad that the Guru has given me this knowledge that there is One Reality both inside and out. Those who know this truth their doubts are removed.

ਬਾਹਰਿ ਭੀਤਰਿ ਏਕੋ ਜਾਨਹੁ ਇਹੁ ਗੁਰ ਗਿਆਨੁ ਬਤਾਈ ॥ (Ang 684)
(*Outside and inside, know that there is only One Reality, the Guru has imparted this wisdom to me.*)

ਸੋ ਅੰਤਰਿ ਸੋ ਬਾਹਰੇ ਬਿਨਸੇ ਤਹ ਭਰਮਾ ॥ (Ang 816)
(*Those who know that He is inside and out both, have all their doubts dispelled.*)

56

**Everything Is Inside Us:**

Everything inside us does not mean inside the body and the mind. The body and mind do not even have independent existence. So when it is said everything is inside us it means that everything is inside the One Reality or Awareness, that we are. The inner world is said to be much bigger than the outer world. In the ultimate analysis this may not be a correct statement either. Gurbani says that there is no outside world. Everything is inside.

ਘਰੈ ਅੰਦਰਿ ਸਭੁ ਵਥੁ ਹੈ ਬਾਹਰਿ ਕਿਛੁ ਨਾਹੀ ॥  (Ang 425)
(*Everything is within the home of your own Self, there is nothing outside it.*)

ਸਭ ਕਿਛੁ ਘਰ ਮਹਿ ਬਾਹਰਿ ਨਾਹੀ ॥
ਬਾਹਰਿ ਟੋਲੈ ਸੋ ਭਰਮਿ ਭੁਲਾਹੀ ॥  (Ang 102)
(*Everything is within the home of the Self, there is nothing outside. One who searches outside is deluded by doubt.*)

A simple way to get a feel of the fact that everything is inside us or inside Awareness, is that when we look at anything we find that we are aware of it, meaning the object we are looking at, is in our Awareness. No matter where we look, we look near or far, low or high, there is nothing outside our Awareness. In fact, we cannot see anything if we are not aware of it. We cannot see outside our Awareness, simply because if something is outside our Awareness, it would be logically unknown to us. Now the Awareness is infinite and as such nothing can be outside it. So we can safely say that everything is in our Awareness. One more point to be made here is that our Awareness is not our personal Awareness, but there is only one Awareness which is shared by all. This point has been discussed eralier in another artcle.

Use of the dream analogy may help to explain it more clearly. We all have dreams at night. When we go to sleep, our mind starts to dream. The mind creates a dream world and then enters in the dream world as a subject in the dream along with other subjects. Everything in the dream world including the subjects in the dream are contained in the mind of the dreamer. Same way the One Reality, Atman or Awareness is dreaming, so to speak, and has created its own dream world, which is our waking state world and we are all subjects in His or Her dream. Just as everything in the night dream is contained in our dreaming mind, similarly everything of the waking world is contained in our dreaming Atman or Awareness. Some readers may not have much trust in the dream analogy. It may be pointed out here that Gurbani has said many times that this world is just a dream and nothing more. There are about fifty specific shabads in Sri Guru Granth Sahib that state that this world is just a dream. In the last Bani "Salok Mahalla Nawan " there are three Slokes in one Bani, saying that the world is just a dream. In our everyday life when we get frustrated with someone who doesn't believe us, we say to him or her "If I have told you once, I have told you a thousand times", that this is so, you better believe me. Guru ji is probably saying the same thing to us that "If I have told you fifty times, I have told you fifty thousand times," that life is like a dream, you better believe me.

ਇਹੁ ਸੰਸਾਰੁ ਸਗਲ ਹੈ ਸੁਪਨੋ ਦੇਖਿ ਕਹਾ ਲੋਭਾਵੈ ॥ (Ang 1231)
(*This whole world is just a dream, why do you get enticed upon seeing it.*)

ਨਾਨਕ ਕਹਤ ਜਗਤ ਸਭ ਮਿਥਿਆ ਜਿਉ ਸੁਪਨਾ ਰੈਨਾਈ ॥ (Ang 1231)
(*Says Nanak, the whole world is totally false, it is like a dream at night.*)

Gurbani says that the nine continents of the earth, the markets, cities and streets are found inside this body. At another place Gurbani says there are countless objects in this body and a Gurmukh who attains the Truth comes to see them. Guru Ji is using the word "body" but He is really implying it to be One Reality, Atman or Awareness.

ਇਸੁ ਕਾਇਆ ਅੰਦਰਿ ਨਉਖੰਡ ਪ੍ਰਿਥਮੀ ਹਾਟ ਪਟਣ ਬਾਜਾਰਾ ॥ (Ang 754)
(*Within this body (Awareness) are the nine continents of the earth, markets, cities and streets.*)

ਕਾਇਆ ਅੰਦਰਿ ਗੜੁ ਕੋਟੁ ਹੈ ਸਭਿ ਦਿਸੰਤਰ ਦੇਸਾ ॥ (Ang 955)
(*Within this body (Awareness) is the Fort of the Lord,
And all lands and countries.*)

Our night dream analogy enables us to understand the fact that everything in the waking world is a grand illusion. There is nothing real in the dream world, similarly there is nothing real in our waking world, since waking world is also a dream. When we wake up in the morning from our night dream, we find that everything in the dream was illusory. There was no world, no dreamed subjects, and no nothing. It was only an imagination. Similarly, when we will wake up from the "waking world dream" we will find that everything in the waking state is illusory too. There is no world, no objects, and no nothing. **This is all a grand illusion.**

One thing I want to add at the end is that even though the waking world and its contents that you see are not real, You, the dreamer, is real. It is just like in the night dream, the dream world and its contents are not real, but the dreamer is real.

◆ ◆ ◆

# EGO, THE
# NONEXISTENT MASTER

ਹਉਮੈ ਵਿਚਿ ਸਭੁ ਜਗੁ ਬਉਰਾਨਾ ॥ ਦੂਜੈ
ਭਾਇ ਭਰਮਿ ਭੁਲਾਨਾ ॥ *(Ang 159)*

*(The entire world has gone insane
in egotism. In the love of duality,
it wanders in delusion.)*

When we talk of ego, generally, we think of people showing off and boasting of their achievements. They may be looking down upon other people and feeling superior to others. While this type of behavior is classified as egoistic, there is more to ego than just pride and arrogance. As we understand the ego more and more we will discover that we all suffer from this disease no matter if we are showing off or not, or if we are acting egoistic or not. In this article we will discuss this egoic phenomena in more detail and will try to understand what ego really is, and how to identify it. Ego is a very illusive and a nonexistent enemy. It stays hidden but it makes its home in everyone of us. We will also discover as we investigate it further that it is just a mirage, meaning it appears to exist but in fact it does not. People are suffering from it nonetheless. Guru Ji says that the whole world is suffering from ego. As a result, all of the humanity is going through a painful cycle of birth and death.

ਹਉਮੈ ਰੋਗਿ ਸਭੁ ਜਗਤੁ ਬਿਆਪਿਆ ਤਿਨ ਕਉ ਜਨਮ ਮਰਣ ਦੁਖੁ ਭਾਰੀ ॥
(Ang 735)
(*The entire world is afflicted by the disease of egotism. As a result, they suffer the terrible pains of birth and death.*)

ਹਉਮੈ ਵਿਚਿ ਜਗਤੁ ਮੁਆ ਮਰਦੋ ਮਰਦਾ ਜਾਇ ॥ (Ang 555)
(*In egotism, the world is dead, it dies again and again.*)

Ego is essentially a form of conditioning that we acquire right from our childhood. It has many layers of conditioning. First and the foremost layer of conditioning is that we believe that we are a body and mind combination. Almost all of us suffer from this. It will be shown, as we discuss it in more detail, that this belief is completely false. Next layer of ego is putting various labels on the body and the mind. We call the body short or tall, handsome or ugly, weak or strong, etc. Other labels we attach to the body mind is that I am a teacher, an engineer or a doctor etc. Once we are done with these labels then we start bragging about our labels and sometimes we brag to the point of arrogance. We consider ourselves superior to other people and start looking down on others. Our conditioning forces us to keep improving on our labels so we can become better than the other person. We normally think that arrogant and heartless behavior is the sign of ego, but it is not limited to that only. This behavior is simply a culmination of the process, which starts from our young age. Root cause of ego in our life is our mistaken belief in our identity, to be something that we are not. We believe ourselves to be bodies and minds which we are not. We will look into this in detail later in the article.

Looking at our daily behavior, we are all trying to get ahead of the other guy. We want to be richer and smarter than anyone else. If we are earning a decent living, we still want to make more. We have one car, we want one more, especially if our neighbor or relative has more than us. We are never satisfied with what we have. Guru ji describes our condition in Sukhmani

Sahib.

ਸਹਸ ਖਟੇ ਲਖ ਕਉ ਉਠਿ ਧਾਵੈ ॥
ਤ੍ਰਿਪਤਿ ਨ ਆਵੈ ਮਾਇਆ ਪਾਛੈ ਪਾਵੈ ॥ (Ang 278)
(*After earning a thousand, one runs after a hundred thousand. Satisfaction is not achieved by chasing after money.*)

We can find a number of examples in our culture that substantiate the claims made in the shabad above. Have you ever noticed a stock, commodity, or mercantile trading floor live? It is unnerving to watch hundreds of people gathered on the trading floor shouting their signals, making gestures with their hands to do buying or selling. There is so much noise over there and the conditions are so poor, one wonders what is wrong with all these guys. It appears that they all have gone mad. Why are they subjecting themselves to all of this? Some, of course, are plainly making their living but others are out there to make a fast buck to climb higher on the social ladder.

We have all seen what happens in political circles. Some people stay in their elected positions for decades until they are 80 or even 90 years old. Their ego won't let them step down. However, they all claim that they are working because they love to serve people. Lately we are seeing in the United States politics that older and older people are getting into races for office of the President, the highest office of the land. The campaign for this high office takes a ridiculous amount of effort, time, and money. It takes almost two years of canvassing across the country. It is extremely tiring and nerve racking. But people still put themselves willingly through all that. One wonders what is pushing them to go through all the hard work. It is clear that they are really serving their "ego". The ego won't let them get off the wheel and rest. They all want to claim the top prize. Recently there have been presidential candidates who are in their seventies trying to run for the office. It is very obvious that they are trying to serve their egos and not their country, by winning the top prize. Normally an old man in his seventies would be enjoying his or her retired life caring less for the top office.

Brokers and politicians are just two glaring examples but serving the ego is not limited to those situations only. We all want to work harder to make more money or keep ahead of the guy. We get up early in the morning and work all day, come home, get some sleep and there we go to work again. Why do we do all this? To make ourselves rich, smart, and famous. Of course, there are exceptions to this. Some people are just working to make a decent living to support their families. But when you see people in their seventies and higher, still working, it is obvious that something else is pushing them. Most of those people probably have enough to live on. This is not their fault because that is the way they have been brought up. Our culture encourages this behavior, because it rewards the people who come out on top in any event. It could be an athletic event, could be an academic event or even a religious event. Gurbani says that the whole of mankind is stuck in ego. Our daily living, our dealings, our statements to others, everything is based on ego. Gurbani says that unless we come to understand what this ego is we cannot find the Truth.

ਹਉ ਵਿਚਿ ਆਇਆ ਹਉ ਵਿਚਿ ਗਇਆ||ਹਉ ਵਿਚਿ ਜੰਮਿਆ ਹਉ ਵਿਚਿ ਮੁਆ ||
ਹਉ ਵਿਚਿ ਦਿਤਾ ਹਉ ਵਿਚਿ ਲਇਆ || ਹਉ ਵਿਚਿ ਖਟਿਆ ਹਉ ਵਿਚਿ ਗਇਆ ||
ਹਉ ਵਿਚਿ ਸਚਿਆਰੁ ਕੁੜਿਆਰੁ || ਹਉ ਵਿਚਿ ਪਾਪ ਪੁੰਨ ਵੀਚਾਰੁ ||
ਹਉ ਵਿਚਿ ਨਰਕ ਸੁਰਗਿ ਅਵਤਾਰੁ || ਹਉ ਵਿਚਿ ਹਸੈ ਹਉ ਵਿਚਿ ਰੋਵੈ ||
ਹਉ ਵਿਚਿ ਭਰੀਐ ਹਉ ਵਿਚਿ ਧੋਵੈ || ਹਉ ਵਿਚਿ ਜਾਤੀ ਜਿਨਸੀ ਖੋਵੈ ||
ਹਉ ਵਿਚਿ ਮੂਰਖੁ ਹਉ ਵਿਚਿ ਸਿਆਣਾ || ਮੋਖ ਮੁਕਤਿ ਕੀ ਸਾਰ ਨ ਜਾਣਾ ||
ਹਉ ਵਿਚਿ ਮਾਇਆ ਹਉ ਵਿਚਿ ਛਾਇਆ ||ਹਉਮੈ ਕਰਿ ਕਰਿ ਜੰਤ ਉਪਾਇਆ ||
ਹਉਮੈ ਬੂਝੈ ਤਾ ਦਰੁ ਸੂਝੈ || ਗਿਆਨ ਵਿਹੂਣਾ ਕਥਿ ਕਥਿ ਲੂਝੈ ||
ਨਾਨਕ ਹੁਕਮੀ ਲਿਖੀਐ ਲੇਖੁ || ਜੇਹਾ ਵੇਖਹਿ ਤੇਹਾ ਵੇਖੁ || (Ang 466)

*(In ego they come, and in ego they go.*
*In ego they are born, and in ego they die.*
*In ego they give, and in ego they take.*
*In ego they earn, and in ego they lose.*

*In ego they become truthful or false.*
*In ego they reflect on virtue and sin.*
*In ego they go to heaven or hell.*
*In ego they laugh, and in ego they weep.*
*In ego they become dirty, and in ego they wash clean.*
*In ego they lose social status and class.*
*In ego they are ignorant, and in ego they are wise.*
*They do not know the value of salvation and liberation.*
*In ego they love maya, and are kept in darkness by it.*
*In ego, mortal beings are created.*
*When one understands ego, then the Lord's Gate is known.*
*Without understanding, they babble and argue.*
*O Nanak, by the Lord's Command the destiny is written,*
*As the Lord blesses us, so we are seen.*

This egotism is not limited to social circles only; it goes deep into religious and spiritual spheres also. I remember one real episode which the writer witnessed himsef. It was a night kirtan get together "Raan Sabai" where a renowned and an accomplished ragi (Gurbani Singer) was doing kirtan. He was a religious man of great wisdom; and would preach others to live their daily life in accordance with the religious principles. The room where he was doing kirtan was packed full. The program was being held in a house where there was no stage and everyone including the ragis were sitting on the floor. It so happened that a child of about five years of age walked behind the ragi as the ragi was doing the kirtan. In doing so the child leaned on the ragi and caused some disturbance. The ragi did not like it and got enraged. He stopped doing kirtan and started saying, take this child away in a loud voice. Someone else in the Sangat, asked the ragi not to mind, saying it was just a little child, and pleaded to him to continue doing the kirtan. At this point the ragi got enraged even more and got up and walked away in anger. The irony of the situation is that the shabad that the ragi was reciting had the main message of telling the mind not to be egoistic. The shabad being recited was:

ਮਨ ਤੂੰ ਮਤ ਮਾਣੁ ਕਰਹਿ ਜਿ ਹਉ ਕਿਛੁ ਜਾਣਦਾ ਗੁਰਮੁਖਿ ਨਿਮਾਣਾ ਹੋਹੁ ॥   (Ang 441)
(*O mind, don't be so proud of yourself, as if you know something, O Gurmukh stay humble.*)

We also know from the history of "Panja Sahib" Gurudwara, where an old fakir Baba Vali Kandhari pushed a boulder off the hill to crush Guru Nanak, under the influence of his ego. He did that just because he did not want another fakir in the area. Baba Vali Kandhari had been meditating for years in that region and had gotten some notoriety among the people of the region. He had achieved some miraculous powers but he still was not able to get over his ego. Due to his "ego" he did not want Guru Nanak to be staying in the area, and as the history says that is the reason he pushed the boulder towards Guru Nanak.

The point of mentioning all these episodes is not to criticize anybody. This is to point out that ego runs deep in every body no matter what level of spiritual progress has been made by the person. It is in the rich and poor, young and old, educated and uneducated, religious and non-religious almost without exception.

ਮਨ ਅੰਤਰਿ ਹਉਮੈ ਰੋਗੁ ਹੈ ਭ੍ਰਮਿ ਭੂਲੇ ਮਨਮੁਖ ਦੁਰਜਨਾ ॥   (Ang 1317)
(*The disease of egotism is deep within the mind; the self willed manmukh and the evil beings are deluded by doubt.*)

ਨਾਨਕ ਹਉਮੈ ਰੋਗ ਬੁਰੇ ॥
ਜਹ ਦੇਖਾ ਤਹ ਏਕਾ ਬੇਦਨ ਆਪੇ ਬਖਸੇ ਸਬਦਿ ਧੁਰੇ ॥ (Ang 1153)
(*O Nanak, the disease of egotism is very deadly. Wherever I look I see the same disease. God Himself saves some by the grace of His Shabad.*

**Understanding The Ego:**

Gurbani's basic principle is that there is only One Reality (ੴ) that is pervading the universe. There is none other whatsoever. One Reality has become everything in the world including

65

ourselve, and whatever else we see around us. That means we as human beings are part and parcel of that One Realty, and not separate from It. But we ignore this fact and believe ourselves to be separate from the One Reality. We, additionally believe ourselves to be independent entities in our own right with a sense of doership. When we think of the One Reality we stand alongside the One Reality as an independent observer. Even though we have no existence of our own we believe that we do. This belief that we have an independent existence in our own right, with a sense of doership, is called ego. Ego is equated to a wall that separates us from the Lord. Gurbani calls us soul brides, and points out that the soul bride and the Lord live at one place but are separated by the wall of ego.

ਧਨ ਪਿਰ ਕਾ ਇਕ ਸੰਗਿ ਹੀ ਵਾਸਾ ਵਿਚਿ ਹਉਮੈ ਭੀਤਿ ਕਰਾਰੀ ॥ (Ang 1263)
(The soul bride and the husband Lord live together as one, but the hard wall of egotism stands between them.)

We not only believe that we have independent existence, we also believe that we have free will and have freedom to do anything we want, which is at odds with the facts.
Gurbani says that we do not have any free will of our own and everything is being done by the Lord.

ਹਾਥਿ ਹਮਾਰੈ ਕਛੂਐ ਨਾਹੀ ਜਿਸੁ ਜਣਾਇਹਿ ਤਿਸੈ ਜਣਾਵਣਾ ॥ (Ang 1086)
(*Nothing is in our hands, he alone knows whom You inspire to know.*)

ਜਿਤੁ ਜਿਤੁ ਲਾਵਹੁ ਤਿਤੁ ਲਗਿਹ ਹਰਿ ਨਾਥ ॥
ਨਾਨਕ ਇਨ ਕੈ ਕਛੂ ਨ ਹਾਥ ॥ ( Ang 271)
(*O Lord, wherever you assign them, they apply themselves,*
*O Nanak, there is nothing in their hands.*)

So the basic problem of ego is ignorance of our real identity. It can be defined as mistaking ourselves for something that we are not. Gurbani tells us that we all are One Reality, Atman or Awareness. But we, the Atman or Awareness, ignore the fact and voluntarily forget our real identity and believe ourselves to be a separate entity consisting of body and mind. We further adopt the limitations that really belong to the body and mind. These limitations are that I am a fragment and vulnerable. I will age and will eventually die.

**This "false belief" that we are body-mind combination and not Atman or Awareness, and the belief that we are separate independent entities in our own right, with a sense of doership, is what is termed as ego. So it is not only the persons that are proud and arrogant, possess ego, but also the others who do not exhibit such behavior, but still believe themselves to be a body-mind combination. They believe themselves to be something that they are not.**

One other point to be made here is that it is our belief, and not the body mind that constitutes ego. There is no problem with the body mind as long as we don't identify with them. Once we believe we are body minds we have created ego self.

Believing ourselves to be a separate independent entity we think of ourselves to be a fragment, and as such we go through the world with two main objectives. First is to acquire the other, objects or relationships to fulfill ourselves, and the second is to protect ourselves from the other, because we feel vulnerable. That is the reason we spend our lives acquiring things, relationships and activities that make us feel fulfilled or make us feel whole again. On the contrary, we spend our lives defending ourselves from the other because we feel the danger of being exterminated or eliminated.

Gurbani explains the problem of ego with an analogy, where a king goes to sleep on his throne and finds himself to be a beggar in his dream. So the king in the dream adapts a false identity of being a beggar, even though he is still the king of his land. Gurbani says just like the king we as Atman or Awareness have gone to sleep, and are in a dream right now. In our dream we have become human beings and have adopted false identities or false egos.

ਨਰਪਤਿ ਏਕੁ ਸਿੰਘਾਸਨਿ ਸੋਇਆ ਸੁਪਨੇ ਭਇਆ ਭਿਖਾਰੀ ॥
ਅਛਤ ਰਾਜ ਬਿਛੁਰਤ ਦੁਖੁ ਪਾਇਆ ਸੋ ਗਤਿ ਭਈ ਹਮਾਰੀ ॥ (Ang 657)
(*It is like the king, who falls asleep on his throne,*
*And dreams that he is a beggar,*
*His kingdom is intact, but separated from it, he suffers,*
*Such has become our condition.*)

To expand on the analogy further, the king in the analogy is our Real Self, Atman or Awareness. But our Real Self has gone to sleep and is right now in the state of dreaming. He has created His dream and has entered His dream as dreamed subjects. We are all the subjects in the dream. Like the king became a beggar in the dream, our Real Self has become human beings in His dream, which is all of us. The king was overcome by the illusion of becoming a beggar in spite of him still being a king. Similarly our Real Self appears to have been overcome by the illusion and has become human beings even though It is still pervading in full glory. When we say our Real Self appears to have been overcome by the illusion, we are talking about Ourselves. We as Real Self have been overcome by illusion and have become human beings. Our essence is Atman or Awareness in spite of the roles we all have assumed as human beings. We have become egos under the spell of our own dream.

**How Is Ego Formed:**

We have seen that ego consists of us believing ourselves to be body minds rather than Atman or Awareness. How did we start believing ourselves to be body minds? If we examine our life closely starting with our birth, we find that our life is full of conditioning. When a child is born he or she is a clean slate. There may be some past life karmas but we are not going to discuss those here. As the child grows up he or she is taught all kinds of things about the family, surroundings and the outside world. One thing else he or she is taught is about who he or she is. This is where things go wrong. There are no specific instructions to tell him or her about who he or she is. The conditioning of the child progresses naturally as the child is brought up. He or she is given a name and when the child is called by that name over and over again, the child comes to know his name and responds accordingly. That is the first label of conditioning that the child receives. The child is then told she or he looks beautiful or handsome, has a fair or dark complexion. The child is also told that he or she is so tall, and how fast he or she is growing. If you notice, everything the child is being told about himself or herself is about his or her physical body. So the child understands, and rightfully so, that he or she is the body. If the body has some sensation like pain or injury the child thinks it is he or she who is having the pain or injury. What has happened is that the child has become conditioned that he or she is a body, which is a completely false belief.

Of course, we cannot blame the child, it is the parents or the teachers and society that is to blame. This conditioning continues throughout the child's life, who has become a grown up person now. The conditioning continues during education through schools and universities. One more piece of conditioning that gets added with the education, is that the person acquires a mind as he or she gets educated, and then becomes a combination of body and mind. Education, of course, develops the mind in the areas of math, science, business etc. for dealing with the world. But it adds conditioning nonetheless. It firms up the belief even further that he or she is not only body but mind also. Nowhere in our education system, a person is given the correct education about who he or she really is. Our education system needs to be reformed to include a course or two to at least inform the person about his true identity.

As we go through our life we pick up additional conditioning. We become engineers, doctors or teachers. We become fathers, mothers, uncles, aunts etc. We keep on adding label after label on top of our bodies and minds. All these labels are like building blocks of the house of ego. We end up with thousands of labels that make our ego so huge that it becomes impenetrable. The first mistake that was made was that we were made to believe that we are bodies and minds. That is like laying a false foundation. We keep adding more and more labels on that false foundation as we get older. That is the reason why older people have bigger egos. You have heard of the phrase "you can't teach an old person new tricks", this is why.

Of course, if you tell anyone that they have an ego, they would never admit it, and they would defend themselves with all their might. If properly understood we find that everyone of us has ego. This is because of our basic belief that we are the body and minds. Until we do away with the belief, we can't really eradicate ego. We see people trying to lead a very humble life to portray themselves to be free of ego. That is a very good characteristic if one is sincere, but that is not getting rid of ego. Believing oneself to be a body; and acting humble, really is a sort of "negative ego". Normally we think ego is showing off and aggrandizing oneself, but ego works the other way too. We can believe ourselves to be worthless and unlucky. That would be classified as a negative ego. Ego is ego, no matter one aggrandizes oneself or one humbles oneself, as long as one adheres to the false identity.

Sant Maskeen Ji talks about this, in one of his Katha episodes. He says that one person he knew, would come everyday to listen to his katha. Sant Ji would exchange greetings with him and ask him every day how he was. He would reply "I am like the dust of your feet" trying to portray himself as very humble and ego free. Sant ji was very smart and recognized that this person was just faking being humble. So next time when Sant ji met this person, Sant Ji asked him the same question, how he was. The person had the same answer, I am like the dust of your feet. Sant ji said, yes, I know that, in a serious tone. The person was shocked to hear Sant ji's words. Sant ji says in his katha that the person never faced him again. The point is that if the person was sincerely humble and free of ego, he would not mind what Sant Ji said and would not avoid him later. One cannot be ego free by just being humble. That is a misunderstanding. Unless one gets rid of the fundamental problem of false identity, there is no dissolution of ego. Thinking that you can do away with ego by just being humble is like killing a tree by cutting its branches. In fact, the tree will become stronger and grow stronger than before. Until the roots of the tree are taken out it will always try to come back. Same is true of ego, unless the basic mistake which created the ego, is corrected, the problem cannot be fixed. If the ego is just superficially suppressed it will come back even stronger.

## Ego Is Really Nonexistent:

Even though most of us suffer from ego, it can be categorically stated that the ego is just an illusion. It is unbelievable how all of us could suffer from something that does not even exist. As stated before, the ego is just a belief, whereby we mistake ourselves to be body and mind and thereby create an egoic self, sometimes called a separate self. Gurbani says that this becomes the cause of one's coming and going.

ਮਨੁ ਤਨੁ ਥਾਪਿ ਕੀਆ ਸਭੁ ਅਪਨਾ ਇਹੋ ਆਵਣ ਜਾਣਾ ॥ (Ang 882)
(*They mistake themselves to be body and minds, this becomes the cause of their transmigration.*)

There is an interesting story about the ego being non-existent. This story has been taken from a video by Rupert Spira, an English Spiritual teacher.

Once a master lived with his servant in a big house on the bank of a river. The master was very elusive and never showed his face to the servant. The servant on the other hand was a very obedient and dedicated person. He was so faithful and loyal to the master that he would do anything for the master. He would do all the chores of the house and cook food for the master. He would fight with other people for his master, and would defend his master if someone said anything negative about him.

The strange thing was that the servant had never seen his master. But he knew the master lived in the house. He never picked up the courage to go inside the house and look for the master. The servant stayed in his own quarter which was also located in one corner of the house. One day, the servant's friend asked him to go inside the house and see what his master looked like. Initially, the servant hesitated to do so but then agreed. So one day he went into one room to look for the master, but he did not see anybody. He did not feel the courage to go into the other rooms so he came out without going further. But his friend pushed him to check the other rooms. So the next day he went into another room and still did not find his master. He checked in the third room and still did not find anybody. Eventually, he went through the whole house and did not find the master. He could not believe himself, so he checked the rooms again and again and still could not find anybody. He was wonderstruck and could not come to terms with this. How could he have served a master all his life that he had never seen, and now he cannot even find? The servant said to himself, It looks like I have fooled myself, and have been serving a non-existing master all my life.

We may laugh at the servant's folly but this is our story too. We are all serving a master called "ego" in us that we have never seen or met. In fact, we are so used to it that we never even think that we are serving our ego. We may not have realized it, but we too have been working to please our nonexistent master. Why is the ego called a nonexistent master? It is because our false belief that we are body minds. We are really Atman or Awareness but we have come to believe that we are body minds. If it can be proven that we are not body minds, it should lead us to conclude that the ego is nonexistent or just a make-believe entity. We will go through a brief exploration of our own experience, that will show that we are not body minds. We have discussed this false identity issue before in other articles but will briefly go through this again to maintain continuity in the article.

We normally believe that we are body minds. Mind can further be broken down into thoughts, feelings, sensations and perceptions. Let us look at these one by one to see if we are body, mind or something else. Look at the body first. All of us know that we are not bodies even though we think otherwise. Body is just an accumulation of food which comes out of the soil. So the body is essentially made out of soil. Gurbani even calls the body simply a lump of clay.

ਮਾਟੀ ਤੇ ਜਿਨਿ ਸਾਜਿਆ ਕਰਿ ਦੁਰਲਭ ਦੇਹ ॥ (Ang 809)
(*He fashioned you from clay, and made you a priceless body.*)

The body is insentient too, meaning it has no awareness of its own. How can we be the body that is made out of clay and is not even sentient? So we can conclude that the body is not what we are for sure.

Now let us look at the mind and analyze all its components like thoughts, feelings, sensations, and perceptions. Look at the thoughts to start with. We experience thoughts that rise in us. When a thought comes up we are aware of it. A few seconds later the thought disappears, we are aware of that too. When the thought disappears we are still there watching it disappear. We are aware of the thoughts hence we are separate and different from thoughts. Looking at the feelings. Let us imagine we are feeling sad. Like the thought we are aware of the feeling of sadness. We can even know when this feeling started and when it disappeared. So we watch the feeling of sadness appear, stay for a while and then disappear. We are aware of all our feelings and hence are separate from them. That proves that we are not feelings either. We can apply the same logic to the other characteristics of the mind and conclude that we are not those either. By proving that we are not the components of mind such as thoughts, feelings, sensations and perceptions, we can conclude that we are not the mind either. **Now we have proven that we are neither body nor mind, which implies that the ego is nonexistent and it's just our imagination. With the understanding that we are not body minds, the ego has nothing to stand upon.** We are really Atman or Awareness, as has been stated before. This Atman or Awareness is the one that is aware of the body and the mind both, and is beyond or higher than both.

We have made a very important discovery that we are not body minds but we are Atman or Awareness. However, as long as we believe ourselves to be body minds, we will suffer from ego. But as soon as we upgrade our belief that we are Atman or Awareness, the ego disappears. That is why Gurbani says the ego is a grave problem but it's cure is found in the ego too. What it means is that it is just a matter of mindset. We have a choice to believe ourselves to be body minds or Atman/Awareness. As long as we believe ourselves to be body minds, there will be ego, but when we believe ourselves to be Atman or Awareness, the ego is no more.

ਹਉਮੈ ਦੀਰਘ ਰੋਗੁ ਹੈ ਦਾਰੂ ਭੀ ਇਸੁ ਮਾਹਿ ॥
ਕਿਰਪਾ ਕਰੇ ਜੇ ਆਪਣੀ ਤਾ ਗੁਰ ਕਾ ਸਬਦੁ ਕਮਾਹਿ ॥ (Ang 466)
(*Ego is a chronic disease, but it contains its own cure as well.*
*If the Lord grants His Grace, they will meditate on the Shabad and thus get rid of their ego*)

The shabad says we can avail of the cure that is contained in the ego, if we are blessed with God's Grace and as a result meditate on Shabad. Shabad here means the Lord, Atman or Awareness. Essentially, what is being said here is that if we identify ourselves with the Lord, Atman or Awareness rather than the body mind, we will eradicate our ego.

One more way to look at the ego and it being nonexistent, is to look at our dreams. We all dream at night. What happens in dreams is that our mind dreams up a world and then the mind gets into the created dream, in the form of a dreamed subject. The dreamed subject thinks of itself to be an independent entity in its own right made of body and mind. It believes itself to be separate from everybody else in the dream. In essence, the dreamed subject exhibits the behavior of an ego just like we do in the waking state. But when we wake up we find that the dreamed subject had no independent existence. There was no person in the dream, it was just a thought or imagination. The question arises that If there was no real person in the dream, how can there be an ego? There was no person, so there could not be any ego in the dream. In other words the ego in the dream was nonexistent. Our real life can be compared to the dream. In fact, Gurbani compares our real life to a dream quite a few times. God, the Infinite Being, Atman or Awareness is having a dream of Her own and has manifested a world in the dream and then has entered in her own dream and has become all of us. Just like the dreamed subject in our dream has no real existence, we as God's dreamed subjects have no real existence. If we don't have real existence, how can there be ego? This proves that the ego is just a misunderstanding and is nonexistent. Gurbani says that our body in the waking state is just like the one we have in our dream at night, it is false.

ਝੂਠਾ ਤਨੁ ਸਾਚਾ ਕਰਿ ਮਾਨਿਓ ਜਿਉ ਸੁਪਨਾ ਰੈਨਾਈ ॥ (Ang 218)
(*The body is false, but they believe it to be true, the body is like the one in the dream at night.*)

Gurbani says that the ego is for those who do not recognize their Real Essence. But for those who recognize their Real Essence and stay with it, there is no ego. This is one way to eradicate the ego.

ਆਪੁ ਪਛਾਣੈ ਘਰਿ ਵਸੈ ਹਉਮੈ ਤ੍ਰਿਸਨਾ ਜਾਇ ॥ (Ang 57)
(*One who recognizes one's Real Essence, and dwells there, his or her ego and thirst for worldly things will disappear*)

◆ ◆ ◆

# WE DO NOT HAVE
# FREE WILL

ਜਿਤੁ ਜਿਤੁ ਲਾਵਹੁ ਤਿਤੁ ਲਗਹਿ ਹਰਿ ਨਾਥ ॥
ਨਾਨਕ ਇਨ ਕੈ ਕਛੂ ਨ ਹਾਥ ॥ (Ang 271)

*(O Lord, wherever You assign them,
they apply themselves. O Nanak,
nothing is in their hands.)*

T his question has been around for a long time. There has
been a lot of discussion on the topic of whether we as
human beings have anything in our hands or it is all
destined for us. Can we do anything to change our destiny or is it
fixed forever? If We have freedom of will, why don't we succeed
in everything we do? We shall look at these questions in detail
to see what our experience tells us, and at the same time reflect
what Gurbani says about it.

Before we get into the heart of discussions we should clarify who
it is we are talking about, who has free will or not. We are talking
about ourselves as human beings. We are defining ourselves as a
body and mind combination which we call a person or a human
being. We further believe that we are independent entities
having a sense of doership. Additionally, we think that we
possess individual awareness. This is what we think ourselves
to be based on our current beliefs. Why is this being brought
up here, because even though we believe ourselves to be body-

mind entities, this assumption is not correct. We will discuss this later in this article. But for now let us proceed with what we think ourselves to be, which is, a body mind entity, with a sense of doership, and having its own parcel of awareness. So when we talk about who has free will or not, we are talking about the body mind entity that we think ourselves to be. Let us look at our daily experience. We do all kinds of activities all day long and we think that we have complete freedom to do something or not to do something. We can make decisions, good or bad, and then feel free to act on our decisions. We feel that freedom is our birthright and think it cannot be taken away from us. If somebody tells us that we can or cannot do something, then we strongly protest against the one who is limiting our freedom. Our social culture gives us all the freedom, only limiting the behaviors that could be harmful to the society. Even our governments grant us constitutional rights for freedom and liberty.

**Even though we feel complete freedom to do anything as we wish, there are some logical arguments that can be made from our experience that prove that our concept of being free may not be fundamentally correct after all.** We will look at some of the arguments based on our experience, that support the fact that our body minds do not have free will. These arguments will be varified and tested from Gurbani's viewpoint. We will also discuss some of the objections that possibly can be raised against the arguments.

First of all, let us look at our body, which is an extremely complicated structure. There are millions of reactions going on in our body simultaneously. There are about a dozen systems in the body such as digestive system, blood circulatory system, nervous system, endocrine, immune etc, etc. There are many chemical reactions going on in each system and the body overall. Last time I googled to look for the number of reactions that are taking place in the body at one time I was shocked to see the number. Even though I knew the number would be a big number, I was still amazed to find the number to be so high. According to one of the science websites, there are thirty seven thousand billion billion (37 with 21 zeros) reactions going on in the body every second. That is really an astronomical number. The number may be off by a million or or a billion but it is still an unimaginably high number. I don't understand how they even measure such a high number. Anyway, now the question is how many of these reactions do we have control over? Most of us have no idea that so many reactions are going on in the body that we call our own. Additionally, we don't know how many reactions we control. The fact that there are so many reactions taking place and we don't even know how many of these we control, should be enough to convince us that we have no free will. If you ask a man on the street how many things you control in your life, he or she will, probably, name two or three items. Many of us believe that we have control over our thoughts and our actions. Control of two or three things out of trillions is no control at all.

First uttering of Siri Guru Granth Sahib is Ek Onkar. Ek Onkar means that there is only One Reality in the universe. What this implies is that everything except this One Reality, is unreal. That includes everything living and non living. It includes all human beings, all the animals, all birds and all the perceived universe. In fact, this one Reality has become everything in the universe, and hence nothing else but this One Reality exists.

ਤਿਸੁ ਬਿਨੁ ਦੂਜਾ ਅਵਰੁ ਨ ਦੀਸੈ ਏਕਾ ਜਗਤਿ ਸਬਾਈ ਹੇ ॥ (Ang 1072)
(*There is no one except Him. The One Lord has become the whole universe.*)

There are many other shabads in Siri Guru Granth Sahib that assert this fact over and over, that there is only Him pervading the universe. It means that there is no stand alone universe out there, it is only Him, God, the One Reality. If nothing is real in the universe except the Lord, then all of us have no existence as individual entities. Consequently, the question of our free will should not even arise. How can there be a free will for an entity that does not even exist?

Let us look at another argument that tells us that we have no free will. If we look closely at our thoughts we find that we do not control them. Let us consider an example. If one could just keep one thought in mind "I do not mind what happens" and live by it sincerely under all circumstances, then he will never have any kind of pain and suffering. Imagine just one thought can make one bear all the problems in life. If some tragedy happens in life, which will normally throw one off completely, but if one could stick to the thought "I don't mind what happens" then there would be no suffering. But we all know that we cannot control our minds and as a result we are at the mercy of the circumstances. This proves that we do not have the free will, otherwise we would avoid suffering just with one simple thought made out of six words.

This idea is similar to the one of surrender to the Will of God (ਭਾਣਾ ਮੰਨਣਾ) emphasized in Gurbani. Surrender to the will of God means, no matter what happens we just accept it. No ifs and buts. We face a tragedy, it was the Will of God, so just accept it. Gurbani also says that one who surrenders to the Will of God will always be happy.

ਭਾਣਾ ਮੰਨੇ ਸੋ ਸੁਖੁ ਪਾਏ ਭਾਣੇ ਵਿਚਿ ਸੁਖੁ ਪਾਇਦਾ ॥ (Ang 1063)
(*One who surrenders to the Lord's Will finds peace and happiness, he finds peace and happiness in the Lord's Will.*)

ਜਿਨੀ ਪਛਾਤਾ ਹੁਕਮੁ ਤਿਨ ਕਦੇ ਨਾ ਰੋਵਣਾ ॥ (Ang 523)
(*Those who recognize His or Her Command, they never have to weep.*)

But how many of us can live by that one thought or surrender to the Will of God. Only the realized souls, who know and believe that everything is happening through the Will of God, can live by it. But for a normal person it is almost impossible to surrender to the will of God.

We all know that all our actions are preceded by thoughts. Anything that is done by us is preceded by the thought to do it. Really, no thought, no action. It is just so simple. So if we could control our thoughts, we could essentially control our actions. We have established earlier that we cannot control our thoughts so how can we control our actions?

We are all familiar with our explosive behavior when someone offends us. Somebody pushes the wrong button and we become resentful or defensive. When someone offends us, why do we become defensive? This is because a thought arises in us automatically that I am being attacked. Now rather than controlling the rising thought we start acting on it and become defensive, and are ready to fight. Most of us are not even aware of the rising thought and our response. If we are not even aware of the situation, how can we control our actions? This is why it is said that we are asleep even while we are awake. We have no control over our behavior because we are sound asleep. That shows that we do not have free will.

We do see that this world is full of rich and poor people and many others at different levels in between. Nobody wants to be poor. Everybody wants to be rich and famous. If we had free will, why would anyone be poor? Everyone would want to become rich if he or she could help it. Since we don't see everyone rich in the world it tells us that it is beyond our control. Gurbani says that if we could get things by our own efforts then everyone would be rich or lucky.

ਆਪਣ ਲੀਆ ਜੇ ਮਿਲੈ ਤਾ ਸਭੁ ਕੋ ਭਾਗਠੁ ਹੋਇ ॥ (Ang 156)
(*If people could get it with their own efforts, then everyone would be rich.*)

Gurbani tells us that there is nothing man can do. Whatever the Lord wants him to do is done by him. The truth is that we do not have anything in our hands. The Lord makes us do whatever He or She wants.

ਕਹੁ ਮਾਨੁਖ ਤੇ ਕਿਆ ਹੋਇ ਆਵੈ ॥
ਜੋ ਤਿਸੁ ਭਾਵੈ ਸੋਈ ਕਰਾਵੈ ॥  (Ang 277)
(*Say what a human being can do.*
*Whatever pleases God is what He causes us to do.*)

It is not only that there is financial inequality among people, there are all kinds of other inequalities. Some people are healthy, others are not, some people are smart, others are not, some people are kind and others are not. It is very obvious that we are all born with some traits specific to us, and these traits are assigned to us by the Lord. I have seen people who want to stay drunk all day long without any regard to their families; and then there are others who hate the idea of drinking. The inequities are sometimes explained by the law of Karma. But the law of karma only shifts the responsibility from this life to previous life, but if you keep going to previous births and end up with the first birth, what was the reason for inequality in that first birth. There is no answer for that except to admit it is all God's Will. This karma theory has been questioned by Gurbani also.

ਸਾਸਤੁ ਨ ਹੋਤਾ ਬੇਦੁ ਨ ਹੋਤਾ ਕਰਮੁ ਕਹਾਂ ਤੇ ਆਇਆ ॥  (Ang 973)
(*When there were no Shastras and no Vedas, then where did the karma come from?*)

That is why life is said to be a dream. In the dream all kinds of characters appear to pop up with different roles at different levels. Some characters in the dream are rich, some poor, some fortunate and others are unfortunate. A character in the dream has no idea why all the disparity. In fact, all the disparity is brought into manifestation by the dreamer's own mind. People in the dream are not poor or rich because of their previous karmas, it is just how the dreamer's dream unfolded. There was no criteria that the rich person did better karma than the poor person. Similarly this life is God's dream where He Himself has become all of us playing different roles at different levels. He has made Himself rich in one person and poor in the other. In essence, all of this is done by the Lord Himself. We have no independent will of our own in this grand show of the Almighty.

Gurbani emphasizes over and over again that nothing is in a person's hand. There are probably hundreds of shabads in Sri Guru Granth Sahib concerning this topic. Gurbani's message is very clear and stern that there is no free will and everything is decided by the Almighty for us. According to Gurbani, our life's program is all preplanned. We are told that we should surrender to the Will of God. In fact, this surrender to the Order (Hukam) of the Lord is one of essential requisites to be able to meet the Lord.

The shabad listed below appears on page one of Sri Guru Granth Sahib. In the shabad Guru Ji gives us insight into our free Will. Guru Ji tells us, unequivocally, that there is no free will for human beings. Everything is in His Command, called Hukam. Guru Ji says by His command the universe is created. This Hukam is indescribable. By His Command human beings are created, and by His Command people get higher or lower status in life. By His command people get comfort and suffering in life. Some people are blessed with His kind Grace but others are made to transmigrate from one incarnation to another forever. Everything, bar none, is within His Command. Guru Ji asserts that if one can truly understand His Command, then he will not boast about his or her ego.

ਹੁਕਮੀ ਹੋਵਨਿ ਆਕਾਰ ਹੁਕਮੁ ਨ ਕਹਿਆ ਜਾਈ ॥
ਹੁਕਮੀ ਹੋਵਨਿ ਜੀਅ ਹੁਕਮਿ ਮਿਲੈ ਵਡਿਆਈ ॥
ਹੁਕਮੀ ਉਤਮੁ ਨੀਚੁ ਹੁਕਮਿ ਲਿਖਿ ਦੁਖ ਸੁਖ ਪਾਇਅਹਿ ॥
ਇਕਨਾ ਹੁਕਮੀ ਬਖਸੀਸ ਇਕ ਹੁਕਮੀ ਸਦਾ ਭਵਾਈਅਹਿ ॥
ਹੁਕਮੈ ਅੰਦਰਿ ਸਭੁ ਕੋ ਬਾਹਰਿ ਹੁਕਮ ਨ ਕੋਇ ॥
ਨਾਨਕ ਹੁਕਮੈ ਜੇ ਬੁਝੈ ਤ ਹਉਮੈ ਕਹੈ ਨ ਕੋਇ ॥   (Ang 1)

(*By His Command the universe is created*, His Command cannot be described.
*By His Command human beings come into existence,*

*By His Command, glory and greatness is achieved.*
*By His Command some are high and some are low,*
*By His written Command, pain, pleasure are encountered.*
*Some, by His Command, are blessed and forgiven,*
*Others, by His Command, wander aimlessly forever.*
*Everyone is subject to His Command, no one is beyond It.*
*O Nanak, one who understands His Command, have no ego)*

Scientist Benjamin Libet of University of California did an experiment in his laboratory in 1983 to research the issue of free will. Libet set up an experiment in his laboratory and asked volunteers to tap a target on a screen with their fingers at will, freely choosing the time of their action. They were, however, asked to note the time when they made a conscious decision to tap the target. The volunteers were simultaneously monitored with an Electroencephalogram (EEG) to study their brain activity during the experiment. The brain activity showed very interesting information. The EEG revealed an electrical activity occurred in their brain "350 milliseconds" before the time they made a conscious decision to perform the action of tapping the target. A graph is shown below for reference.

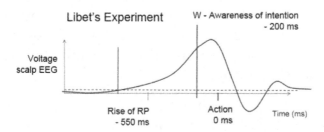

Conclusion: The brain shows signs of being about to produce muscle motion about 0.4 seconds before we report that we are AWARE of having made a decision to move our muscles.

Analysis of the Libet research showed that the decision was made by the brain, before the volunteer made a conscious decision to tap the target. It only made it into the consciousness of the volunteer three hundred fifty milliseconds later.

The graph above shows the subject's brain voltage as he or she goes through the experiment. The brain voltage is called rising potential (RP). In the graph the subject becomes aware of his or her intention to act at point "W", which 200 milliseconds before the action is complete at point 0 milliseconds (ms). But the brain signal starts rising at 550 milliseconds before the action is complete; which is 350 milliseconds before the subject becomes aware of his intention to act. So the experiment shows that the activity in the subject's brain starts 350 milliseconds before the subject consciously decides to initiate the action. Does this experiment show that we do not make our decisions ourselves, but there is some mysterious force acting on our brains which makes the decision for us before we even decide to do something? It appears that we just follow this mysterious force which is making the decision for us. This mysterious force is acting on our brains, informing it of the decision already made. Once the brain gets the information then it just compiles with it. But at the same time the subject believes that he or she is really making the decision. Now this experiment by Benjamin Libet has been a topic of discussion among scientists for a long time. Some scientists have confirmed the results and others have picked at the conclusions drawn. We won't go into the discussions between the scientists but we will review this finding from Gurbani's point of view.

There are many shabads in Sri Guru Granth Sahib that emphasizing that everything is being done by God Himself. Here are a few listed below.

ਜੋ ਕਿਛੁ ਕਰੇ ਸੋ ਆਪੇ ਆਪੈ ॥
ਬੁਧਿ ਸਿਆਣਪ ਕਿਛੁ ਨ ਜਾਪੈ ॥ (Ang 107)
(*Whatever He does, He does it by Himself,*
*No one else's intellect and wisdom works there.*)

ਆਪੇ ਹੁਕਮੁ ਚਲਾਇਦਾ ਜਗੁ ਧੰਧੈ ਲਾਇਆ ॥ (Ang 789)
(*He Himself directs the world with His Command, and assigns them to worldly tasks.*)

ਆਪੇ ਕਰੇ ਕਰਾਏ ਕਰਤਾ ਜਿਉ ਭਾਵੈ ਤਿਵੈ ਚਲਾਇਦਾ ॥ (Ang 1061)
(*The Creator Himself acts and inspires all to act; as He wills, He leads us on.*)

These shabads above tell us that the Lord Almighty Himself directs all of us in our life and assigns us to various tasks. We think we are planning and controlling what happens in our life but Gurbani says that is just wishful thinking. Could it be that Benjamin Libet's experiment is confirming what Gurbani is saying in the shabads above? Could this mysterious force that instigates action in the brain in Libet's experiment, be the Force that is being referred to in the shabads? Could it be the Lord's secret Command working through our neurological system to direct us to do things? In the shabads above we are being told that the Lord makes us move according to His will. He directs us to do various things. We act like robots, being controlled by a WiFi type signal that comes directly from something beyond.

ਨਕਿ ਨਥ ਖਸਮ ਹਥ ਕਿਰਤੁ ਧਕੇ ਦੇ ॥
ਜਹਾ ਦਾਣੇ ਤਹਾ ਖਾਣੇ ਨਾਨਕਾ ਸਚੁ ਹੇ ॥ (Ang 653)
(*Lord has our noose in His hand, and our karmas push us on,*
*Wherever our food is, there we go to eat it,*
*O Nanak, this is the truth.*)

Gurbani calls this signal appearing in our brains, a kind of noose that is used in India to control the movement of animals. We all are directed by this signal to do things. It appears that the signal comes to us in the form of a thought. We make statements like "I didn't do something because I didn't think of it". Or "I did something because I thought of it" or "thought came to me out of the blue at the appropriate time". We all know that every action we do, is preceded by a thought to do that action. There would be no action done by us if there was no thought that prompted us to do it. Essentially, a thought can be said to be a controlling signal that is fed into the human brain to direct his or her actions and behavior. It is like a WiFi signal which we are so familiar with these days.

**Have you ever wondered, when you get a thought where does it come from? We say this thought occurred to me but we never think about or know where it came from. Let us explore where these thoughts come from?**

We all say that I got this thought or that idea. In fact, when we get a good idea we put a claim on it, verbally or even in writing that it is my idea. People put patent rights on their thoughts and ideas, and if someone's idea is stolen, it can end up in lawsuits and big court fights. When we say that I got this thought or the idea, we imply that this body mind that we consider ourselves to be, generated the idea. That is not true. We make this claim without completely understanding it. The thoughts being fed to us are generated by something beyond the body mind. To have a clear understanding of where the thoughts are coming from, we will explore what is this something beyond body mind. One thing we are sure of is, that we call this something as "I". We make statements like "I" thought of this idea or that idea. So to explore this something we have to explore what this "I" is.

When we think of "I", we normally think of it as the body. On further analysis we include our thoughts, feelings and sensations etc. also to be part of me or "I". So we think of ourselves to be a combination of thoughts, feelings and sensations all locked up in one package called mind and residing in the body. But we don't have a clear idea what this "I" is. Let us look at what this "I" is. We use this word "I" all the time. When we were a child we used to call ourselves "I", when we become a middle age person or an old age person, we call ourselves "I". In fact, there was not a moment in our life when we did not call ourselves "I". It has stayed with us all our life. One thing more about this "I" is that this "I" has not increased or decreased in shape or size throughout our life. The knowledge of "I" has stayed steady and constant irrespective of our age. So we have to find out what has stayed with us all our life; and has also stayed constant and steady throughout. That something that we call "I" has to satisfy these two conditions. Let us look at the body first. Body has stayed with us all our life but it has changed all through our life. The body was small when we were children and grew to be much bigger when we got to be adults. Since the body has changed throughout our life, the body cannot be called "I".

Let us look at the thoughts if they qualify to be called "I". We all know that when we get a thought, in a few seconds it disappears, only to be replaced by another thought. We see thoughts stream in us throughout the day. They come and go one after the other all day long. No thought stays with us forever. So thought is not what we can call "I", since it stays with us for a few seconds, instead of staying with us all our life. Similarly, when we look at feelings and sensations they don't last very long either. They may stay longer than the thoughts but not long enough to qualify to be called "I". In conclusion, we find that the thoughts, feelings and sensations, a combination of which is called the mind, do not make what we call "I". So it can be said that both body and mind do not qualify to be called "I".

We have been believing all our life that "I" in me represents a combination of the body and mind, but we find that belief to be false. "I" is not body and mind. When the writer understood this fact that he was not the body and mind, it was an eye opening experience, to say the least. We find that "I" is something beyond body and mind. Upon closer look we find that this "I" has no objective qualities meaning it does not have a shape or a form. That is the reason it cannot be located in us. Being formless it is without any boundaries. So it is limitless or infinite. There is only one Infinite entity and that is God. So what we are finding is that "I" is the God's Presence or Divine Presence in us and is beyond the body and the mind. It has stayed with us all our life and has not changed. It is called by many other religious names like Atman, Guru, Satguru, Parmatma etc. In philosophy this Divine Presence is termed as Awareness or Consciousness.

This "I", the Divine Presence in us, is the one which is generating thoughts and feeding them into our brains to make our body do various actions. So it can be safely said that we as body minds do not have any free will. Essentially, the body mind combination is being used as a robot to carry out various life functions. The thoughts are not being generated by the robot but are being fed to it from the Divine Presence, Atman or Awareness. But because of ignorance, the body mind robot thinks that it is generating thoughts and imagines itself to be an independent entity. Believing itself to be an independent entity it then thinks it has freedom to act. This is the birth of an ego. Notice that ego is just thinking of ourselves to be something that we are not.

Gurbani tells us that the Divine Presence pervades all human beings. It pervades everything living and non living. Divine Presence is the only acting agent in everything. We, being ignorant of the presence of Divinity in us, think ourselves, you or me, to be the doer of deeds.

ਅਕੁਲ ਪੁਰਖ ਇਕੁ ਚਲਿਤੁ ਉਪਾਇਆ ॥
ਘਟਿ ਘਟਿ ਅੰਤਰਿ ਬ੍ਰਹਮੁ ਲੁਕਾਇਆ ॥
ਜੀਅ ਕੀ ਜੋਤਿ ਨ ਜਾਨੈ ਕੋਈ ॥
ਤੈ ਮੈ ਕੀਆ ਸੁ ਮਾਲੂਮੁ ਹੋਈ ॥   (Ang 1351)
(The Almighty has staged this play.
The Divine Presence is hidden deep within each heart.
But no one knows about the Divine Presence in them,
So it appears that "you" and "me" are the doers.)

Gurbani emphasizes this point throughout Sri Guru Granth Sahib. There are many Shabads that impart similar messages. Some shabads are very straightforward, some are blunt. But we are so insensitive that we read them, listen to them and then move on with our life without giving them any more thought. Even the smallest episodes of life are controlled by the Lord. Guru ji says that no problem of any kind can appear in one's life until the Lord allows it. This also implies that there are no coincidences in life. Everything is controlled and done by the Lord.

ਭਾਈ ਮਤ ਕੋਈ ਜਾਣਹੁ ਕਿਸੀ ਕੈ ਕਿਛੁ ਹਾਥਿ ਹੈ ਸਭ ਕਰੇ ਕਰਾਇਆ ॥
ਜਰਾ ਮਰਾ ਤਾਪੁ ਸਿਰਤਿ ਸਾਪੁ ਸਭ ਹਰਿ ਕੈ ਵਸਿ ਹੈ ਕੋਈ ਲਾਗਿ ਨ ਸਕੈ
ਬਿਨ ਹਰਿ ਕਾ ਲਾਇਆ ॥   (Ang 168)
(O brother, let no one think that they have anything in their hand. All act as Lord causes them to act.
Old age, death, fever, headache etc. all kinds of ailments are in Lord's hand.
Nothing can touch anyone without the Lord's Will.)

Guru Arjan Dev ji writes in Sukhmani Sahib that as long as one thinks he is the doer, he cannot taste peace in his life. Also as long as he thinks he can do something, he will continue to transmigrate into the birth and death cycle.

ਜਬ ਲਗੁ ਜਾਨੈ ਮੁਝ ਤੇ ਕਛੁ ਹੋਇ ॥ (Ang 278)
ਤਬ ਇਸ ਕਉ ਸੁਖੁ ਨਾਹੀ ਕੋਇ ॥
ਜਬ ਇਹ ਜਾਨੈ ਮੈ ਕਿਛੁ ਕਰਤਾ ॥
ਤਬ ਲਗੁ ਗਰਭ ਜੋਨਿ ਮਹਿ ਫਿਰਤਾ ॥
(As long as one thinks that he can do something, he will have no peace.
As long as one thinks that he is the one who does things, He shall wander in reincarnation through the womb.)

This shabad portrays our situation very clearly. We never give up our belief that we are not the doers. So we never find lasting peace in our life and continue to wander in the cycle of reincarnation. If we would ever let go of our belief of being a doer, there may be peace in our life and we may escape from the cycle of reincarnation.

A Maharashtra Saint Balsekar, an advocate of non-doership, says that everything happens by the Will of God. Knowing that everything happens by the Will of God, one is relieved of the immense burden on his or her shoulders of doing this or doing that. He says if one can believe this, his life will become full of happiness and peace. He asks us to develop this understanding and just enjoy our lives without any worries. Guru Ji says in the next shabad that his Guru has told him that everything happens by the Will of God. Guru Ji says, believing that everything happens by the Will of God, I don't mind the daily ups and downs of life, and I sleep soundly without any worry.

ਗੁਰਿ ਕਹਿਆ ਜੋ ਹੋਇ ਸਭੁ ਪ੍ਰਭ ਤੇ ॥
ਤਬ ਕਾੜਾ ਛੋਡਿ ਅਚਿੰਤ ਹਮ ਸੋਤੇ ॥ (Ang 1140)
(*The Guru told me that whatever happens, happens through God. So I have abandoned worrying; and now I sleep worry free.*)

The whole thing can be explained through an analogy. In this analogy, life is compared to a movie playing on a TV screen or the cinema screen. Everything that is in the movie, people, cars, houses, animals etc. are all modulations of the light. All the objects in the screen have no reality of their own. They are just modulations of the light and all the movements and actions in the movie are just light movements too. In exactly the same way, this world we see is made of modulations of the Divine Presence. No object in the world, like people, cars, houses etc are real in their own right, and nothing that is happening in the world is being done by the individuals. Everything is made out of Divine Presence and everything is being done by the Divine Presence. This analogy explains in an indirect way that human beings do not have free will of their own, it is all God's will.

**Possible Objections:**

Some people may disagree with the conclusion that an individual made of the body-mind combination does not have free will. They may have many objections. We will go through some obvious ones. Their objection may be that if we don't have free will then we will see no progress in life. People will become lazy and just throw up their hands that I am not free to do anything, so why do anything. Why not let destiny decide what I get or not get. This objection on its face may look plausible but does not stand to reason. There are two answers to this objection.

First answer is that when you say, that if I have no free will, then I am going to throw up my hands and I am not going to do anything, there are two contradictions in this statement. First contradiction is that the argument goes against what we have just proved. We just proved that the body and mind does not have free will. It is the Divine presence in us which has free will and makes the body mind do certain activities. So how can you, as body mind say I am not going to do anything. We just proved that doing things is not in the body mind control. Body mind is being directed by something beyond, to do whatever it is doing. So how can it do or not do anything on its own? Divine Presence in you will create thoughts in your mind and those thoughts will force you to do whatever needs to be done. One other way to look at it would be to just try not doing anything for a while and see how long you will last in non-doing mode. I am sure, one will be forced by his or her spouse or any other family member to get up and do something. The second contradiction in the statement is that when you say that you are not going to do anything, you have already done something. Your "non-doing" has become an act of doing and is based on a thought that arose in your mind before you decided not to do anything. Anything you do or not do is going to be decided not by you but by the thought that arises in your mind. We have already established that the thoughts that arise in our mind do not belong to us, the body and mind.

There is a short Indian story of an old lady who lived in a small village. She had a rooster who would crow in the morning when the sun rose. The lady thought that the sun rose because of the rooster's crowing. The villagers would make fun of the lady and she would get very upset. One day she got so upset that she told the villagers that I am going to move to another village and take my rooster with me. Since there would be no rooster crowing in the village anymore, the sun will stop rising in your village. The lady did just that and moved to another village. Of course, like before, the sun did rise in the village anyway.

Our thinking is like that of the lady. We think whatever is happening is happening because of our doing, like the lady thought that the sun rose because of her rooster's crowing. That is absolutely incorrect as per Gurbani. Following shabad makes this clear that everything is God's play and no one else, meaning everything is being done by Him and Him alone.

ਆਪਨ ਖੇਲੁ ਆਪਿ ਵਰਤੀਜਾ ॥
ਨਾਨਕ ਕਰਨੈਹਾਰ ਨ ਦੂਜਾ ॥   (Ang 291)
(*He Himself has staged His own drama,*
*O Nanak, there is no other doer.*)

The second answer to the objection, is that if you believe you have free will, you can keep working in your life with that mindset. Just keep in mind that you don't. This may sound a little ambiguous and needs further explanation. The fact that you do not have free will, does not stop you from working in our old ways, believing that we do have free will. We have free will or not, does not depend upon what we think about it. It is what it is. In fact, as long as one is not convinced, one should not assume that there is no free will. As a result, one should not hesitate to do whatever he or she feels like doing. However, one should keep an open mind to having no free will, while working with the old mindset of having free will. Then, at one point in their life when they have made some spiritual progress, they may be able to see the hidden hand of the Almighty in everything. So the goal would be to go ahead and do whatever one feels like doing, but always keep the higher truth in mind, that we are not the doer and whatever has happened or is happening, was destined to happen. Gurbani says that it is not we, but the Divine in us, who is working through our body minds. Guru ji says in Sukmani Sahib:

ਜੋ ਹੋਆ ਹੋਵਤ ਸੋ ਜਾਨੈ ॥
ਪ੍ਰਭ ਅਪਨੇ ਕਾ ਹੁਕਮੁ ਪਛਾਨੈ ॥   (Ang 286)
(*Whatever happens, understand that it had to happen; and recognize the happening to be the Lord's own Command*)

There is a saying by Lord Buddha which has been used in spiritual literature repeatedly, "Events happen, deeds are done but there is no doer thereof." Implied in this quote is that there are deeds happening but there is no individual doer of the deeds. Only doer is God Himself or Herself.

If we can recognize the real Doer, God in us, our life will change for the better. The implications of this understanding are immense. Our lives will become peaceful and worry free. We will stop throwing blame around if things don't go our way. With this understanding that I am not the doer, one's ego will start falling away. It may take some time for it to fall away completely, but it definitely will. Once the ego disappears, one attains mukti.

ਜਿਹਿ ਪ੍ਰਾਨੀ ਹਉਮੈ ਤਜੀ ਕਰਤਾ ਰਾਮੁ ਪਛਾਨ ॥
ਕਹੁ ਨਾਨਕ ਵਹੁ ਮੁਕਤਿ ਨਰੁ ਇਹ ਮਨ ਸਾਚੀ ਮਾਨ ॥   (Ang 1427)
(*The person who forsakes his egotism,
and recognizes Lord as the Doer,
says Nanak, that person is liberated,
O mind know this as the truth.*)

I want to mention here that the tenth Guru, Guru Gobind Singh Ji lived his life with this attitude. He did everything to meet the challenging circumstances of his times, but he always kept in mind that everything was being done by the Almighty. In fact, he coined a slogan for us that we use all the time: "Waheguru ji Ka Khalsa, Waheguru ji Ki Fateh". Even though he fought all the battles in his life, he always credited the Almighty (Waheguru) for the wins. He never took credit Himself. This is the attitude we need to adopt in our lives too, where we do everything required of us, but should always keep in mind that God is the real doer. We should give credit to Waheguru instead of taking credit ourselves. We have met people in life who say that whatever they did was not their own doing. They would say that it was Guru's doing or the Guru ji gave them the guidance to do that. This is the mindset we should have when we do anything. If we do that we will certainly get glimpses of the real Doer at one point in our life.

One more objection that may be raised, is that if I don't have free will then I don't need to react to bad things happening around me. If something unjustified happens around me, I am going to say that I don't have freedom to act so I am going to ignore it. Answer to this objection is the same as before. You may think you are not going to react to the situation but it is not in your hand as a body mind, to react. You are making the same mistake that we all made before this understanding, that we are all free to act. Again you cannot do anything, since you are not the doer. The real doer is the Divine Presence in us beyond the body and mind. If you are not the doer what can you do or not do? The Doer will make you do whatever is required to be done under the circumstances. The Lord is doing everything through you and He will do whatever is necessary. That means if you feel like protesting the bad act, go ahead and do it with all your might. If you do so then that was God's plan. The Lord is acting through you to fight it. So you are being used as an instrument by the Lord to play his drama. If you feel no action is necessary then the Lord is deciding that too and not you. So having no free will does not mean you become a slave to circumstances and get beaten down by others. Look at Guru Gobind Singh Ji's life. He is called a Soldier Saint. He was a saint in one way, one who is supposed to do only meditation. But he fought for human rights and justice for all beings. He had realized that it was the Lord who was working through him and, in spite of that knowledge he never refrained from the battles that he had to fight against injustice and cruelty of his times.

I would like to mention an episode in Sant Maskeen Ji's life, he recited himself during one of his Gurbani Vichar sessions. During the aftermath of 1984 riots in Punjab and Delhi against sikhs, in which thousands of sikhs were massacred and the government did not do anything to protect them. Many sikh leaders were speaking against the government criticizing its lack of action. Maskeen Ji was one of those leaders who was speaking against the government too. In his normal katha sessions Sant Ji would advocate that everything happens by God's Will and the best thing to do is to surrender to His Will. After the 1984 riots, he made speeches and criticized the government for not protecting the sikhs from the rioters. One day a renowned media reporter stopped Sant Ji outside the Gurdwara, where Sant Ji had just spoken. The reporter asked Sant Ji, why was he blaming the Indian government for the riots and not considering it as an act of God. The reporter said to Sant Ji that you have always said that nothing happens without God's Will and we should surrender to His Will rather than finding fault with it. Why are you now finding fault with the government and not considering the riots as an act of God? Maskeen Ji says that he got very worried for a moment after hearing the unexpected question. Sant ji acknowledges in his own words that he did not know how to answer the question. He states that he felt very nervous and a heartfelt prayer arose from his heart to the Guru for guidance in answering the question. Sant Ji's prayer worked and this is how Sant ji answered the question. The riots against sikhs were in God's Will and so is my criticism of the government for not protecting sikhs. He said to the reporter that you burn fire under my feet and expect me not to react. Protest is the natural outcome of excessive unjust use of force and it is all God's will. So my criticism of the government is also God's Will. The reporter said to Sant Ji that we thought we were going to trap you today but we failed. Conclusion drawn from this episode is that the action and the reaction both are happening according to God's Will. So next time someone attacks you unjustly, it is ok to fight back. Don't think the attack was God's will and your reaction is not. Both are in His Will.

Only thing to watch is that your reaction should not be out of anger or a knee jerk reaction, but a genuine protest against the injustice being done to you.

Guru ji is saying in the following shabads that everything is in the Lord's control. We don't have the power to do anything. He has created us all and puts us to work whatever way it pleases Him. Everything is being done by Him; and there is nothing that is in our hands.

ਮੇਰੇ ਹਰਿ ਜੀਉ ਸਭੁ ਕੋ ਤੇਰੈ ਵਸਿ ॥
ਅਸਾ ਜੋਰੁ ਨਾਹੀ ਜੇ ਕਿਛੁ ਕਰਿ ਹਮ ਸਾਕਹ ਜਿਉ ਭਾਵੈ ਤਿਵੈ ਬਖਸਿ ॥ (Ang 736)
(*O my Lord, everything is in your Power. I have no power to do anything at all. Accept us as it pleases you.*)

ਜੀਅ ਜੰਤ ਸਭਿ ਤੁਧੁ ਉਪਾਏ ॥
ਜਿਤੁ ਜਿਤੁ ਭਾਣਾ ਤਿਤੁ ਤਿਤੁ ਲਾਏ ॥
ਸਭ ਕਿਛੁ ਕੀਤਾ ਤੇਰਾ ਹੋਵੈ ਨਾਹੀ ਕਿਛੁ ਅਸਾੜਾ ਜੀਉ ॥ (Ang 103)
(*You have created all beings and creatures. As it pleases you, you assign tasks to one and all. Everything is being done by You; we are not capable of doing anything*)

We don't consider night dreams to be very important but they provide a window into understanding of our waking life. In fact, a dream is a microcosm of a macro event of our waking state. When we look at the dream closely, the subject in the dream feels that he or she has free will and can do anything. But when we wake up and look at the dream we find that the subject in the dream had no free will at all. All the activities of the subject in the dream were really the activities of the dreamer's mind. The subject in the dream does not know that. So he or she thinks that he or she is the independent doer of the activities. Our waking state is similar to our dreaming state. God has projected this world like a dream and we all are subjects in His dream. As the subjects in our night dream have no free will, similarly we, the waking state subjects in God's dream, do not have any free will. Essentially, all our activities in this life are really the activities of God's Mind. Gurbani has asserted many times that this life we are living is like a dream. In the Following shabad Gurbani makes it clear that the world is like a dream. As in the dream there is nothing real, the same way whatever we see, feel etc. in the waking state is unreal too. Only thing present in the waking state is God Himself.

ਜਿਉ ਸੁਪਨਾ ਅਰੁ ਪੇਖਨਾ ਐਸੇ ਜਗ ਕਉ ਜਾਨਿ ॥
ਇਨ ਮੈ ਕਛੁ ਸਾਚੋ ਨਹੀ ਨਾਨਕ ਬਿਨੁ ਭਗਵਾਨ ॥ (Ang 1427)
*(Know the world is like a dream that we see at night. There is no truth in it without God.)*

Another objection that could be raised is that if we don't have free will then why do we feel that we have free will? Everyone feels free to act and or not to act. The reason we feel freedom of will, is because we have Divine Presence in each one of us. This Divine Presence in us is our Essence and that is what is asserting itself in our daily life. Our real Essence is that we are Divine Being and not body minds. That is what is coming to the forefront and giving us the feeling that we have free will. But the irony of the situation is that we do not believe ourselves to be a Divine Being. We believe ourselves to be body minds. As long as we think ourselves to be body minds, we will have no free will, even though we feel we do.

Another objection may be raised that if there is nothing in my hand then why am I held responsible for my karmas or actions? Why I have to suffer the consequences of my actions, as pointed out in the following shabad:

ਪੁੰਨੀ ਪਾਪੀ ਆਖਣੁ ਨਾਹਿ ॥
ਕਰਿ ਕਰਿ ਕਰਣਾ ਲਿਖਿ ਲੈ ਜਾਹੁ ॥
ਆਪੇ ਬੀਜਿ ਆਪੇ ਹੀ ਖਾਹੁ ॥
ਨਾਨਕ ਹੁਕਮੀ ਆਵਹੁ ਜਾਹੁ ॥ ( Ang 4)
*(Vice and virtue are not a mere talk,*
*whatever actions are done, are written and go with us,*
*What we sow so shall we reap,*

*O Nanak, by the Command of the Lord we come and go in incarnation.)*

The reason for this is that as long as we think we are the doer of deeds, the deeds will bind us, and we will have to suffer the consequences of our deeds. Once we rise above the doership and believe everything is being done by the Lord, then nothing will bind us. It is not the deed that binds us but it is the belief, that we are the doer of the deed, that binds us. This is the old question of ego. As long as we have an ego that I am the doer, then we will have to face the consequences of our deeds. Gurbani calls a person a fool who claims that he is the doer and forgets the real doer.

ਹਮ ਕੀਆ ਹਮ ਕਰਹਗੇ ਹਮ ਮੂਰਖ ਗਾਵਾਰ ॥
ਕਰਨੈ ਵਾਲਾ ਵਿਸਰਿਆ ਦੂਜੈ ਭਾਇ ਪਿਆਰੁ ॥   (Ang 39)

*("I have done this, and I will do that"; I am an idiot for saying that. I have forgotten the real Doer, I am caught in the net of duality.)*

As long as we have an ego, we think we have free will and accordingly, we think ourselves to be the doer. When we make some progress in our spiritual life, our ego begins to fade and we start having a glimpse of our non-doership. We find everything is being done by the Lord. **Fact of the matter is that it is only the Lord's Will that is being done all the time, no matter whether we know it or not or whether we have ego or not.** Only difference is that if we have ego we don't know that it is God's Will and if we don't have ego then we know it is God's Will. Even the free will that one thinks he or she has, can be said to be not his or hers. Whatever one is doing is based on one's prior conditioning, one has gone through in his life. Everybody's mind has been programmed for years by the parents, teachers and the culture. So the truth of the matter is that instead of having a free will one has a "conditioned" will, which, technically, is also not his or her will.

Another objection that may be raised is that if we don't have free will, why would Guru Ji tell us to do certain things and not to do the others. Gurbani instructs us in many ways how to live our life, how and why to remember the Lord's Name. It also instructs us to stay away from bad company and bad deeds. It even employs blunt language at times to scare us from doing bad deeds. I, personally, have struggled with this for years. I could not reconcile Guru ji telling us in one shabad to do certain things, and then in another shabad would say there is nothing in a person's hand to do or not do. Following two shabads seem to show a contradiction, which is not a contradiction when understood properly.

ਨਾਮੁ ਜਪਹੁ ਨਾਮੇ ਆਰਾਧਹੁ ਗੁਰ ਪੂਰੇ ਕੀ ਸਰਨਾਈ ॥ (Ang 630)
(*Chant the Name of the Lord, worship the Name in adoration, and enter the Sanctuary of the Perfect Guru*)

ਜਾ ਆਪਿ ਕ੍ਰਿਪਾਲੁ ਹੋਵੈ ਹਰਿ ਸੁਆਮੀ ਤਾ ਅਪਣਾ ਨਾਉ ਹਰਿ ਆਪਿ ਜਪਾਵੈ ॥ (Ang 555)
(*When the Lord Master Himself becomes merciful, the Lord Himself causes His Name to be chanted.*

The first shabad above is an instruction to the disciple to do the Naam Simran. This shabad implies that the disciple has free will to do what has been asked of him. But the second shabad says that one can do Naam Simran only when the Lord Himself becomes merciful and then causes the disciple to chant His Name. There seems like a contradiction between the first shabad and the second shabad. But when understood properly the seeming contradiction disappears.

The answer to this seeming contradiction is really a matter of context. Since we all claim to have free will to do anything, with that context in mind, Guru Ji asks us to do certain things and not to do the others. The first shabad where we are being instructed to do Naam Simran, it is being done because of our claim that we can do things on our own. The operative word here is "claim". We all claim that we have free will, so Guru ji challenges us with that context in mind, to do certain things and not others. In fact, in the following shabad Guru Ji throws such a challenge at us, to do something since we claim that we have free will.

ਪੰਚ ਤਤੁ ਕਰਿ ਤੁਧੁ ਸ੍ਰਿਸਟਿ ਸਭ ਸਾਜੀ ਕੋਈ ਛੇਵਾ ਕਰਿਉ
ਜੇ ਕਿਛੁ ਕੀਤਾ ਹੋਵੈ ॥ (Ang 736)
(O Lord, You have created the entire universe out of five elements, if anyone can do something, let him or her come up with the sixth element.)

In the second shabad Guru Ji is speaking of the higher understanding that nothing can happen without His blessing, or without God's Will. He is asking us to create the sixth element, if we believe we can do something. Of course, we all know that is not possible. He is making the body and mind do Naam Simran through His Grace. So the seeming contradiction between the two shabads is not really a contradiction but just a matter of context.

### There Is Free Will Beyond Body Mind:

Even though the arguments made above show that the human being as a body mind does not have any free will, still it is not all a lost cause. There is hope of attaining free will. One can raise oneself spiritually to a higher level and one can attain free will. Like the proverbial phrase "if the mountain won't come to Mohammed, then Mohammed must go to the mountain". The way to attain free will is to be more and more conscious and eventually get to be completely conscious. It is like in a dream, normally we have no control over our dreams, but if we learn to do lucid dreaming, we can develop a degree of control over the dream. In lucid dreaming the dreamer is conscious while dreaming and because of being conscious one is able to control the dream. Similarly, becoming conscious in the waking state, sometimes called lucid waking, we can start getting control over our life and thus command free will.

Being conscious means being conscious of our own Being,

while dealing with the world. In our normal lives we are so much absorbed or lost in the objects and our actions, that we completely are unaware of our own Being. Most of us go through our whole life without ever being conscious of ourselves. If we look closely and estimate the time we are unconscious, it would be easy to say that we are unconscious, on the order of 99% of the time. Being unconscious does not mean that we are unaware of our surroundings. It means that we are aware of our surroundings, but we are unaware of ourselves. It is like when we are so focused on the surroundings that we forget ourselves completely. When we see objects of the world we get lost in them totally. We all have an experience watching movies. If the movie is interesting, we get so absorbed in the movie that we completely lose awareness of the surroundings and, most importantly, awareness of ourselves.

Being conscious or aware essentially, gives oneself control over our actions and reactions; and one does not have knee jerk reactions. We see everyday, episodes where people get so mad with just trivial things and end up doing things that they would not do if they were conscious of what they were doing. Being conscious all the time is a great achievement. What is happening is that when we become conscious, we get closer to our Divine Presence. Not only do we get closer, but we become the Divine Presence, where we start to have a free will. As evident from the following shabad the difference between us and the Lord is that we are completely asleep or unconscious and the Lord is completely awake or conscious.

ਏਕਾ ਸੇਜ ਵਿਛੀ ਧਨ ਕੰਤਾ ॥
ਧਨ ਸੂਤੀ ਪਿਰੁ ਸਦ ਜਾਗੰਤਾ ॥ (Ang 737)
(*The soul bride and the Husband Lord are laying on one bed, the bride is sleeping while the Husband Lord is always awake*)

What is implied from this shabad is that if one becomes completely conscious or awake, then he or she becomes one with God. In that state there is no difference between her and God.

Then her will becomes God's will. Her success becomes God's success and her failure becomes God's failure.

ਰਾਮ ਸੰਤ ਮਹਿ ਭੇਦੁ ਕਿਛੁ ਨਾਹੀ ਏਕੁ ਜਨੁ ਕਈ ਮਹਿ ਲਾਖ ਕਰੋਰੀ ॥ (Ang 208)
(*Between the Lord and the Saint, there is no difference at all. There is scarcely one such Saint in hundreds of thousands of people*)

ਇਸੁ ਗ੍ਰਿਹ ਮਹਿ ਕੋਈ ਜਾਗਤੁ ਰਹੈ ॥
ਸਾਬਤੁ ਵਸਤੁ ਓਹੁ ਅਪਨੀ ਲਹੈ ॥ (Ang 182)
(*Those who remain awake in themselves, even though rare, receive the whole Divine Treasure by staying awake*)

Gurbani puts a lot of emphasis on the person becoming conscious or aware. Being conscious is also described as being awake in Gurbani. This is not the same thing as being awake during our waking time. Gurbani says that we are asleep even during our waking hours. We mistakenly call persons who are awake during the day, awake. According to Gurbani they are really asleep meaning that they are not alert or aware of themselves during the day. These people are doing things during the day like some people do during sleep walking. They are doing things but they are not aware of themselves. Everything is being done unconsciously and as such there is no control of the will. That is the reason that Gurbani pleads with us to wake up, to be conscious. Guru Ji even encourages us that nothing is lost, and it is not too late to do so even now.

ਜਾਗਿ ਲੇਹੁ ਰੇ ਮਨਾ ਜਾਗਿ ਲੇਹੁ ਕਹਾ ਗਾਫਲ ਸੋਇਆ ॥ (Ang 727)
(*Wake up, O mind, wake up. Why are you sleeping unaware.*)

ਕਹਾ ਭੁਲਿਓ ਰੇ ਝੂਠੇ ਲੋਭ ਲਾਗ ॥
ਕਛੁ ਬਿਗਰਿਓ ਨਾਹਨਿ ਅਜਹੁ ਜਾਗ ॥ (Ang 1187)
(*Why are you deluded and attached to falsehood and greed? Nothing is lost yet, there is still time to wake up.*)

Osho says that it is always God's will. Man is unconscious so man thinks it is his will. But when man wakes up and becomes conscious, then he discovers that his will is really God's will.

"In unconsciousness there is false self, but no free will, in consciousness there is free will but no false self". False self here means body mind entity that we believe ourselves to be.

May the Lord wake us all up so we can live our life consciously and get a taste of free will.

◆ ◆ ◆

# COME HOME MY FRIEND

ਤੁਮ ਘਰਿ ਆਵਹੁ ਮੇਰੇ ਮੀਤ ॥ ਤੁਮਰੇ ਦੋਖੀ ਹਰਿ
ਆਪਿ ਨਿਵਾਰੇ ਅਪਦਾ ਭਈ ਬਿਤੀਤ ॥ *(Ang 678)*

*(Come Home my friend, Lord*
*will end your suffering and*
*eliminate your misfortunes)*

Guru Arjan Dev Ji is asking us, in a friendly way, to come home, and telling us that all our suffering and misfortunes will be eliminated when we come home. There are many shabads in Sri Guru Granth Sahib, asking us to come home and to stay home. Guru Ji addresses this in many different ways. Sometimes He addresses the mind as a foreigner, who is traveling all the time like nomads. Other times he addresses the mind as a friend and implores it to come home. At times Guru Ji is a bit harsh and calls the mind foolish and ignorant, and asks it to come home and stay there. It is said that our mind went out of its home a long time ago and got lost in the attractions of the world. It has been lost for many lifetimes and has not returned home. That is the reason Guru Ji calls mind a foreigner. Guru Ji asks the mind in a very friendly way, to come back home.

ਮੇਰੇ ਮਨ ਪਰਦੇਸੀ ਵੇ ਪਿਆਰੇ ਆਉ ਘਰੇ ॥ *(Ang 451)*
*(O my dear foreigner mind, come back home.)*

ਅਹਿ ਰਹੁ ਰੇ ਮਨ ਮੁਗਧ ਇਆਨੇ ॥ (Ang 1030)
(*O my foolish and ignorant mind, remain in your own home.*)

Guru Ji says that our home is full of all kinds of treasures, consisting of jems, jewels and rubies but we cannot find them because our minds, instead of staying home, are always wandering outside. Our home is full of Divine Nectar but the manmukhas, whose minds are turned away from the Guru who lives in our home, cannot get the taste of the Nectar.

ਘਰਿ ਰਤਨ ਲਾਲ ਬਹੁ ਮਾਣਕ ਲਾਦੇ ਮਨੁ ਭ੍ਰਮਿਆ ਲਹਿ ਨ ਸਕਾਈਐ ॥ (Ang 1179)
(*This House is loaded with countless gems, jewels, rubies and emeralds, but the wandering mind cannot find them.*)

.

ਘਰ ਹੀ ਮਹਿ ਅੰਮ੍ਰਿਤੁ ਭਰਪੂਰੁ ਹੈ ਮਨਮੁਖਾ ਸਾਦੁ ਨ ਪਾਇਆ ॥ (Ang 644)
(*The home within is filled with Ambrosial Nectar, but the self-willed manmukhas do not get to taste it.*)

Ultimately, Guru Ji says that not only the treasures, Divine Nectar, peace and happiness are found in this Home, even the Lord Himself is found in the same home. All the mind has to do is go inside and stay there, it will find the Lord. Guru Ji scolds our immature minds, why do you feel so proud? The Lord lives in your own home and you don't even experience His Loving and Blissful Company.

ਇਆਨੜੀਏ ਮਾਨੜਾ ਕਾਇ ਕਰੇਹਿ ॥
ਆਪਨੜੈ ਘਰਿ ਹਰਿ ਰੰਗੋ ਕੀ ਨ ਮਾਣੇਹਿ ॥ (Ang 722)
(*O ignorant soul-bride, why are you so proud? The Lord lives in your own home, why don't you enjoy his sweet Love.*)

These claims being made about coming home are amazing. There are many more shabads in Sri Guru Granth Sahib making similar claims. It behooves us to explore here as to what home Guru Ji is talking about. The home offers all the treasures of the world, all the peace and happiness and even the company of the Lord Himself or Herself. To find such a home will be a dream come true. The first thing that comes to mind that Guru Ji is asking us to do, is to bring our mind under control and keep it from wandering all over the place. This will no doubt bring us some peace and happiness but it may be temporary and limited. So we will search deeper to understand what home Guru ji is talking about.

Our attention throughout our life has been going out looking for the objects, the scenes and other attractions of the world. Our culture has never told us to look inwards. Not only does our culture tell us to look outwards, it also tells us to go out, if you want to achieve anything and be successful in life. The education system right from our kindergarten to the graduate school, has taught us about the external world. Due to our education and social conditioning, our minds have been trained to the point of addiction, to always look out. We never get tired of looking out. Gurbani says that our senses are never tired of going out in persuing their own respective interests. Our mouth is never satisfied talking, the ears are never tired of hearing and our eyes are never satisfied seeing.

ਆਖਣੁ ਆਖਿ ਨ ਰਜਿਆ ਸੁਨਣਿ ਨ ਰਜੇ ਕੰਨ ॥
ਅਖੀ ਦੇਖਿ ਨ ਰਜੀਆ ਗੁਣ ਗਾਹਕ ਇਕ ਵੰਨ ॥   (Ang 147)
(*The mouth is not satisfied speaking, and the ears are not satisfied hearing. The eyes are not satisfied seeing, each organ is lost in its own activity.*)

In summary, we are so occupied with the other that we forget ourselves completely. We never look inwards . How can we ever access our real home that is located inside us. There is a story in Vedantic literature that makes this point clear. The story is about ten people going from one village to another village. There was a river they had to cross to reach the other village. There was no bridge or boat to take them to the other side. Only way to cross the river was to wade through the raging water which they did. When they got to the other side they said let us count to make sure that all of us made it through the river. So one of them stood in front of the group and started counting one by one. He counted the group and came up with a count of nine. What he did was that he counted everybody else but not himself. Another person from the group tried to count and came up with nine also because he made the same mistake of not counting himself. So they got really worried that one of their companions had drowned in the river. They sat down and started wailing about their loss. A wise man was passing by and saw the group wailing and asked what was wrong. They told him that they had lost one of their friends in the river while crossing it. They told him they were a group of ten friends and now there are only nine. The wise man quickly counted them and figured out what the problem was. So he said you all stand in line and I will do the counting. Of course, when he counted them he came up with ten of them and explained to them their mistake.

We may laugh at the story but that really is our story too. We are counting ourselves out all the time. If one would sincerely review at the end of the day, how long one was aware of himself or herself during the day, one may be surprised to find that there was absolutely no time at all when one was aware of oneself. We are so heavily conditioned to look outwards in our life that we never even think of ourselves. No one has ever told us to look inside during our school or college days. Nobody is ever told to be aware of themselves while doing the daily business. It is never a topic of discussion at any time amongst people in general. Almost all of us go through our entire life without ever thinking about our inner self. All our education or training is geared towards material achievements. Education teaches us how we can make more money or which is the best profession to make money etc. Gurbani says that we make all kinds of endeavors for the material things that we are going to leave here when we go; and we just shun the One who is with us all the time.

ਛੋਡਿ ਜਾਇ ਤਿਸ ਕਾ ਸ੍ਰਮੁ ਕਰੈ ॥
ਸੰਗਿ ਸਹਾਈ ਤਿਸੁ ਪਰਹਰੈ ॥   (Ang 267)

*(They strive for what they must leave eventually,
They turn away from their Real Self, their Help and Support, who is
always with them.)*

When Guru Ji talks about coming home he is not talking of some
far off home, He is asking us to come back to our own home
inside us, and live there. Guru Ji further says that if we stay at
home, we will find peace and happiness; and the messenger of
death will not touch us.

ਆਪਨੈ ਘਰਿ ਤੂ ਸੁਖਿ ਵਸਹਿ ਪੋਹਿ ਨ ਸਕੈ ਜਮਕਾਲੁ ਜੀਉ ॥ (Ang 569)
*(Dwell in peace in the Home of your own Self, and the messenger of
death will not touch you)*

Of course, Gurbani does not stop anybody from attending to
worldly engagements and relations as long as we do not get lost
into the world. Not getting lost means we do not forget our
own self like pointed out in the story above. Gurbani says that a
person can do any business with alertness and awareness.

ਗੁਰਮੁਖਿ ਸਭੁ ਵਾਪਾਰੁ ਭਲਾ ਜੇ ਸਹਜੇ ਕੀਜੈ ਰਾਮ ॥ (Ang 569)
*(All the dealings of the Gurmukh are good, if they are accomplished
with natural awareness.)*

To understand what home Guru Ji is referring to we have to first
discover who we are. Once we know ourselves then we will be
able to know our home. In fact, Gurbani says that those who
have recognized themselves or have known themselves, not only
find their real home but they automatically become residents of
their real home. They do enjoy peace and happiness in their real
homes. Following shabads tell us that those people who have
recognized their True Self, find residence in their True Home.

ਮੂਲੁ ਪਛਾਣਨਿ ਤਿਨ ਨਿਜ ਘਰਿ ਵਾਸਾ ਸਹਜੇ ਹੀ ਸੁਖੁ ਹੋਈ ॥ (Ang 1334)
*(Those who recognize their own origin, dwell within the Home of
their inner Being and they find peace there)*

ਗੁਰਮਤੀ ਆਪੈ ਆਪੁ ਪਛਾਣੈ ਤਾ ਨਿਜ ਘਰਿ ਵਾਸਾ ਪਾਵੈ ॥ (Ang 565)
*(Under Guru's instructions, one comes to recognize his own self, and*

*then he comes to dwell in the Home of inner Being)*

We will now explore and understand who we really are and where our home is. Currently, we believe ourselves to be a combination of body and mind consisting of thoughts, feelings, sensations and perceptions. But Gurbani tells us that we are Divine Light or Divine Presence.

ਮਨ ਤੂੰ ਜੋਤਿ ਸਰੂਪੁ ਹੈ ਅਪਨਾ ਮੂਲੁ ਪਛਾਣੁ ॥ (Ang 441)
*(O my mind, you are the Divine Light, recognize your own origin.)*

So Gurbani does not agree with our concept that we are a combination of body and mind. It says that we are Divine Light. We will try to understand what Gurbani is saying and try to get an experiential feel of our Divine Presence by doing a short exercise in introspection. This simple exercise will give us an understanding of who we really are and lead us to explore our home Guru Ji is talking about. This exercise has been explained in detail in the article "Know Yourself and meet the Lord" but we will briefly discuss it again to maintain link in the article. Imagine we are listening to a piece of music from an electronic device or listening to it live. Listening to music can be conceptualized as a process where there is a listener on one side and the music being played on the other side; and they are connected by a process of listening. Now instead of focusing our attention on listening to music, let us focus our attention on the "listener" in us, meaning who in us, is listening to the music. Is our body listening to music, or is it the mind or something else? This question may come as a surprise to some people because they have probably never thought about such a question.

If we ask any person about the listener in him or her, probably a great number of people won't be able to answer the question. They might even have difficulty in understanding the question. Once the question has been understood and they try to look for the listener inside them, they may be confused to decide what in them is doing the listening. Is the body doing the listening or the mind doing the listening; or is it a combination of body and mind? I remember my personal experience years ago when I was taking a walk in the evening by myself. A thought popped into my head, "who am I really". Am I the body or the mind? I found myself very confused. I could not define who I really was? I was not able to put my finger on anything specific in me to call it "myself".

To explore the Listener in us, first we will explore the body and then the mind. The body cannot be the listener because the body is not sentient. It is really made out of food which is essentially made out of clay. As such it is not even aware and cannot be the listener. To be a listener one has to be sentient and aware. Let us look at the mind next. The mind cannot be the listener too because it is not aware either. Mind consists of thinking, sensing and perceiving. None of these can do the listening. Let us take a thought, any thought. We can see that this thought by itself cannot do the listening, or seeing or knowing. On the contrary, the thought is something which is known. The other faculties of the mind like the sensing, tasting, touching and smelling are not aware either. They cannot know or listen. On the contrary, they are known by something else. So all the faculties of the mind and hence the mind is not the listener either.

So we conclude that both body and mind are not capable of listening because they lack awareness or listening quality. But we know for sure that something in us is doing the listening? If we try to look for this listening entity in us, we will not be able to find it. This is because this entity is without any objective qualities. Being without objective qualities, it has no shape or form and hence is limitless. Being limitless it is infinite. This infinite entity without objective qualities is referred to as Infinite Being. Since it is Infinite, there can be only one Being in the universe. In other words the listener or the knower in us is the only Entity in the universe. This is what Gurbani has called Ek Onkar (ੴ), One Reality. Our finite mind cannot grasp it. Ek

Onkar or the One Reality is beyond the body mind, is the real listener. This One Reality has been called by many other names too like Atman, Awareness, Real Self or the Divine Presence etc.

Now we have discovered that this One Reality (ੴ) is the real listener in us. On the other hand, if someone asks us who is listening to music we say that I am listening to music. Putting these simple statement together proves "that the listener in us, the One Reality (ੴ) and the "I" that we call ourselves to be, is one and the same entity". To repeat this finding, "I" that we all call ourselves to be is the same entity as the One Reality (ੴ). This One Reality resides in us or has its Home in all of us and has become us. We address this Reality as "I". How to locate the One Reality in us? All we have to do is to find "I" in us. Sometimes this "I" is referred to as "I am". As pointed out before, this Reality is without objective qualities. It cannot be grasped by our mind. It can be felt though. If one tries to locate the "I" or "I am" in oneself sincerely, one will be able to feel Its presence in the heart area. This is the Home of One Reality or God or the Divine Presence in us. Even though God is infinite and is present everywhere, His Presence crystallizes in our hearts. To use an analogy, the internet we use at home is present in the whole internet space but it shows its presence only when it activates a device like a computer or a phone. Similarly God's Presence is everywhere, but when it touches our hearts it generates a feeling of Its Presence in our hearts. Gurbani tells us to look for Him in our hearts because that is the only place God lives.

ਵਸੀ ਰਬੁ ਹਿਆਲੀਐ ਜੰਗਲੁ ਕਿਆ ਢੂਢੇਹਿ ॥  (Ang 1378)
(*The Lord abides in the heart, why are you looking for him in the jungle.*)

ਦਖਨ ਦੇਸਿ ਹਰੀ ਕਾ ਬਾਸਾ ਪਛਿਮਿ ਅਲਹ ਮੁਕਾਮਾ ॥
ਦਿਲ ਮਹਿ ਖੋਜਿ ਦਿਲੈ ਦਿਲਿ ਖੋਜਹੁ ਏਹੀ ਠਉਰ ਮੁਕਾਮਾ ॥  (Ang 1349)
(*God of the Hindus lives in the southern lands, and the God of the Muslims lives in the west,*
*Search in the heart, look deep into your heart of hearts; this is the*

*home and the place where God lives.)*

Hindus in old days believed that their God lived in the south; and the Muslims believed that their God lived in the west. But Bhagat Kabir says that God lives in our own hearts and asks us to search Him there.

**So when Guru Ji asks us to come home, He is talking about the Home in our own hearts. This is where all the treasures are found. This is where Ambrosial Nectar is found. This is where the Lord resides. It also happens to be the place where our Real Essence resides which we call "I", beyond body and mind. In fact, our Real Essence and the Lord are one and the same. So we just need to come back to our own Real Self, feel It and abide in Its Presence. This is our real Home. If we come to live in our Home, we not only find all the treasures, the Nectar, the peace and happiness, but will also meet the Lord.**

Guru ji calls this coming home a merger of our attention (Surat) with the sound (Shabad). First Guru, Guru Nanak had discussions with the yogis in Batala, a small town near Gurdaspur in Punjab. These discussions between Guru Ji and the yogis are called Sidh Gosht. Yogis asked Guru Nanak many questions about God realization. One of the questions asked of Guru Nanak was, who is your guru and whose disciple are you? Guru Nanak's answer to that question was, Shabad (Sound) is the Guru and surat (attention) is the disciple.

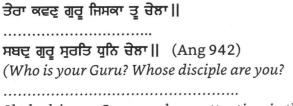

ਤੇਰਾ ਕਵਣੁ ਗੁਰੂ ਜਿਸਕਾ ਤੂ ਚੇਲਾ ॥

.................................

ਸਬਦੁ ਗੁਰੂ ਸੁਰਤਿ ਧੁਨਿ ਚੇਲਾ ॥ (Ang 942)
*(Who is your Guru? Whose disciple are you?*

.............................................

*Shabad is my Guru, and my attention is the disciple of shabad's sound.)*

Sant Maskeen Ji explains the concept of Shabad Surat in one

of his katha episodes. He says that Shabad Surat merger is the meeting of the disciple with the Guru. Sant ji explains in detail in the katha how to merge Surat in Shabad. Sant Ji states that navel is the center of the body and is called dhunni (ਧੁੰਨੀ) in the Punjabi language. This navel or the dhunni is the place, where the Shabad or the dhun (ਧੁਨ) originates in the human body. That is why the navel is called dhunni, meaning the place where sound (dhun) originates from. When the diaphragm inside the body pushes the air against the dhunni or the navel, air moves through the body's vocal system to produce the sound. So the sound is produced due to the activity at the navel. Sant ji says that we have to lock our attention on this sound and then take it back to the source of the sound at the navel. Once the attention has been taken back to the naval location and held there, then the merger of the Surat and Shabad has been achieved. This is called the Shabad Surat merger. In essence, what is being done here is the attention is being brought inwards by listening to the sound to unite it with the One Reality, our Real Self that resides at the heart navel level. Gurbani talks about uniting Surat and Shabad to achieve peace and happiness. It says that when attention (Surat) and the Word (Shabad) unite in the heart, then one is bestowed with the joy of drinking Ambrosial Nectar.

ਸੁਰਤਿ ਸਬਦੁ ਰਿਦ ਅੰਤਰਿ ਜਾਗੀ ਅਮਿਉ ਝੋਲਿ ਝੋਲਿ ਪੀਜਾ ਹੇ ॥ (Ang 1074)
(*Awareness of the Word of the Shabad has awakened within my heart. I drink Ambrosial Nectar with joy.*)

ਸਬਦ ਸੁਰਤਿ ਸੁਖੁ ਊਪਜੈ ਪ੍ਰਭ ਰਾਤਉ ਸੁਖ ਸਾਰੁ ॥ (Ang 62)

(*Focusing your attention on the Shabad, happiness wells up. Attuned to God, most blissful peace is found.*)

Guru ji further explains in Jap Ji Sahib, pauris 8-11, benefits of listening or listening to shabad. The word "ਸੁਣਿਐ" means listening, but this listening is not ordinary listening that we do everyday. This listening is from the platform that we have just established above. It is not done at the thought level of the body and mind but at the level of the Listener beyond the body and mind, at our Real Self level. The listening is done with complete awareness. Guru ji says that if one listens at the Real Self level, one attains to the status of Siddha, Pir, Shiva, Brahma and Inder. One comes to understand the sacred books like Shastras, Simrities and Vedas etc. They also begin to understand the mysteries of earth, sky and other celestial bodies. He or she becomes truthful, contented and spiritually wise. Above all, one becomes always blissful and his troubles and sins are all wiped away. These are just a few of the positive characteristics that are developed with this deeper level of Listening. Shabad below documents an amazing list of transformations that come to fruition as a result of this Listening.

ਸੁਣਿਐ ਸਿਧ ਪੀਰ ਸੁਰਿ ਨਾਥ ॥ ਸੁਣਿਐ ਧਰਤਿ ਧਵਲ ਆਕਾਸ ॥
ਸੁਣਿਐ ਦੀਪ ਲੋਅ ਪਾਤਾਲ ॥ ਸੁਣਿਐ ਪੋਹਿ ਨ ਸਕੈ ਕਾਲੁ ॥
ਨਾਨਕ ਭਗਤਾ ਸਦਾ ਵਿਗਾਸੁ ॥ ਸੁਣਿਐ ਦੂਖ ਪਾਪ ਕਾ ਨਾਸੁ ॥

ਸੁਣਿਐ ਈਸਰੁ ਬਰਮਾ ਇੰਦੁ ॥ ਸੁਣਿਐ ਮੁਖਿ ਸਾਲਾਹਣ ਮੰਦੁ ॥
ਸੁਣਿਐ ਜੋਗ ਜੁਗਤਿ ਤਨਿ ਭੇਦ ॥ ਸੁਣਿਐ ਸਾਸਤ ਸਿਮ੍ਰਿਤਿ ਵੇਦ ॥
ਨਾਨਕ ਭਗਤਾ ਸਦਾ ਵਿਗਾਸੁ ॥ ਸੁਣਿਐ ਦੂਖ ਪਾਪ ਕਾ ਨਾਸੁ ॥

ਸੁਣਿਐ ਸਤੁ ਸੰਤੋਖੁ ਗਿਆਨੁ ॥ ਸੁਣਿਐ ਅਠਸਠਿ ਕਾ ਇਸਨਾਨੁ ॥
ਸੁਣਿਐ ਪੜਿ ਪੜਿ ਪਾਵਹਿ ਮਾਨੁ ॥ ਸੁਣਿਐ ਲਾਗੈ ਸਹਜਿ ਧਿਆਨੁ ॥
ਨਾਨਕ ਭਗਤਾ ਸਦਾ ਵਿਗਾਸੁ ॥ ਸੁਣਿਐ ਦੂਖ ਪਾਪ ਕਾ ਨਾਸੁ ॥

ਸੁਣਿਐ ਸਰਾ ਗੁਣਾ ਕੇ ਗਾਹ ॥ ਸੁਣਿਐ ਸੇਖ ਪੀਰ ਪਾਤਿਸਾਹ ॥
ਸੁਣਿਐ ਅੰਧੇ ਪਾਵਹਿ ਰਾਹੁ ॥ ਸੁਣਿਐ ਹਾਥ ਹੋਵੈ ਅਸਗਾਹੁ ॥
ਨਾਨਕ ਭਗਤਾ ਸਦਾ ਵਿਗਾਸੁ ॥ ਸੁਣਿਐ ਦੂਖ ਪਾਪ ਕਾ ਨਾਸੁ ॥ (Ang 2)

*(Listening, one attains the stature of Siddhas, the spiritual guides, the angels and Supreme master,*
*Listening, one gets an understanding about the earth, it's support and the sky,*
*Listening, one gets understanding about the oceans, the lands of the world and the nether regions of the underworld,*
*Listening, death cannot even touch you.*
*O Nanak, the devotees are forever in bliss,*

*Listening, pain and sin are erased.*

*Listening, one attains the stature of Shiva, Brahma and Indra,*
*Listening, even foul mouthed people praise Him,*
*Listening, one attains understanding of yoga, and the secrets of the body,*
*Listening, one gets understanding of Shastras, Simrities and Vedas,*
*O Nanak, the devotees are forever in bliss,*
*Listening, pain and sin are erased.*

*Listening, one attains Truth, Contentment and Spiritual Wisdom,*
*Listening, one gets a bath at the sixty eight sacred places of pilgrimage,*
*Listening, one attains to the honor that the well read people get,*
*Listening, one is established in the steady meditation,*
*O Nanak, the devotees are forever in bliss,*
*Listening, pain and sin are erased.*

*Listening, one attains to the ocean of goodness,*
*Listening, one attains to the stature of shaykhs, religious scholars, spiritual teachers and emperors,*
*Listening, even the blind find the path,*
*Listening, the Unreachable comes within grasp,*
*Nanak, the devotees are forever in bliss,*
*Listening, pain and sin are erased.)*

Gurbani stresses in many shabads that we should remember the Lord with conscious Awareness. Conscious Awareness implies that our remembrance should come not from our mind level but from our gut level, from our heart, our Real Home. Bhagat Kabir Ji says if one does this, there can be no doubt that one will attain the highest status.

ਕੋਈ ਗਾਵੈ ਕੋ ਸੁਣੈ ਹਰਿ ਨਾਮਾ ਚਿਤੁ ਲਾਇ ॥
ਕਹੁ ਕਬੀਰ ਸੰਸਾ ਨਹੀ ਅੰਤਿ ਪਰਮਗਤਿ ਪਾਇ ॥ (Ang 335)
(*Whoever sings or listens to the Lord's Name with conscious Awareness,*
*Says Kabir, without a doubt, will attain the highest spiritual status.*)

Contemporary spiritual philosophers in the west are discovering this secret too and are advocating it to their followers. Here is a quote from Eckhart Tolle from his book, "The Power of Now" "When listening to another person, don't listen with your mind, listen with your whole body. Feel the energy field of your inner body as you listen. That takes attention away from thinking and creates a still space that enables you to truly listen without the mind interfering."

Eckhart is talking about the same thing, that the listening should be done from a place which is beyond the body and the mind, even though he says listening should be done with the whole body. We know that the body cannot listen. He is implying that one should listen from the level of our Real Self.

Gurbani mentions the same thing from another angle. We have proven above that we are not the body or the mind. So Gurbani says, in an unusual way, in the following shabad that we should not listen from the perspective of the body or the mind. In fact Gurbani even goes further asking us not to even see, speak or do anything else from the perspective of the body or mind.

ਅਖੀ ਬਾਝਹੁ ਵੇਖਣਾ ਵਿਣੁ ਕੰਨਾ ਸੁਨਣਾ ॥
ਪੈਰਾ ਬਾਝਹੁ ਚਲਣਾ ਵਿਣੁ ਹਥਾ ਕਰਣਾ ॥
ਜੀਭੈ ਬਾਝਹੁ ਬੋਲਣਾ ਇਉ ਜੀਵਤ ਮਰਣਾ ॥ (Ang 139)
(*See without eyes, listen without ears,*
*Walk without feet, work without hands,*
*Speak without tongue, thus be dead while alive*)

This shabad is written in the context of our belief that we are body minds. We think we are body minds and as a result, we employ the body and its senses to conduct activities like seeing, listening and speaking etc. Gurbani is saying we need to rise above the level of the senses, to the Real Self or Awareness level to do our daily chores. That is why Guru Ji is asking us not to see with eyes, not to listen with ears etc. Essentially, the message is that we need to go beyond our body minds and operate from a deeper level, our Divine Home. As pointed out earlier our Divine Home is in the heart or near the heart and not in the head. If we make a home in our head, then we would just be strengthening our ego, which is not what Guru Ji meant.

Someone once said, "our real journey in life is only from head to heart." meaning we are living in our heads and we need to move to our heart. This is very important to understand because this statement, very appropriately emphasizes Gurban's message of coming home. If we watch our attention, we will find it is always in our head and is operating from there all the time. Most of our senses like seeing, speaking, listening etc. are located in the head too. The thinking machine, the brain, where the mind resides is also located in the head. There is a nonstop thinking process going on in our heads. Essentially, our operational headquarters are located in the head, so to speak. We have to move our headquarters out of our head and move it down to the heart location which our real Home is. We need to operate from our real home all the time.

Why it is so important to move from head to heart is because the head deals in duality. Its nature is to see the world in duality, good and bad, happiness and suffering, love and hate etc. The mind can never see the world as a non-dualistic phenomenon. But when one operates from the heart level there is no duality. It is only oneness and everything is based on love. One can try to get a feel of this just by taking one's attention to the heart level and stay there for a while. One will easily discover that there is no duality there. All the thinking stops when one's attention is at the heart or the naval level. Thinking is only possible when the attention is in the head. Since there is no thinking at the heart level, there is no duality at that level either. Thinking and duality go hand in hand. So at the heart level there is only love, no thinking and no duality. That is why when we see a baby our attention immediately drops to the heart level. Baby has no duality in him or her and is purely an embodiment of love. When we see a baby we see love and we respond with love. In fact, we even start talking to the baby in the baby language, out of love. This love is what Guru Ji wants us to embrace and enjoy by "coming home".

Even though all of us are so immersed in pursuing worldly objects and pleasures, we are in fact, searching for our real home all the time, whether we know it or not. All our actions in this world are for one thing only and that is to achieve happiness. All of us are in search of peace and happiness right from our early life. Why do we want a good job, a good house, a good car, a good relationship etc; because we are all looking for happiness. Everyone, no matter what one is doing, is doing it to make his or her life more comforting and enjoyable to attain happiness. Only problem is that our efforts are misguided. We think happiness can be achieved by going out and by acquiring worldly objects and relationships. But Guru Ji says that real happiness lies inside us and not outside. Gurbani says that everything is inside our real Home and not outside it. Those who search outside are misguided. We need to go to the place where happiness is found.

ਸਭ ਕਿਛੁ ਘਰ ਮਹਿ ਬਾਹਰਿ ਨਾਹੀ ॥ ਬਾਹਰਿ ਟੋਲੈ ਸੋ ਭਰਮਿ ਭੁਲਾਹੀ ॥
ਗੁਰਪਰਸਾਦੀ ਜਿਨੀ ਅੰਤਰਿ ਪਾਇਆ ਸੋ ਅੰਤਰਿ ਬਾਹਰਿ ਸੁਹੇਲਾ ਜੀਉ ॥ (Ang 102)
(*Everything is within the Home of the Self, there is nothing outside. One who searches outside is misguided.*
*By Guru's Grace, one who has found the Home within, is happy inside and outside.*)

ਜਿਥੈ ਵਥੁ ਹੋਵੈ ਤਿਥਹੁ ਕੋਇ ਨ ਪਾਵੈ ਮਨਮੁਖ ਭਰਮਿ ਭੁਲਾਵਣਿਆ ॥ (Ang 117)
(*Where happiness resides, no one looks for it there. The manmukhs are just deluded by doubt.*)

Instead of coming home we are always going away from it. If we watch our life closely we notice that our attention is always moving outward. It never, I mean never goes inwards. With the mind always moving outwards, how can we expect to know our

Real Self, and find our Divine Home? Gurbani describes this state of our mind:

ਇਸੁ ਮਨ ਕਉ ਬਸੰਤ ਕੀ ਲਗੈ ਨ ਸੋਇ ॥
ਇਹੁ ਮਨੁ ਜਲਿਆ ਦੂਜੈ ਦੋਇ ॥
ਇਹੁ ਮਨੁ ਧੰਧੈ ਬਾਂਧਾ ਕਰਮ ਕਮਾਇ ॥
ਮਾਇਆ ਮੂਠਾ ਸਦਾ ਬਿਲਲਾਇ ॥  (Ang 1176)
(*This mind is not even touched by the spring,*
*This mind is burnt by duality and double mindedness.*
*This mind is entangled in worldly affairs, creating more and more karma,*
*Enticed by Maya, it cries out in suffering.*)

ਉਰਝਿ ਰਹਿਓ  ਬਿਖਿਆ ਕੇ ਸੰਗਾ ॥
ਮਨਹਿ ਬਿਆਪਤ ਅਨਿਕ ਤਰੰਗਾ ॥
ਮੇਰੇ ਮਨ ਅਗਮ ਅਗੋਚਰ ॥
ਕਤ ਪਾਈਐ ਪੂਰਨ ਪਰਮੇਸਰ ॥  (Ang 759)
(*O my mind, you are always entangled in corrupt associations;*
*And so many thought waves pass through you.*
*Under these conditions how can the Unapproachable and Incomprehensible Lord be found.*)

So we need to watch our mind constantly to keep it from indulging in useless outward activity, and bring it back and make it stay in its Divine Home. Gurbani compares our mind to a musk deer who is wandering all over the forest to find the kasturi smell, that is really from his own navel. The musk deer has a kasturi smell coming from a gland near his navel, but the deer is ignorant of the fact that the smell is coming from his own self. The deer thinks the smell is coming from outside, and wanders around looking for it in the forest in the bushes. That is the case with us too that we are looking for peace and happiness outside, while it is located right in our own home.

ਘਰ ਹੀ ਮਹਿ ਅੰਮ੍ਰਿਤੁ ਭਰਪੂਰੁ ਹੈ ਮਨਮੁਖਾ ਸਾਦੁ ਨ ਪਾਇਆ ॥
ਜਿਉ ਕਸਤੂਰੀ ਮਿਰਗੁ ਨ ਜਾਣੈ ਭ੍ਰਮਦਾ ਭਰਮਿ ਭੁਲਾਇਆ ॥  (Ang 644)
(*The home within is filled with Ambrosial Nectar, but the self-willed*

*manmukhas do not get to taste it. He is like a deer, who does not recognize its own musk scent, and wanders around deluded by doubt.)*

ਵਿਚੁ ਕਾਇਆ ਜਿ ਹੋਰ ਥੈ ਧਨੁ ਖੋਜਦੇ ਸੇ ਮੂੜ ਬੇਤਾਲੇ ॥
ਸੇ ਉਝੜਿ ਭਰਮਿ ਭਵਾਈਅਹਿ ਜਿਉ ਝਾੜ ਮਿਰਗੁ ਭਾਲੇ ॥ (Ang 309)

*(Those who search for this treasure outside themselves, in other places, are foolish and mentally deranged, They wander around deluded by doubt, like the deer who searches for the musk in the bushes.)*

Bhagat Ravidas Ji calls this Divine Home Begumpura, "City without Sorrow" and says that there is no suffering or anxiety in that City. There are no troubles like taxes, fear, blemish or downfall there. He says now I have found this beautiful city where there is peace and safety all the time.

ਬੇਗਮ ਪੁਰਾ ਸਹਰ ਕੋ ਨਾਉ ॥  ਦੂਖੁ ਅੰਦੋਹੁ ਨਹੀ ਤਿਹਿ ਠਾਉ ॥
ਨਾਂ ਤਸਵੀਸ ਖਿਰਾਜੁ ਨਾ ਮਾਲੁ ॥  ਖਉਫੁ ਨ ਖਤਾ ਨ ਤਰਸੁ ਜਵਾਲੁ ॥
ਅਬ ਮੋਹਿ ਖੂਬ ਵਤਨ ਗਹ ਪਾਈ ॥  ਊਹਾਂ ਖੈਰਿ ਸਦਾ ਮੇਰੇ ਭਾਈ ॥
ਕਾਇਮੁ ਦਾਇਮੁ ਸਦਾ ਪਾਤਿਸਾਹੀ ॥  ਦੋਮ ਨ ਸੇਮ ਏਕ ਸੋ ਆਹੀ ॥
ਆਬਾਦਾਨੁ ਸਦਾ ਮਸਹੂਰ ॥  ਊਹਾਂ ਗਨੀ ਬਸਹਿ ਮਾਮੂਰ ॥
ਤਿਉ ਤਿਉ ਸੈਲ ਕਰਹਿ ਜਿਉ ਭਾਵੈ ॥  ਮਹਰਮ ਮਹਲ ਨ ਕੋ ਅਟਕਾਵੈ ॥
ਕਹਿ ਰਵਿਦਾਸ ਖਲਾਸ ਚਮਾਰਾ ॥  ਜੋ ਹਮ ਸਹਰੀ ਸੁ ਮੀਤੁ ਹਮਾਰਾ ॥ (Ang 345)

*(Baygumpura, the city without sorrow, is the name of the town.
There is no suffering or anxiety there,
There are no troubles or taxes on commodities,
There is no fear, blemish and downfall there.
Now, I have found the most beautiful city,
There is lasting peace and safety there, my brother.
God's Kingdom is steady, stable and eternal,
There is no second or third citizen, all are equal there,
That city is populous and eternally famous,
Those who live there are wealthy and contented,
They stroll about freely, just as they please,
They know the Manson of the Lord's Presence, and no one blocks*

*their way,*
*Says Ravi Dass, the emancipated shoe maker,*
*Whosoever is a citizen there, is a friend of mine.*

Bhagat Ji, further goes on singing the praises of this Home. In that Home he says, is God's Kingdom, which is steady, stable and eternal. Everyone there is equal and free, and one who lives there is wealthy and contended. People stroll about freely wherever they please.

May God bless us all to find our real Home of Divine Presence and grant us residence there.

# WHY THERE IS SUFFERING

ਪਰਮੇਸਰ ਤੇ ਭੁਲਿਆਂ ਵਿਆਪਨਿ
ਸਭੇ ਰੋਗ॥ *(Ang 135)*

*(Forgetting the Lord, all sorts of
illnesses are contracted)*

W hy is there so much suffering in the world? This
question has been asked for a long long time. There
are many ways this question has been asked. Why
is there suffering in the world? If God is merciful and most
forgiving, then why does he allow suffering? Why some people
who do bad deeds, are not suffering and those who do good
deeds are suffering? There are many questions like these that
have been asked. There have been many answers given for these
questions too. These questions on suffering are very hard to
answer. However, in this article we will try to look at the broader
picture of suffering and will try to find answers from Gurbani
point of view.

There is all kind of suffering in the world. Normally, the cause
of suffering is thought to be not having enough worldly things,
but other times it may be having too many things. Suffering
can happen because of many factors. Some are suffering because
they are lonely but others are suffering because they have too
much company. Some may have nothing to do and are getting

bored, while others may have too many engagements and are always hustling to keep up. There are no hard and fast criteria for suffering in the world. There is a lot of suffering caused by egos clashing with each other. There is suffering because of jealousy and hate. Following shabad in Gurbani lists a number of causes that people have suffered from in the past. The entire Shaba has not been listed for the sake of brevity. At the end of the shabad the conclusion is that everyone in the world is suffering.

ਰੋਵਹਿ ਕਿਰਪਨ ਸੰਚਹਿ ਧਨੁ ਜਾਇ ॥ ਪੰਡਿਤ ਰੋਵਹਿ ਗਿਆਨੁ ਗਵਾਇ ॥
ਬਾਲੀ ਰੋਵੈ ਨਾਹਿ ਭਤਾਰੁ ॥      ਨਾਨਕ ਦੁਖੀਆਂ ਸਭ ਸੰਸਾਰ ॥ (Ang 954)
*(The miser weeps, because he is hurt when his accumulated wealth*
*leaves him, The Pundit, the religious scholar, loses his knowledge,*
*The young woman weeps because she has no husband,*
*O Nanak, the whole world is suffering.)*

If we look closely into the causes listed, we see that most of the suffering listed in shabad is due to one's ego getting hurt for some trivial reason. That would be true for current times also. There are, of course, many more causes of suffering.

Why there is so much suffering in the world. It looks like God does not care any more. You watch the evening news on the television; and all we see is how many people died that day, how many tornadoes hit the ground, how floods and fires are causing enormous damages and suffering. On the other hand all religions claim that God loves every human being unconditionally. So how to reconcile the enormous suffering and God's Love. There is physical suffering and there is psychological suffering. The psychological suffering can lead to physical ailments. Normally, the cause of suffering is said to be our own actions which are termed as Karmas. According to the "Theory of Karma" it is believed that our past actions are the cause of our present fortunes or misfortunes. While this may be true, it cannot explain how the cycle of karma started. Where did the karma come from in the first cycle of incarnation? Gurbani questions the theory of karma too. Bhagat Namdev says that in the beginning when there was no world, no mother, no father and no body, and there were no religious books to declare good and bad karma, then where did the Karma come from?

ਮਾਇ ਨ ਹੋਤੀ ਬਾਪੁ ਨ ਹੋਤਾ ਕਰਮੁ ਨ ਹੋਤੀ ਕਾਇਆ ॥

..........................................

ਚੰਦੁ ਨ ਹੋਤਾ ਸੂਰੁ ਨ ਹੋਤਾ ਪਾਨੀ ਪਵਣੁ ਮਿਲਾਇਆ ॥
ਸਾਸਤੁ ਨ ਹੋਤਾ ਬੇਦੁ ਨ ਹੋਤਾ ਕਰਮੁ ਕਹਾ ਤੇ ਆਇਆ ॥  (Ang 973)

(*When there was no mother and no father, no karma and no body,*

.............................................................

*When there was no moon and no sun; and water and air were not even separated,*
*When there were no Shastras and no Vedas, then where did the karma come from?*)

It is very hard to point out the exact cause of suffering. Overall, Gurbani describes this whole cosmos as His Play, in which He Himself is the Player and He Himself is the sufferer. He Himself has become a beggar at one place and the king at the other. He Himself has become the oppressor and the oppressed.

ਸਭੁ ਜਗੁ ਖੇਲੁ ਰਚਾਇਓਨੁ ਸਭੁ ਵਰਤੈ ਆਪੇ ॥  (Ang 789)
(He created the whole world as a play, and He Himself is pervading in all of it)

Even in this Play of the Lord which is beyond comprehension, Gurbani gives us some insight into the causes and remedies for the suffering. We will take a broader view of these insights and will address what causes suffering and how that comes into our life. How can we remedy this suffering in our lives?

## Main Causes Of Suffering:

### Separation From The Source:

ਪਰਤਖਿ ਪਿਰੁ ਘਰਿ ਨਾਲਿ ਪਿਆਰਾ ਵਿਛੁੜਿ ਚੋਟਾ ਖਾਇ ॥  (Ang 234)
(*Your Beloved Husband Lord is clearly with you in your own home,*

*but you have separated yourself from Him, and you suffer because of that.)*

This shabad says that our suffering is mainly caused by our separation from our Source. Gurbani says even though we are always in touch with our Source, we still suffer, thinking that we are separate from It. Separation from our Source is considered to be the root cause of suffering. By imagining ourselves to be separate entities, we develop egos which leads to suffering. Guru Ji details in the shabad below, the types of suffering that are being encountered by the human beings. He is saying in this shabad that the main cause of our suffering is the separation from our Source. Then there are other forms of suffering like insatiable hunger for worldly objects, fear of death and diseases of the body. Guru Ji is implying here that the main cause of suffering is separation from our Source; and that then results into the other forms of suffering. Guru Ji says to the doctor not to treat these forms of suffering with any medicine because they can't be treated by medicine. Their treatment lies in eradication of the separation from our Source.

ਦੁਖੁ ਵੇਛੋੜਾ ਇਕੁ ਦੁਖੁ ਭੂਖ ॥
ਇਕੁ ਦੁਖੁ ਸਕਤਵਾਰ ਜਮਦੂਤ ॥
ਇਕੁ ਦੁਖੁ ਰੋਗੁ ਲਗੈ ਤਨਿ ਧਾਇ ॥
ਵੈਦ ਨ ਭੋਲੇ ਦਾਰੂ ਲਾਇ ॥  (Ang 1256)

*(Human being's main suffering is separation from its Source,*
*One suffering is never ending hunger for material world,*
*One suffering is fear of death,*
*One suffering is disease of the body,*
*O foolish doctor, don't give me medicine for these.)*

If we look closely we find the real reason for our suffering is that we have been separated from our Source or God. Our Source (ੴ), also called Atman, Awareness or Infinite Being is embodiment of peace and happiness; and is free from suffering. This Source is sometimes described as Sat, Chit Anand, meaning it is Truth, Consciousness and Bliss. This Source or Awareness is Bliss or

Happiness Itself. But when this Source manifests itself into the world, it forgets its True Nature and assumes the limitations of the body and mind. When it forgets its True Nature, it forgets that it is the embodiment of peace and happiness,, and as such it experiences unhappiness and lack of peace. This can be made clearer by using an analogy of the dream world. Manifestation of our waking world is similar to the manifestation of the dream at night. In fact, Gurbani equates our current life to no more than a dream at night. Gurbani stresses over and over again that this life is like a dream and advises us to wake up from this dream. There are a number of shabads in Sri Guru Granth Sahib that state this fact.

ਜਗਿ ਜੀਵਨ ਐਸਾ ਸੁਪਨੇ ਜੈਸਾ ਜੀਵਨ ਸੁਪਨ ਸਮਾਨੰ ॥ (Ang 482)
(*This life of the world is like a dream, life is just equivalent to a dream*)

Everybody experiences dreams at night. In a dream, one person who is having the dream, manifests himself or herself into a world of multiple persons, animals and objects. At the same time the dreaming person, the dreamer, gets into his or her own dreamed world as the dreamed subject, from whose viewpoint the dreamer sees the dreamed world. The dreamed subject considers itself to be a separate and independent entity in its own right. **This dreamed subject, believing itself to be an independent entity, has, in fact, separated itself from its source, the dreaming subject.** This is generally defined as the establishment of ego. As a result of its separation from the source, it loses its peace and happiness. This point needs to be understood clearly. While the dreaming subject is sleeping in his or her bed peacefully, the separated subject in the dream is dealing with the ups and downs of the dreamed life. Since the dreamed subject is unaware that he is a dreamed subject, life seems real to her or him. The dreamed subject has the same worries and heartaches that we all have in our daily life. At times the dream can be a nightmare where the dreamed subject goes through a terrifying episode or tragic event in the dream, which causes great pain and suffering. In the mean time, the dreamer is sleeping peacefully, almost unaffected. All this suffering is happening because the dreamed subject has separated herself or himself from its source, and believes itself to be an independent entity. This is how the separation from one's real source becomes the cause of suffering.

In our waking life the dreamer is Atman or Awareness. It has manifested the world in Its dream, and we are all the dreamed subjects in His or Her dreamed world. As in the dream, the dreamed subject considered himself or herself an independent entity in its own right, and established separation from its source, we all consider ourselves as independent entities, and as such have separated from our Source, Atman or Awareness. We have in essence, established little egos as a result of separation which is the cause of our suffering. As a result of this separation, we have lost our peace and happiness which was inherent in our Source. We all have become individual egos in the dream of Atman. In this dream we do have nightmares just like the nightmares in the night dreams. These nightmares essentially are the suffering we face in our waking state. These nightmares can end only if we wake up from the dream that we are in, and end our separation from our Source. Bhagat Ravidas Ji describes our plight very appropriately in the following shabad:

ਨਰਪਤਿ ਏਕੁ ਸਿੰਘਾਸਨਿ ਸੋਇਆ ਸੁਪਨੇ ਭਇਆ ਭਿਖਾਰੀ ॥
ਅਛਤ ਰਾਜ ਬਿਛੁਰਤ ਦੁਖੁ ਪਾਇਆ ਸੋ ਗਤਿ ਭਈ ਹਮਾਰੀ ॥ (Ang 657)
(*A king falls asleep on his throne, and dreams that he is a beggar;*
*In spite of possessing the kingdom, but separated from it in his dream, he faces suffering. Such is our condition.*)

Just like the king goes to sleep on his throne and starts dreaming, we as Atman or Awareness have gone to sleep and are currently in a dream state. Bhagat Ji says that the king suffers in his dream in spite of him still being a king and possessing his kingdom. The suffering is caused by his imagined separation from his kingdom, since he forgets that he is still a king. He believes himself to be a beggar. Our condition is similar to that of the king. We are embodiments of peace and happiness as Atman or Awareness, and have become separated from our Source because of the dream. As a result we have lost our peace and happiness. We have forgotten our true identity like the king had forgotten that he was a king. Hence we are suffering like the king. Gurbani says that those who are separated from the True Guru, the Source, suffer tremendously.

ਸਤਿਗੁਰ ਤੇ ਵਿਛੁੜੇ ਤਿਨੀ ਦੁਖ ਪਾਇਆ ॥
ਅਨਦਿਨੁ ਮਾਰੀਅਹਿ ਦੁਖ ਸਬਾਇਆ ॥ (Ang 1063)
(*Those who are separated from the True Guru, suffer in misery.*
*Night and day they are punished, and they suffer from all kinds of ailments.*)

Have you noticed that when a child is born, he or she cries like crazy. Wise men have wondered why a child who is not sick or hungry cries at birth. Look at other species like the birds and animals, all their offspring take birth without crying or any noise. In fact, the birds come out of the eggs chirping and supposedly happy. Why do human's children cry at birth? Bhai Gurdas Ji points out in the following shabad that the child cries at birth because of it's separation from the its Source. The child enjoys Divine Peace in its Source in the mother's womb but loses it at his or her birth.

ਰੋਵੈ ਰਤਨੁ ਗਵਾਇ ਕੈ ਮਾਇਆ ਮੋਹੁ ਅਨੇਰੁ ਗੁਬਾਰਾ ॥
ਓਹੁ ਰੋਵੈ ਦੁਖੁ ਆਪਣਾ ਹਸਿ ਹਸਿ ਗਾਵੈ ਸਭ ਪਰਵਾਰਾ ॥ (Vaar 37)
(*Losing the jewel (Name of the Lord), the child cries (at birth) in the utter darkness of Maya and infatuation.*
*The child cries because of his own suffering, but the whole family sings with happiness.*)

Once we believe ourselves to be independent entities separated from our Source, over time we completely forget our Source. Like it is said "out of sight out of mind". When we believe ourselves to be independent entities we don't even think about our Source. Our daily life has become so busy that we don't find any time to do any introspection. Gurbani emphasizes remembrance of the Lord on a daily basis by following a disciplined protocol of doing Naam Simran and Nitnem. This is essentially trying to reconnect with our Source. Gurbani reminds us that if we forget the Lord, we fall prey to all sorts of illnesses. So our effort should be to eradicate this separation from our Source, so our inherent peace and happiness can prevail in our life. Gurbani asserts that we need to remember the Lord, or reconnect with the Source, if we want to protect ourselves from suffering.

ਪਰਮੇਸਰ ਤੇ ਭੁਲਿਆਂ ਵਿਆਪਨਿ ਸਭੇ ਰੋਗ ॥ (Ang 135)
(*Forgetting the Lord, all sorts of illnesses are contracted.*)

**Believing Oneself To Be A Fragment:**

One other cause for suffering is that when we start believing ourselves to be an independent entity, we also start believing that we are a fragment and feel incomplete. So we start going out to acquire things to fulfill ourselves and to put an end to this misery of being a fragment. That is the reason we see everyone running after the accumulation of wealth and worldly things. Have you noticed that nobody, I mean nobody is ever content with what they have. Everyone wants more money, more fame, more status, more fun, the list goes on and on. We may not be aware of this but this is why we are all working so hard in our lives. If we ask anyone why he or she is working so hard, the most common answer to that question would be to have a good life. There may be some exceptions but the majority of the respondents will have that kind of answer. If asked a follow up question, why do you want a good life, the answer generally would be to be happy. No matter what anyone is doing, the goal is the same, that is to be happy. This happiness is really getting rid of the pain of incompleteness. So we are all working hard everyday to fulfill ourselves to achieve happiness, whether we are aware of it or not. The irony of the situation is that it is a misguided effort, because this void cannot be filled with worldly things or worldly achievements. This void can be filled only by going back to our Source, because that is what we are missing as a fragment. We just have to change our mindset that we are Atman or Awareness, and not the person that we think ourselves to be. Gurbani says that it is very rare that one's desires are satisfied. No matter how much money we have we still want more.

ਤ੍ਰਿਸਨਾ ਬਿਰਲੇ ਹੀ ਕੀ ਬੁਝੀ ਹੇ ॥
ਕੋਟਿ ਜੋਰੇ ਲਾਖ ਕ੍ਰੋਰੇ ਮਨੁ ਨ ਹੋਰੇ ॥
ਪਰੈ ਪਰੈ ਹੀ ਕਉ ਲੁਝੀ ਹੇ ॥ (Ang 213)
(*The thirst for fulfillment of desires is rarely quenched,*
*People may accumulate hundreds of thousands, millions, tens of millions, yet the mind is not restrained.*
*They only yarn for more and more.*)

Associated with the run after money and fame is suffering and heartaches that make one's life miserable. We can see everyday life of a typical person, it is full of stress, worry and disappointment. People are fighting, cultures are fighting, nations are fighting, it has become the survival of the fittest. The stress and worries lead to ailments of the body. Bhagat Kabir Ji says that people who look for happiness from the worldly objects, they instead get more suffering. That is why, he says I don't want to ask for such happiness. He is implying that peace and happiness cannot be found in this outside world.

ਸੁਖ ਮਾਂਗਤ ਦੁਖੁ ਆਗੈ ਆਵੈ ॥
ਸੋ ਸੁਖੁ ਹਮਹੁ ਨ ਮਾਂਗਿਆ ਭਾਵੈ ॥
(*People beg for the happiness but get suffering instead,*
*I would rather not ask for such happiness.*)

The reason that suffering comes from worldly objects when we ask for happiness, is because we live in the world of duality.

The creation or manifestation of the world is based on duality. If duality is eliminated there would be no world, so to speak. The hypothesis of manifestation is that One Reality has divided Itself into two, so everything we find has two polar opposites like good and bad, beautiful and ugly, rich and poor etc. So when we ask for happiness, suffering comes with it because there is no single pole in this world. That is why Guru Ji tells us that we should get rid of duality, so when we ask for happiness we will really get happiness only, and not the happiness laced with suffering.

ਜੋ ਇਸੁ ਮਾਰੇ ਤਿਸਹਿ ਵਡਿਆਈ ॥
ਜੋ ਇਸੁ ਮਾਰੇ ਤਿਸ ਕਾ ਦੁਖੁ ਜਾਈ ॥   (Ang 237)
(*One who eradicates duality, obtains glorious greatness,*
*One who eradicates duality, is freed of suffering.*)

**Remedies For Suffering:**

**End Separation From The Source:**

ਮਿਲਿ ਸਤਿਗੁਰ ਸਭੁ ਦੁਖੁ ਗਇਆ ਹਰਿ ਸੁਖੁ ਵਸਿਆ ਮਨਿ ਆਇ ॥   (Ang 46)
(*Meeting the Sat Guru, all sufferings come to an end,*
*And Peace of the Lord comes to dwell in the minds.*)

As we have discussed earlier, the main cause of our suffering is that we have separated from and have forgotten our True Source. We are Atman or Awareness but we believe ourselves to be bodies and minds. So the first and foremost thing we need to change is our mindset. We have to turn towards our Source and recognize it. As we have separated ourselves from our Source, the same way we have to retrace our way back again. After recognizing our Source we have to meditate on It and be one with it. In other words we have to eradicate our separation. This eradication of separation is rather simple because we are not talking about separation between two different entities. The fact is that there is one entity Atman or Awareness that has voluntarily ignored its own identity and has become human beings. So all we have to do as Atman or Awareness is to get rid of this self imposed ignorance, that we are a human being and re-establish our true identity. Once we do that our life will change for the better. Guru Ji has carved a path for us which is called Naam Simran. Naam Simran is the way to end our separation from the Guru or our Source. Guru Ji defines Naam Simran as follows:

ਹਰਿ ਨਾਮਾ ਹਰਿ ਰੰਞੁ ਹੈ ਹਰਿ ਰੰਞੁ ਮਜੀਠੈ ਰੰਞੁ ॥
ਗੁਰਿ ਤੁਠੈ ਹਰਿ ਰੰਗੁ ਚਾੜਿਆ ਫਿਰਿ ਬਹੁੜ ਨ ਹੋਵੀ ਭੰਞੁ ॥ (Ang 731)
(*Lord's Naam is the Love of the Lord. The Lord's Love is the permanent color.*
*When the Guru is pleased, He colors us with His Love, this color will never fade away.*)

Guru Ji is saying that the Naam is the love of the Lord. When we are asked to do Naam Simran, it means that we should love the Lord with utmost intensity. It is like we should color ourselves in His Love. Love is a force that dissolves the individual's ego and as the ego dissolves, a person becomes one with the Source, and ends the separation from the Source. Ego is considered to be a wall between the person and its Source. Gurbani says in the following shabad that the soul bride and the husband Lord live together as one, but are separated by the wall of ego, which is a very tough wall.

ਧਨ ਪਿਰ ਕਾ ਇਕ ਹੀ ਸੰਗਿ ਵਾਸਾ ਵਿਚਿ ਹਉਮੈ ਭੀਤਿ ਕਰਾਰੀ ॥ (Ang 1263)
(*The soul bride and the Husband Lord live together as one, but the hard wall of egotism has come between them.*)

So Naam Simran with love eradicates the ego and hence the wall of separation between the person and his or her Source. As a result, the suffering in one's life is eliminated.

Gurbani says that Naam Simran is the panacea for all kinds of suffering because once we become one with our Source, there is no more separation and hence no more suffering.

ਸਰਬ ਰੋਗ ਕਾ ਅਉਖਧੁ ਨਾਮੁ ॥ (Ang 274)
(*Naam is the panacea, the remedy to cure all ills.*)

Guru Gobind Singh Ji also speaks of the Love of Lord and says that the truth of the matter is that only the people who love the Lord shall meet the Lord. The tenth Guru goes even farther by saying that there is no benefit of meditating with closed eyes, taking bath at all kinds of holy places, while performing evil actions. Guru Ji puts love of the Lord ahead of any other endeavor to meet our Source.

ਕਹਾ ਭਯੋ ਜੋ ਦੋਉ ਲੋਚਨ ਮੂੰਦ ਕੈ ਬੈਠਿ ਰਹਿਓ ਬਕ ਧਿਆਨ ਲਗਾਇਓ ॥
ਨ੍ਹਾਤ ਫਿਰਿਓ ਲੀਏ ਸਾਤ ਸਮੁੰਦ੍ਰਨ ਲੋਕ ਗਇਓ ਪਰਲੋਕ ਗਵਾਇਓ ॥
ਬਾਸੁ ਕੀਓ ਬਿਖਿਆਨ ਸੋ ਬੈਠ ਕੈ ਐਸੇ ਹੀ ਐਸੇ ਸੁ ਬੈਸ ਬਿਤਾਇਓ ॥
ਸਾਚੁ ਕਹੋ ਸੁਨ ਲੇਹੁ ਸਭੈ ਜਿਨ ਪ੍ਰੇਮ ਕੀਓ ਤਿਨ ਹੀ ਪ੍ਰਭੁ ਪਾਇਓ ॥ (Akal Ustat Ang 13)
(*Of what use it is if:*
*One sits with both eyes closed and meditates,*
*One takes bath at seven seas, he loses this world and the next too,*
*One spends one's life in performing evil actions and wastes his life in such pursuits,*
*I speak the Truth, everyone listen, those who love the Lord shall realize the Lord.*)

When we make contact with our Source through Naam Simran with love, we essentially achieve real happiness without its polar opposite, unhappiness. That is because that is what our Source is made of. There is no duality there, so there is no unhappiness. Source is full of happiness and bliss only.

ਆਨਦ ਮੂਲੁ ਜਗਜੀਵਨ ਦਾਤਾ ਸਭ ਜਨ ਕਉ ਅਨਦੁ ਕਰਹੁ ਹਰਿ ਧਿਆਵੈ ॥
(Ang 494)
(*Lord is the Source of Bliss, the Life of the world, great Giver and brings Bliss to all who meditate on Him.*)

ਅਨੰਦ ਬਿਨੋਦੀ ਖਸਮੁ ਹਮਾਰਾ ॥ (Ang 384)
(*My Husband Lord, is blissful and playful.*)

This can be explained from our personal experience that we have every night. We all love to go to sleep at night. The main reason why we love to go to sleep is, because we get to taste the end of the separation from our Source. Every night during our sleep, we go into a deep sleep state for some time. This deep sleep state is when we are one with the Source or more accurately, we are our own Self. There is no thought, no feeling, no body, no mind and no world. We are by ourselves or we are completely merged in God. This is the reason deep sleep is the most restful and blissful state. This is the state we want to achieve all the time, so we do not fall prey to suffering.

**Acceptance Of God's Will: (ਭਾਣਾ ਮੰਨਣਾ)**

Acceptance of the Will of God has been very strongly advocated in Gurbani. Gurbani says that suffering is happening in accordance with the will of the Almighty. Acceptance of the Will of God has been given great importance in spiritual advancement and also in getting rid of suffering. Sikh history is full of examples of martyrs including the fifth Guru, Guru Arjan Dev Ji and the ninth Guru, Guru Teg Bahadur Ji, who sacrificed their lives as a protest, and accepted their sacrifices as the Will of God. Then there are hundreds of Gursikhs who laid down their lives to protect the Sikh Nation by accepting it as the Will of God. They never shed a single tear while sometimes, being cut to pieces by the enemies. There are episodes in history where the Gursikhs happily accepted the inhuman treatment given to them by their torturers and murderers; and they even taunted their tortures to be tougher than they were.

Acceptance advocated by Gurbani finds its roots in the hypothesis that it is all God's Will that is being carried out everywhere. Nobody can do anything unless God wills it. In fact, it is not that nobody can do anything, but there is nobody else other than God who is doing anything. It is all God's doing, and Gurbani says that if one really understood this one thing "that it is only God who is the doer of all things", then his or her ego will be obliterated. Once ego is gotten rid of, acceptance of His will becomes automatic. Fifth Guru Arjan Dev Ji in Sukhmani Sahib says that whatever happens had to happen because it is God's Command.

ਜੋ ਹੋਆ ਹੋਵਤ ਸੋ ਜਾਨੈ ॥
ਪ੍ਰਭ ਅਪਨੇ ਕਾ ਹੁਕਮੁ ਪਛਾਨੈ ॥ (Ang 286)
(*Whatever has happened, know that it had to happen,*
*Recognize it as the Lord's Command.*)

Guru Nanak Dev Ji, in Jap Ji Sahib says that everything is happening because of God's Hukam.

ਹੁਕਮੈ ਅੰਦਰਿ ਸਭੁ ਕੋ ਬਾਹਰਿ ਹੁਕਮ ਨ ਕੋਇ ॥
ਨਾਨਕ ਹੁਕਮੈ ਜੇ ਬੁਝੈ ਤ ਹਉਮੈ ਕਹੈ ਨ ਕੋਇ ॥ (Ang 1)
(*Everything is subject to His Command, nothing is outside His Command,*
*O Nanak, one who understands His Command, has no ego.*)

Why is Guru Ji saying that everything is done according to His Hukam or Will? We will try to understand it from our daily experience. We will try to understand why He is the only doer. Because as long as we believe that we are the doer there cannot be a surrender or acceptance of His Will. So we will address this issue of who is the real doer in our lives. Let use the analogy of our dreams at night employed earlier in the article to explain our separation from our Source. In our dream we have a dreamer who dreams a world and then the dreamer gets into his own dream as a dreamed subject. Analogous to the night dream, Atman or Awareness is the dreamer, this waking world is Atman's dreamed world and we all are the dreamed subjects of His or Her dream. Now the dreamed subject in the dream world believes itself to be an independent entity in its own right and an independent doer. It is only when the dream ends that we find that the dreamed subject was not the doer at all. It was the dreamer who was the only doer working through the dreamed subject. In fact, the dreamed subject was an imaginary figure and had no existence at all. Similarly, we as the dreamed subjects in the waking state believe that we are independent doers. But like the subjects in the night dream, we are not the real doers. Everything that is happening in our life is being done by the dreamer Atman or Awareness. Not only are we not the doers, we do not even have an independent existence of our own similar to the subjects in our night dreams. This is a very important discovery that we are not the doer of deeds. When this fact is realized or becomes our own experience, ego will be eradicated. Once the ego is dead, the acceptance of the will of God will become a reality. As a result, our suffering will end automatically.

One more point to make here is, the fact that we are not the doers is unbelievably obvious, but because of our conditioning it is difficult to grasp.. Gurbani states that there is only One God or One Realty (ੴ). In fact, that is the first uttering of Sri Guru Granth Sahib. This statement means that there is only one Entity that is real and everything else is unreal. This One Reality has become the universe and all of us; and is working through all of us. We are like robots, and this Reality is the driver in us. So we cannot call ourselves to be doers because all our doing is being done by this One Reality or God. It can be said that our life is being lived by this Reality. With that in mind we should let our ego go, because nothing is being done by us.

ਸਭ ਕਿਛੁ ਕੀਤਾ ਤੇਰਾ ਹੋਵੈ ਨਾਹੀ ਕਿਛੁ ਅਸਾੜਾ ਜੀਉ ॥ (Ang 103)
(*All things are Your Doing, nothing is done by us.*)

Acceptance is defined as having no resistance to whatever the situation may be. If there is resistance, the mind is rejecting the current experience. Suffering is not caused by the situation but by the resistance to the situation. Suffering is, mathematically, proportional to resistance to the experience. Higher the resistance, higher will be suffering and vice versa. So, logically, if the resistance is brought down to zero there would be no suffering. No resistance implies saying yes to the situation. That is what acceptance (ਭਾਣਾ ਮੰਨਣਾ) is. It reduces the resistance down to zero and offers relief from suffering. I have been in situations where people have suffered loss of loved ones but they have accepted it to be the Will of God; and have borne the loss with peace and tranquility. Gurbani also tells us that one who accepts whatever happens and believes it to be the Will of the Almighty, will find peace, and will not have to suffer.

ਜਿਨੀ ਪਛਾਤਾ ਹੁਕਮੁ ਤਿਨ ਕਦੇ ਨ ਰੋਵਣਾ ॥ (Ang 523)
(*Those who recognize the Lord's Command, they never have to weep.*)

ਭਾਣਾ ਮੰਨੇ ਸੋ ਸੁਖੁ ਪਾਏ ਭਾਣੇ ਵਿਚਿ ਸੁਖੁ ਪਾਇਦਾ ॥ (Ang 1073)
(*One who surrenders to the God's Will, finds peace,*
*He finds peace in the Lord's Will.*)

Not only acceptance of the Will of God reduces suffering, as an added benefit it helps in our life's goal of meeting our True Guru (Satguru). Guru ji says that our True Guru is like the ship to cross the world ocean to reach the Lord. Those who accept the Will of Satguru or God, automatically get a seat in that Ship.

ਸਤਿਗੁਰੁ ਬੋਹਿਥ ਹਰਿ ਨਾਵ ਹੈ ਕਿਤੁ ਬਿਧਿ ਚੜਿਆ ਜਾਇ ॥
ਸਤਿਗੁਰ ਕੈ ਭਾਣੈ ਜੋ ਚਲੈ ਵਿਚਿ ਬੋਹਿਥ ਬੈਠਾ ਆਇ ॥ (Ang 40)
(*Satguru is the Ship of Lord's Naam, how can one climb on board?*
*One who accepts the Will of the God, will come to sit in the Ship.*)

### Understanding That Suffering Is An Illusion:

Someone once said "There is suffering but there is no sufferer." This is a very controversial statement and probably will not be believed by most of the readers, but it is not untrue. Suffering is built on the false foundation of ego. The author is not minimizing the gravity of suffering by any means, by suggesting that the suffering is an illusion, but is just trying to offer the facts. This understanding is based on the fact that the person who is suffering has no independent entity of his own. If the person does not exist then how can there be suffering?

Let us use the dream analogy referred to earlier in the article to make it clear. If the subject in the dream has a nightmare it will suffer and scream like it was real to him or her. The dreamed subject in the dream, would feel suffering much the same way we do in our waking state. But upon waking up from the dream we find that the suffering in the dream was unreal. Not only the suffering was unreal, the subject in the dream was also unreal. In the same way our suffering in this waking state is unreal too even though it feels very much real. It is not our Real Self but the imaginary self that suffers. The imaginary self is our false identity that we call "ego". If one becomes convinced that the ego is false, then for him or her suffering will become false too. In that case suffering will just fade away or be minimized. One thing needs to be pointed out here is that we are talking about psychological suffering and not physical pain.

If we can look at the Reality of the world beyond the veil of Maya, we find that it is God Himself or Herself that we are looking at. God Himself or Herself has become the world. No matter whether we know it or not, one thing is certain that we are surrounded by the Lord Almighty. Gurbani states this fact many times in Sri Guru Granth Sahib.

ਜਹ ਜਹ ਦੇਖਾ ਤਹ ਤਹ ਸੁਆਮੀ ॥
ਤੂ ਘਟਿ ਘਟਿ ਰਵਿਆ ਅੰਤਰਜਾਮੀ ॥ (Ang 96)
(*Wherever I look, there I see my Lord and Master.*
*You are permeating everything, O all knowing.*)

Gurbani also tells us that the Reality is the Embodiment of Bliss Itself and nothing else. So what we are looking all the time around is Bliss Itself which Gurbani calls Anand (ਅਨੰਦ).

ਅਨੰਦ ਰੂਪ ਰਵਿਓ ਸਭ ਮਧੇ ਜਤ ਕਤ ਪੇਖਉ ਜਾਈ ॥ (Ang 673)
(*The Lord, the embodiment of Bliss, is pervading and permeating in all, wherever I go I see Him there.*)

What is implied by these shabads is that "God which is

138

the "Embodiment of Bliss" is pervading everything and seen everywhere. Everything is made out of happiness and bliss. Similarly even the suffering we face is made of God Himself, which is happiness and bliss. There is nothing else which suffering could be made out of. He has become everything in the universe and even the suffering itself. But because of the veil of Maya we cannot see the happiness and bliss behind what we see. We instead interpret it according to our own conditioning. It is a case of mistaking happiness and bliss for sorrow and suffering. That is why Gurbani says that if the teaching is understood properly, one will find there is no suffering.

ਕਹਨ ਕਹਾਵਨ ਕਉ ਕਈ ਕੇਤੇ ॥
ਐਸੋ ਜਨ ਬਿਰਲੋ ਹੈ ਸੇਵਕੁ ਜੋ ਤਤ ਜੋਗ ਕਉ ਬੇਤੈ ॥
ਦੁਖੁ ਨਾਹੀ ਸਭੁ ਸੁਖੁ ਹੀ ਹੈ ਰੇ ਏਕੈ ਏਕੀ ਨੇਤੈ ॥
ਬੁਰਾ ਨਹੀ ਸਭੁ ਭਲਾ ਹੀ ਹੈ ਰੇ ਹਾਰ ਨਹੀ ਸਭ ਜੇਤੈ ॥ (Ang 1302)
(*There are many who talk and incite others to talk,*
*But one is rare who understands the essence of teaching.*
*There is no suffering, there is only peace, just see One and only One.*
*There is no evil, there is only good. There is no defeat, there is only*
*victory.*)

## Coming And Staying Home:

One thing Gurbani has stressed heavily is that we should all come back to our real home and stay there if we want peace and happiness. The home that is referred to here is not the home where we live, but it is our spiritual home. Gurbani says that our heart is our real Home, because that is where God lives. When we stay at our real home, we are in the company of the Lord. This Divine Company gets rid of all our suffering. Gurbani pleads with us to come home and abide there. Gurbani further says that if we come home we will not only solve all our problems but will get rid of our misfortunes.

ਤੁਮ ਘਰਿ ਆਵਹੁ ਮੇਰੇ ਮੀਤ ॥
ਤੁਮਰੇ ਦੋਖੀ ਹਰਿ ਆਪਿ ਨਿਵਾਰੇ ਅਪਦਾ ਭਈ ਬਿਤੀਤ ॥ (Ang 678)

*(O my friend, come back to your home, God Himself will eliminate all your problems and will do away with the misfortunes.)*

How do we find our real home? For detailed discussion on this topic please refer to the article titled "Come Home My Friend". How does staying home get rid of suffering? Guru Arjan Dev Ji says in the following shabad that in our Real Home reside the Peace, Poise and Bliss. If we become a resident of that Home, our cycle of coming and going will also come to an end because there is no birth and death there.

ਸੁਖ ਸਹਜ ਆਨੰਦ ਵੁਠੇ ਤਿਤੁ ਘਰਿ ॥
ਆਵਣ ਜਾਣ ਰਹੇ ਜਨਮੁ ਨ ਤਹਾ ਮਰਿ ॥ (Ang 524)
*(Peace, Poise and Bliss reside in that House,*
*Coming and going ends, there is no birth and death there.)*

Coming home means to go deep into our hearts and feel the Divine Presence there, melt into it and be one with it. All our circumstances originate from this one Source, the Divine Presence.

When we come home and abide in this Peaceful Place, we will begin to notice that our outside circumstances are beginning to calm down too. We all know that our outside circumstances are a reflection of our inner state of mind. So as we abide more and more in our Home in the company of our Divine Self, our outside circumstances start to get better and better and life becomes more peaceful and trouble free. Guru Ji emphasizes this point through many shabads, and instructs us to stay steady in our home. By doing so we will not have to endure a painful life.

ਏ ਮਨ ਮੇਰਿਆ ਤੂ ਥਿਰੁ ਰਹੁ ਚੋਟ ਨ ਖਾਵਹੀ ਰਾਮ ॥ (Ang 1113)
*(O my mind, remain steady and stable, and you will not have to endure pain in life)*

Guru Ji gives an analogy to emphasize the benefit of staying centered at home. In the old days people employed two round slabs of grindstones to grind corn at home. In this setup the bottom slab is fixed and the upper slab is rotated manually around an axle in the center. The top stone has an opening around the center axle where the corn is added during the process. The corn grinding process consists of rotating the top slab and simultaneously adding corn into the opening in the top slab. As the top slab is spun around, the corn passes between the two stones and comes out grounded around the periphery. The corn that passes between the two stones is crushed and ground, but the corn that sticks close to the center axle is not touched at all, and is spared from being ground. That is what Guru Ji is saying in the following shabad. The people who stay close to their center meaning who stay in their Divine Home are spared from worldly problems. But the people who go away from the center are subject to the rough and tumble of worldly life.

ਦੁਇ ਪੁੜ ਚਕੀ ਜੋੜਿ ਕੈ ਪੀਸਣ ਆਇ ਬਹਿਠੁ ॥
ਜੋ ਦਰਿ ਰਹੇ ਸੁ ਉਬਰੇ ਨਾਨਕ ਅਜਬੁ ਡਿਠੁ ॥ ( Ang 142)

(*People sit and grind the corn by placing it between the two grindstones.*
*Corn that sticks to the central axis is spared from being ground, Nanak has seen this wonder.*)
*Let us all spend some time every day in our heart, feeling the Divine Presence and try to be one with It. Do it earnestly. This will bring peace and happiness not only in our life, but in the life of our families and neighbors. Bhagat Kabir Ji says that the mouth that utters the Lord's Name, is a blessed one. The uttering of the Lord's Name, not only purifies one's body, it purifies the whole village.*

ਕਬੀਰ ਸੋਈ ਮੁਖੁ ਧੰਨਿ ਹੈ ਜਾ ਮੁਖਿ ਕਹੀਐ ਰਾਮੁ ॥
ਦੇਹੀ ਕਿਸ ਕੀ ਬਾਪੁਰੀ ਪਵਿਤੁ ਹੋਇਗੋ ਗ੍ਰਾਮੁ ॥ (Ang 1370)

(Kabir, blessed is the mouth, which utters the Lord"s Name. It purifies the body, and the whole village as well.)

## Suffering Is Self Made:

This is another difficult point to make and probably more difficult to comprehend. This point is being made with all sincerity and there is no intent here to minimize one's suffering. Once understood it would be easier to accept. This may be coupled with the law of karma, but I think it goes deeper than that. Gurbani says that whatever we have done, we have to suffer the consequences of that. We should not blame anybody else.

ਜੋ ਮੈ ਕੀਆ ਸੋ ਮੈ ਪਾਇਆ ਦੋਸੁ ਨ ਦੀਜੈ ਅਵਰ ਜਨਾ ॥ (Ang 433)
(*Whatever I did, for that I have suffered,*
*I should not blame anyone else.*)

Doing does not mean doing only physical deeds. It also includes deeds done through thinking and speaking. Gurbani includes three things in the process of doing. Thought, word and deed are the three forms of actions that are considered to be "doing".

ਮਨ ਬਚ ਕ੍ਰਮ ਰਸ ਕਸਿਹ ਲੁਭਾਨਾ ॥ (Ang 487)
(*In thought, word and deed, people are attached to attractions.*)

We need to be aware of these three modes of karma so we do not create further suffering. When we dream at night we sometimes have bad dreams or even nightmares. The nightmares are not created by anybody else but by ourselves. If we nourish frightening thoughts during waking state, it will lead to bad dreams at night. Frightening thoughts not only lead to bad dreams at night, they also cause further disturbance in waking life. No matter if the dream is good or bad, it is still, one hundred percent our responsibility. Gurbani says that this waking life is like our night dream. So whatever happens in our waking life is also our own responsibility. This is because our waking life is a dream too. Only difference is that waking life is a dream of our Atman or Awareness that is our real Self. We, as real Self are creating the waking life dream, where we face ups and downs of life. So the waking world and its problems are our own creation. This is a subtle point and needs to be understood clearly. It will be explained with a story.

There was a lady who went to sleep at night and had a dream. In her dream the lady went to the neighborhood park for a walk.

She had her purse hanging by her shoulder. A young boy passing by the lady, snatched her purse and ran off with it. She was really shaken up by the incident and it woke her up. This story of the lady shows that the incident that shook her up, was really her own making, created by herself. She herself became the boy in her dream, who snatched her purse. The suffering that she suffered from the incident was her own making. This is a simple story but reveals a great truth. Our life is like that. Gurbani says that our life is like a dream, but we are not aware of it, since we are all sleeping. We are sleeping while awake. This phenomenon is explained in more detail in the article " Wake Up My Mind". In our sleep, we are creating all kinds of dreams, some good and some bad. Please note that we are not just having dreams by coincidence, but we are creating them ourselves. At night when we have a dream we brush it off. But analyzing it closely we find that we just did not have a dream, we created the dream. If it was a nightmare we created it too. There was no one else in our bed infusing the dream in our head. So the dream, good or bad, was our own making. Similarly this daily life is a dream of our Real Self, which is not different from you. Everything that is happening in our life is a dream of our own Real Self. So all our suffering, no matter what level it may be, is created by our own Real Self, in other words, by us alone. Being unaware of it, we just blame it on our circumstances or luck etc..

ਇਹੁ ਸੁਪਨਾ ਸੋਵਤ ਨਹੀ ਜਾਨੈ ॥
ਅਚੇਤ ਬਿਵਸਥਾ ਮਹਿ ਲਪਟਾਨੈ ॥ (Ang 740)
(*This life is a dream, but the sleeper does not know that,*
*In his or her unconscious state, he clings to it.*)

That is why Gurbani wants us to keep our mind steady in our own Real Self. This way the mind will calm down and will generate less disturbance, resulting in our waking life dream to be more peaceful. This will minimize our day to day problems that cause us suffering. Gurbani asks us to keep our mind steady and as a result our problems will get resolved..

ਥਿਰੁ ਘਰਿ ਬੈਸਹੁ ਹਰਿ ਜਨ ਪਿਆਰੇ ॥
ਸਤਿਗੁਰਿ ਤੁਮਰੇ ਕਾਜ ਸਵਾਰੇ ॥
ਦੁਸਟ ਦੂਤ ਪਰਮੇਸਰਿ ਮਾਰੇ ॥
ਜਨ ਕੀ ਪੈਜ ਰਖੀ ਕਰਤਾਰੇ ॥  (Ang 201)

*(Remain steady in the home of your own Self, O beloved servant of God,*

*Sat Guru will resolve all your problems, The Lord will strike down your wicked enemies, God will preserve the honor of His Servant.)*

# PURPOSE OF LIFE

ਪ੍ਰਾਣੀ ਤੂੰ ਆਇਆ ਲਾਹਾ ਲੈਣਿ ॥ ਲਗਾ ਕਿਤੁ
ਕੁਫਕੜੇ ਸਭ ਮੁਕਦੀ ਚਲੀ ਰੈਣਿ ॥ *(Ang 43)*

*(O man, you came here to benefit
from life. What useless activities
are you engaged in, Your life's
night is coming to an end.)*

S ant Maskeen Ji used to say in his katha that he can predict
the future of every man and woman in the world. One
of his followers in New Delhi called Sant Ji by phone and
asked him if it was true that he could predict a person's future.
Sant Ji replied "yes, that is true". The follower said that he would
like to know his own future next time, when Sant Ji came to New
Delhi. Sant Ji responded, you don't need to wait for me to come
to New Delhi, I can tell you your future right now on the phone.
Your future, Sant Ji said, is to become God. This is not only your
future but the future of everyone. What Sant Ji was saying is that
we all have come from one Source, that is God and in the end we
all will go back into It. Gurbani says that we have come from God
and we will become Him again.

ਜਿਸ ਤੇ ਉਪਜਿਆ ਨਾਨਕਾ ਸੋਈ ਫਿਰ ਹੋਆ ॥ (Ang 1193)
(O Nanak, from whom we came, into Him we merge again.)

Guru Gobind Singh Ji says in Bachittar Natak that there is no
question whatsoever, about the oneness of the Lord and His

145

devotee. Guru Ji explains this with an analogy of a wave that rises from the water and merges back into the water. While the wave looks different from the water, it is nothing but water. Similarly, all of us, even though we believe ourselves to be different and separate from God, we are in fact, one with the Almighty.

ਹਰਿ ਹਰਿਜਨ ਦੁਇ ਏਕ ਹੈ ਬਿਬ ਬਿਚਾਰ ਕਛੁ ਨਾਹਿ ॥
ਜਲ ਤੇ ਉਪਜ ਤਰੰਗ ਜਿਉ ਜਲ ਹੀ ਬਿਖੈ ਸਮਾਹਿ ॥60॥ (Sri Dasam Granth Ang 58)
(*The two, Lord and His devotee are one, there is no question about that at all.*
*Just as the wave of water rises in water and merges back in water.*)

In another shabad the tenth Guru gives analogies of fire, dust and water waves to point out that everything we see living and non-living has come out of the Supreme Lord and will eventually go back into Him. Guru Ji writes in Akal Ustat that everything animate and inanimate comes out of the One Reality and eventually, goes back into It again.

ਜੈਸੇ ਏਕ ਆਗ ਤੇ ਕਨੂਕਾ ਕੋਟ ਆਗ ਉਠੇ ਨਿਆਰੇ ਨਿਆਰੇ ਹੁਇਕੈ ਫੇਰ ਆਗ ਮੈ ਮਿਲਾਹਗੇ ॥
ਜੈਸੇ ਏਕ ਧੂਰ ਤੇ ਅਨੇਕ ਧੂਰ ਪੂਰਤ ਹੈ ਧੂਰ ਕੇ ਕਨੂਕਾ ਫੇਰ ਧੂਰ ਹੀ ਸਮਾਹਗੇ ॥
ਜੈਸੇ ਏਕ ਨਦ ਤੇ ਤਰੰਗ ਕੋਟ ਉਪਜਤ ਹੈ ਪਾਨ ਕੇ ਤਰੰਗ ਸਬੈ ਪਾਨ ਹੀ ਕਹਾਹਗੇ ॥
ਤੈਸੇ ਬਿਸੂ ਰੂਪ ਤੇ ਅਭੂਤ ਭੂਤ ਪ੍ਰਗਟ ਹੋਇ ਤਾਹੀ ਤੇ ਉਪਜ ਸਬੈ ਤਾਹੀ ਮੈ ਸਮਾਹਗੇ ॥
(*Just as millions of sparks are created from the fire; although they are different entities, they again merge in the same fire,*
*Just as many insects and creatures are born in dirt and eventually become dirt again,*
*Just as millions of waves are created on the surface of a river;*
*All the waves are called the waves of water,*
*Similarly the animate and the inanimate objects come out of the Supreme Lord;*
*They come out of, and merge in the same Lord.*)

We are Divine and have voluntarily forgotten our origin. We

have mistaken ourselves for the body, and have adopted body's limitations and become body minds. Additionally, we have embraced cultural and other conditioning and have become completely trapped in the drama of the world. Once we let go of these self imposed limitations and cultural conditioning, we will realize our True Identity, which is none other than God. So our purpose in life is to discover our True Identity, or recognize who we really are. There are several shabads in Sri Guru Granth Sahib telling us to recognize our True Identity or Real Self. Gurbani says those who do not recognize their own origin are like fools and wasting their life in the duality of the world.

ਮੂਰਖ ਦੁਬਿਧਾ ਪੜ੍ਹਹਿ ਮੂਲ ਨ ਪਛਾਣਹਿ ਬਿਰਥਾ ਜਨਮੁ ਗਵਾਇਆ ॥ (Ang 1133)
(*The fools live in duality, do not recognize their origin and they waste their lives uselessly.*)

One thing needs to be emphasized here is the word "recognize" (ਪਛਾਣ). This word has been used many times in Gurbani. The dictionary meaning of the word "recognize" is "to know again". So when Guru Ji tells us to recognize our origin He is telling us to know our origin again. That means that we have known our origin before, and Guru Ji is asking us to know it again. We are Divine Being but we have forgotten it temporarily. So Guru Ji is saying that we should know our Divinity again as we did before forgetting it.

Why do we need to recognize our True Nature? The answer is we will regain our peace and happiness that we have lost, as a result of forgetting our True Identity. The Divinity, which is our True Nature, is the embodiment of Peace and Happiness. But when we forget our True Nature and start believing ourselves to be body minds having separate entities, we lose this inherent Peace and Happiness too. This is our current situation. That is why there is so much unhappiness and suffering in the world. So the purpose of our life is to regain that Peace and Happiness by recognizing our True Nature. That is the only way to get permanent Peace and Happiness. There is no other way.

Many philosophers claim that the sole purpose of life is to gain happiness. They do not care about realizing our true identity. The reason for this claim is the fact that happiness is the most sought after object by everyone in the world. Ask anybody and he or she will tell you that they want peace and happiness above anything else. They may be doing different things in their life but their goal is the same which is to acquire happiness. A person who does good deeds has the same goal of attaining happiness as a person who is cheating others. A person who gets up very early in the morning to go to work, has the same goal of being happy as a person who gets up very early to do meditation. We are looking for only one thing in life that is peace and happiness, but going at it in different ways to find it. But if we look closely, happiness cannot be achieved by possessing the outer objects, no matter what the objects may be. We do get some happiness in the beginning when we get the object, but as soon as the honeymoon is over, the happiness is over too. When the object does not bring the same happiness anymore, we start searching for a new object, thinking that it will bring us happiness again. The new object offers happiness for a while but the cycle repeats itself and the permanent peace and happiness is never achieved. That is why Gurbani says that there is no peace and happiness in making bundles of money, watching shows of the world or conquering other countries but it is found in remembering the Lord.

ਸੁਖੁ ਨਾਹੀ ਬਹੁਤੈ ਧਨਿ ਖਾਟੇ ॥
ਸੁਖੁ ਨਾਹੀ ਪੇਖੇ ਨਿਰਤਿ ਨਾਟੇ ॥
ਸੁਖੁ ਨਾਹੀ ਬਹੁ ਦੇਸ ਕਮਾਏ ॥
ਸਰਬ ਸੁਖਾ ਹਰਿ ਹਰਿ ਗੁਣ ਗਾਏ ॥  (Ang 1147)

(There is no peace and happiness in earning lots of money,
There is no peace and happiness in watching dances and plays,
There is no peace and happiness in conquering lots of countries,
All the peace and happiness emanate from singing the Praises of the Lord.)

Additionally, Gurbani says that without remembering the Satguru, our own Real Self we cannot expect to find real Peace and Happiness. The word "remember" is similar to the word "recognize" (ਪਛਾਣ). Remember can be written as re-member, meaning we become a member again or become Real Self again.

ਬਿਨੁ ਸਤਿਗੁਰ ਸੇਵੇ ਸੁਖੁ ਨ ਪਾਏ ਦੂਖੋ ਦੂਖ ਕਮਾਵਣਿਆ ॥ (Ang 114)
(*Without remembrance of the Satguru, they don't find peace and happiness, they earn only pain and misery.*)

So Gurbani does not disagree with the philosophers that the sole purpose of life may be achieving happiness, but it disagrees with the place from which this happiness can be attained. Gurbani also disagrees with the definition of happiness. Gurbani's version of happiness is "Anand" or "Parmanand", which emanates from the union with our Real Self, Guru or God; while general happiness is something that is caused by the possession of worldly objects or relationships. Gurbani defines Anand in the following shabad.

ਅਨਦੁ ਸੁਣਹੁ ਵਡਭਾਗੀਹੋ ਸਗਲ ਮਨੋਰਥ ਪੂਰੇ ॥
ਪਾਰਬ੍ਰਹਮੁ ਪ੍ਰਭੁ ਪਾਇਆ ਉਤਰੇ ਸਗਲ ਵਿਸੂਰੇ ॥
ਦੂਖ ਰੋਗ ਸੰਤਾਪ ਉਤਰੇ ਸੁਣੀ ਸਚੀ ਬਾਣੀ ॥
ਸੰਤ ਸਾਜਨ ਭਏ ਸਰਸੇ ਪੂਰੇ ਗੁਰ ਤੇ ਜਾਣੀ ॥ (Ang 922)
(Listen up the fortunate ones, "*Anand*" is
*Where all the longings are fulfilled,*
*Where Supreme Lord has been realized,*
*Where all the sorrows have been eradicated,*
*Where illness and suffering have departed by listening to True Bani,*
*Where the Saints and their friends are in ecstasy, learning it from the Perfect Guru.*)

So while Gurbani agrees with the achievement of happiness as the purpose of life, it asserts that true happiness which is Anand cannot be had from the objective world. True happiness can only be acquired through union with your Real Self, Guru or God. In the following shabad Gurbani makes it clear that Anand is

149

realized upon meeting with the True Guru.

ਅਨੰਦੁ ਭਇਆ ਮੇਰੀ ਮਾਏ ਸਤਿਗੁਰੂ ਮੈ ਪਾਇਆ ॥
ਸਤਿਗੁਰੁ ਤ ਪਾਇਆ ਸਹਜ ਸੇਤੀ ਮਨਿ ਵਜੀਆ ਵਾਧਾਈਆ ॥ (Ang 917)
(*I am in ecstasy, O my mother, for I have met my True Guru,*
*I have met the True Guru, with intuitive ease, and my mind is*
*overjoyed with bliss.*)

Why does one realizes Anand when one meets the Guru or Real
Self? This is because Supreme Bliss (ਪਰਮਾਨੰਦ) is the real nature of
the True Guru or our Real Self. So by simply meeting the True
Guru one is blessed with the highest form of happiness. The
other reason why we become ecstatic upon meeting our Real
Self or the Guru is that we have separated from our Real Self
for times unknown, and have been longing for it all this time.
Our longing is in the form of running after happiness twenty
four seven. As stated earlier, no matter what anybody is doing,
he or she is doing it to achieve happiness. So when we get to
meet the Source of Happiness, the Bliss wells up in us, we feel
overwhelmed with the Joy of Union with our Source.

ਸੁਖ ਸਾਗਰ ਪ੍ਰੀਤਮ ਮਿਲੇ ਉਪਜੇ ਮਹਾ ਅਨੰਦ ॥
ਕਹੁ ਨਾਨਕ ਸਭ ਦੁਖ ਮਿਟੇ ਪ੍ਰਭ ਭੇਟੇ ਪਰਮਾਨੰਦ ॥ (Ang 431)
(*Those who meet the Lord, the Ocean of Peace and Happiness,*
*Supreme Bliss wells up within them,*
*Says Nanak that all their suffering is eradicated upon meeting with*
*God, the Lord of Supreme Bliss.*)

**So the main purpose of our life is to recognize our Divine
Self. Recognition and awareness of our Divinity will shower
Supreme Bliss (ਪਰਮਾਨੰਦ) upon us. Guru Ji says that by meeting
the ocean of Peace, my Divine Self; Supreme Bliss has welled up
in me and all my problems have been solved.**

Gurbani calls the mind as a "jote" (ਜੋਤ) whose Origin is the Divine
Light "Jote", meaning the mind emanates from the Divine Light.
Mind is made of the Divine Light but has forgotten its origin. So
the mind has to remember its Origin, the Divine Light and has to

merge back into It. With that context in mind, Sant Maskeen Ji defines purpose of life in a more specific way as follows:

**"Purpose of our life is to make our jote (mind) to merge into Jote (Divine Light) before our body, which is dust, merges into dust."**

As per Gurbani Divine Light is shining in everyone of us bar none. Gurbani also says that one who investigates himself or herself, recognises himself or herself, and his or her mind merges into the Light of the Divine.

ਸਭ ਮਹਿ ਜੋਤਿ ਜੋਤਿ ਹੈ ਸੋਇ ॥
ਤਿਸਦੈ ਚਾਨਣਿ ਸਭ ਮਹਿ ਚਾਨਣੁ ਹੋਇ ॥ (Ang 13)
(*In all is pervading the Light of Divine,*
*Everyone is illuminated by this Divine Light.*)

ਚੀਨੈ ਆਪੁ ਪਛਾਣੈ ਸੋਈ ਜੋਤੀ ਜੋਤਿ ਮਿਲਾਈ ਹੇ ॥ (Ang 1024)
(*One who investigates oneself, recognizes himself or herself,*
*and his or her Light merges into the Divine Light.*)

Gurbani is telling us that we have gotten this body in this life, this is our turn to realize the Lord.

ਭਈ ਪਰਾਪਤਿ ਮਾਨੁਖ ਦੇਹੁਰੀਆ ॥
ਗੋਬਿੰਦ ਮਿਲਣ ਕੀ ਇਹ ਤੇਰੀ ਬਰੀਆ ॥
ਅਵਰਿ ਕਾਜ ਤੇਰੈ ਕਿਤੈ ਨ ਕਾਮ ॥
ਮਿਲੁ ਸਾਧਸੰਗਤਿ ਭਜੁ ਕੇਵਲ ਨਾਮ ॥
ਸਰੰਜਾਮਿ ਲਾਗੁ ਭਵਜਲ ਤਰਨ ਕੈ ॥
ਜਨਮੁ ਬ੍ਰਿਥਾ ਜਾਤ ਰੰਗਿ ਮਾਈਆ ਕੈ ॥ (Ang 12)
(*This human body has been given to you,*
*This is your chance to meet the Lord,*
*Doing any other deeds is of no use,*
*Join the company of the Holy, only meditate on Naam.*
*Make every effort to cross over this world ocean,*
*This life is being squandered away uselessly in the Love of Maya.*)

Gurbani says that other tasks of life are not going to help, you should only remember Him in the company of Sadh Sangat. Sadh Sangat here does not mean one has to go out and live with the sadhus. It means the company of your True Inner Self, the Satguru. Gurbani calls Satguru as sadh, as is evident from the following shabads.

ਜਿਨ ਐਸਾ ਸਤਿਗੁਰੁ ਸਾਧੁ ਨ ਪਾਇਆ ਤੇ ਹਰਿ ਦਰਗਹ ਕਾਢੇ ਮਾਰੀ ॥ (Ang 1135)
(*Those who do not find their True Guru, are expelled from the Court of the Lord.*)

ਜਿਨ ਐਸਾ ਸਤਿਗੁਰੁ ਸਾਧੁ ਨ ਪਾਇਆ ਤੇ ਧ੍ਰਿਗੁ ਧ੍ਰਿਗੁ ਨਰ ਜੀਵਾਈਐ ॥ (Ang 1179)
(*Those who do not find their True Guru, their lives are cursed.*)

We are being warned that those who do not meet the Satguru in this life have just wasted their life away. Guru Ji calls those people cynics dying of regretful death who do not find the company of the Satguru.

ਜਿਨੀ ਦਰਸਨੁ ਜਿਨੀ ਦਰਸਨੁ ਸਤਿਗੁਰ ਪੁਰਖ ਨ ਪਾਇਆ ਰਾਮ ॥
ਤਿਨ ਨਿਹਫਲੁ ਤਿਨ ਨਿਹਫਲੁ ਜਨਮੁ ਸਭੁ ਬ੍ਰਿਥਾ ਗਵਾਇਆ ਰਾਮ ॥
ਨਿਹਫਲੁ ਜਨਮੁ ਤਿਨ ਬ੍ਰਿਥਾ ਗਵਾਇਆ ਤੇ ਸਾਕਤ ਮੁਏ ਮਰਿ ਝੂਰੇ ॥
ਘਰਿ ਹੋਦੈ ਰਤਨਿ ਪਦਾਰਥਿ ਭੂਖੇ ਭਾਗਹੀਨ ਹਰਿ ਦੂਰੇ ॥ (Ang 574)
(*Those who have not obtained the blessed vision of the Sat Guru,*
*They have fruitlessly, fruitlessly wasted away their whole lives in vain.*
*They have wasted away their whole life in vain; those faithless cynics die a regretful death,*
*They have the jewel-treasure in their own homes, but they are still hungry,*
*Those unlucky wretches are far away from the Lord.*)

Guru ji is using very harsh language to make sure that we do listen to what is being said here. In spite of all this harsh language, we keep going our old merry ways of ignoring what Guru Ji is saying. If we look at our daily life we are so engrossed in the worldly life that we never think what our purpose in life is. Our mind is always running out after worldly objects. Guru Ji, very appropriately, describes our state of mind in the following shabad. He says to the mind that you are entangled in sinful associations, and innumerable thought waves are going through you all the time. In this state, how can you attain to the Lord, who is normally beyond reach and beyond understanding.

ਉਰਝਿ ਰਹਿਓ ਬਿਖਿਆ ਕੈ ਸੰਗਾ ॥
ਮਨਹਿ ਬਿਆਪਤ ਅਨਿਕ ਤਰੰਗਾ ॥
ਮੇਰੇ ਮਨ ਅਗਮ ਅਗੋਚਰ ॥
ਕਤ ਪਾਇਐ ਪੂਰਨ ਪਰਮੇਸਰ ॥  (Ang 759)
(*The mind is entangled in sinful Associations,*
*Innumerable thoughts rise in it,*
*O my mind, how can you attain to the perfect Lord,*
*Who is unapproachable and incomprehensible.*)

Unless the mind stops running around after the shiny objects of the world it cannot find its Source. The mind has to wake up and stop losing itself in all kinds of thoughts, then and only then there is hope of getting to the Lord. Gurbani calls this dying while living. It means that we have to die to the world or have to stop our attention from going outward. Simply stated if our attention is going out it is going away from our Real Self or the Guru, which is inside us. So how can we meet our Real Self?

ਕਿਨ ਬਿਧਿ ਸਾਗਰੁ ਤਰੀਐ ॥
ਜੀਵਤਿਆ ਨਹ ਮਰੀਐ ॥  (Ang 877)
(*How can we cross the ocean of the world?*
*Unless we die while living.*)

Gurbani compres life in the world to an ocean, which we have to cross to meet the Lord. The shabad is saying that unless we can turn away from the attractions of the world how can we get to the other end. I want to interject here that Gurbani is not asking us to become renunciates. It is just pointing to our attachment to the world. We have to live in the world but not be attached to it.

Gurbani talks about this purpose of life another way by addressing duality in the world. We believe in the duality of people, of animals and of the objects of the world. We think ourselves to be individual entities, and consider ourselves to separate from one other. This is not true. It is all One Reality both inside and out. If we can get rid of duality in our life, we will attain the One Reality, God. Gurbani says that we should eradicate this duality from our minds. If we do that we can reap so many additional benefits from doing this. These benefits are beautifully detailed in the following shabad:

ਜੋ ਇਸੁ ਮਾਰੇ ਸੋਈ ਸੂਰਾ ॥      ਜੋ ਇਸੁ ਮਾਰੇ ਸੋਈ ਪੂਰਾ ॥
ਜੋ ਇਸੁ ਮਾਰੇ ਤਿਸਹਿ ਵਡਿਆਈ ॥      ਜੋ ਇਸੁ ਮਾਰੇ ਤਿਸ ਕਾ ਦੁਖੁ ਜਾਈ ॥
ਐਸਾ ਕੋਇ ਜਿ ਦੁਬਿਧਾ ਮਾਰਿ ਗਵਾਵੈ ॥      ਇਸਹਿ ਮਾਰਿ ਰਾਜ ਜੋਗੁ ਕਮਾਵੈ ॥

ਜੋ ਇਸੁ ਮਾਰੇ ਤਿਸ ਕਉ ਭਉ ਨਾਹਿ ॥      ਇਸੁ ਮਾਰੇ ਸੁ ਨਾਮਿ ਸਮਾਹਿ ॥
ਜੋ ਇਸੁ ਮਾਰੇ ਤਿਸ ਤ੍ਰਿਸਨਾ ਬੁਝੈ ॥      ਜੋ ਇਸੁ ਮਾਰੇ ਸੁ ਦਰਗਹ ਸਿਝੈ ॥

ਜੋ ਇਸੁ ਮਾਰੇ ਸੋ ਧਨਵੰਤਾ ॥      ਜੋ ਇਸੁ ਮਾਰੇ ਸੋ ਪਤਿਵੰਤਾ ॥
ਜੋ ਇਸੁ ਮਾਰੇ ਸੋਈ ਜਤੀ ॥      ਜੋ ਇਸੁ ਮਾਰੇ ਤਿਸੁ ਹੋਵੈ ਗਤੀ ॥

ਜੋ ਇਸੁ ਮਾਰੇ ਤਿਸ ਕਾ ਆਇਆ ਗਨੀ ॥      ਜੋ ਇਸੁ ਮਾਰੇ ਸੁ ਨਿਹਚਲੁ ਧਨੀ ॥
ਜੋ ਇਸੁ ਮਾਰੇ ਸੋ ਵਡਭਾਗਾ ॥      ਜੋ ਇਸੁ ਮਾਰੇ ਸੁ ਅਨਦਿਨੁ ਜਾਗਾ ॥

ਜੋ ਇਸੁ ਮਾਰੇ ਸੁ ਜੀਵਨ ਮੁਕਤਾ ॥      ਜੋ ਇਸੁ ਮਾਰੇ ਤਿਸ ਕੀ ਨਿਰਮਲ ਜੁਗਤਾ ॥
ਜੋ ਇਸੁ ਮਾਰੇ ਸੋਈ ਸੁਗਿਆਨੀ ॥      ਜੋ ਇਸੁ ਮਾਰੇ ਸੁ ਸਹਜ ਧਿਆਨੀ ॥

ਇਸੁ ਮਾਰੀ ਬਿਨੁ ਥਾਇ ਨ ਪਰੈ ॥      ਕੋਟਿ ਕਰਮ ਜਾਪ ਤਪ ਕਰੈ ॥
ਇਸੁ ਮਾਰੀ ਬਿਨੁ ਜਨਮੁ ਨ ਮਿਟੈ ॥      ਇਸੁ ਮਾਰੀ ਬਿਨੁ ਜੰਮ ਤੇ ਨਹੀ ਛੁਟੈ ॥

ਇਸੁ ਮਾਰੀ ਬਿਨੁ ਗਿਆਨੁ ਨ ਹੋਈ ॥      ਇਸੁ ਮਾਰੀ ਬਿਨੁ ਜੂਠਿ ਨ ਧੋਈ ॥
ਇਸੁ ਮਾਰੀ ਬਿਨੁ ਸਭੁ ਕਿਛੁ ਮੈਲਾ ॥      ਇਸੁ ਮਾਰੀ ਬਿਨੁ ਸਭੁ ਕਿਛੁ ਜਉਲਾ ॥

ਜਾ ਕਉ ਭਏ ਕ੍ਰਿਪਾਲ ਕ੍ਰਿਪਾ ਨਿਧਿ ॥      ਤਿਸੁ ਭਈ ਖਲਾਸੀ ਹੋਈ ਸਗਲ ਸਿਧਿ ॥
ਗੁਰਿ ਦੁਬਿਧਾ ਜਾ ਕੀ ਹੈ ਮਾਰੀ ॥      ॥ ਨਾਨਕ ਸੋ ਬ੍ਰਹਮ ਬੀਚਾਰੀ ॥      (Ang 237)

*(One who kills duality, is a hero,*
*One who kills duality, is perfect one,*
*One who kills duality, becomes great,*
*One who kills duality, is freed of suffering.*
*It is very rare that someone kills and gets rid of his duality,*
*Killing it, he or she attains Raja Yoga.*

*One who kills duality, has no fear,*
*One who kills duality, is absorbed in Naam,*

*One who kills duality, his desires die away,*
*One who kills duality, is approved in the Court of the Lord.*

*One who kills duality, is wealthy and prosperous,*
*One who kills duality, is honorable,*
*One who kills duality, is truly a celibate,*
*One who kills duality, attains salvation.*

*One who kills duality, his coming is auspicious,*
*One who kills duality, is steady and powerful,*
*One who kills duality, is very fortunate,*
*One who kills duality, remains awake night and day.*

*One who kills duality, is liberated while alive,*
*One who kills duality, lives a pure lifestyle,*
*One who kill duality, is spiritually wise,*
*One who kills duality, meditates intuitively.*

*Without killing duality, one is not accepted,*
*Even though one may perform millions of rituals, chants and austerities.*
*Without killing duality, one does not escape the cycle of reincarnation,*
*Without killing duality, one does not escape death.*

*Without killing duality, one does not obtain spiritual wisdom,*
*Without killing duality, impurities are not washed away,*
*Without killing duality, everything is dirty,*
*Without killing duality, everything is considered separate.*

*When the Lord, the Treasurer of Mercy, bestows his Mercy,*
*One obtains release, and attains total perfection.*
*One whose duality has been obliterated by the Guru,*
*Says Nanak, he contemplates on God.)*

Eradication of duality is the natural outcome of realizing that there is only One God. Once the duality has been eradicated, there is no me, no you, no mine, no thine. So there is nothing to be jealous about, no reason to hate anybody and no racism etc.

The world will become a haven where everybody would respect and love everyone else as they would do themselves. One thing needs to be emphasized here, as stated in the shabad, one can do all kinds of rituals, religious ceremonies and austerities, unless one attains an experiential understanding of non-duality, one cannot make any spiritual progress and until then the purpose of life is not achieved.

**Discussion:**

Gurbani says that God is both inside us and outside us; and there is no place anywhere that is devoid of Him. As such our goal is to see Him everywhere. So the purpose of our life is two fold. One is to see Him inside ourselves, and also to see Him outside ourselves.

ਬਾਹਰਿ ਭਿਤਰਿ ਏਕੋ ਜਾਨਹੁ ਇਹੁ ਗੁਰ ਗਿਆਨੁ ਬਤਾਈ ॥ (Ang 684)
(*Outside and inside, know that there is only the One God, the Guru has imparted this wisdom to me.*)

ਅੰਤਰਿ ਬਸੇ ਬਾਹਰਿ ਭੀ ਓਹੀ ॥
ਨਾਨਕ ਦਰਸਨੁ ਦੇਖਿ ਸਭ ਮੋਹੀ ॥ (Ang 294)
(*He dwells inside, and outside as well,
O Nanak, beholding His Vision, everyone is fascinated.*)

**God Inside Us:**

There is a lot of emphasis given in Gurbani for going inwards and trying to find Him in our hearts. Talking of God inside us, Gurbani says that God lives inside us but we are looking for him outside. Unless we go inside there is no chance of meeting him. It is like if you want to meet a person who is at a particular place inside a building, and you never go inside that building, how can you ever meet the person. Ragi Jaspal Singh Ji in one of the shabads, while doing kirtan says that we never go to the place where God resides. He is inside us but we never go there. Hence there is no chance of meeting Him. It is only when we will go inside ourselves we will make contact with Him. We will talk in more detail a little later about what going inside really means. Gurbani says that the Lord is present in everybody. So one part of our purpose in life is to realize Him inside us.

ਤੂੰ ਘਟ ਘਟ ਅੰਤਰਿ ਸਰਬ ਨਿਰੰਤਰਿ ਜੀ ਹਰਿ ਏਕੋ ਪੁਰਖੁ ਸਮਾਣਾ ॥  (Ang 10)
(*You reside in each and every heart, You are the only One present there.*)

**Experiencing God Inside Us:**

Shabad after shabad in Granth Sahib stresses that God lives in our heart. One does not have to go to the forest to find Him. Gurbani tells us that He is right where we are, very very near; and in fact, He has become us. He is right there with us all, listening and seeing everything. Difference between the Lord and us is like the gold; and the bracelet which is also made out of gold or between the water and its waves which are also made out of water. Essentially, there is no difference between the Lord and us.

ਸੁਨਤ ਪੇਖਤ ਸੰਗਿ ਸਭ ਕੈ ਪ੍ਰਭ ਨੇਰਹੂ ਤੇ ਨੇਰੇ ॥  (Ang 547)
(*The Lord hears and beholds with us all, He is nearest of the near.*)

ਤੋਹੀ ਮੋਹੀ ਮੋਹੀ ਤੋਹੀ ਅੰਤਰੁ ਕੈਸਾ ॥
ਕਨਕ ਕਟਿਕ ਜਲ ਤਰੰਗ ਜੈਸਾ ॥  (Ang 93)
(*What is the difference between You and me, me and You,*
*It is like the difference between gold and bracelets, or water and its waves.*)

If we check our daily experience closely, we can get an experiential understanding of God within us. Looking at our current experience. If we are reading this page, someone in us knows this experience of reading this page. Let us explore who in us is reading this page. We say that I am reading this page. So we need to find what in us is called "I". There are three possibilities of who the "I" is. It could be the body, mind or something else. Let us look at the body first. Body does not have any intelligence of its own to know anything. In fact, it is a non-conscious, non-sentient material made of food or eventually the soil. Gurbani calls a body a clay doll. We all know that clay cannot be the reader. So we can conclude that body is not the one reading this page.

Next we will analyze the mind. Mind, like the body, does not have its own intelligence either. It is like a computer. It works great but it has to be programmed and it works according to its programming. Mind is made out of thoughts. If there is no thought then there is no mind. So the mind does not even have a continual existence. How can the mind which does not have a continual existence, can be the reader? So we can say that the mind cannot be the reader of the page either.

We have discovered that both body and mind are not the readers of the page. The question arises if body and mind are not the readers, then who is it? We know for sure that something in us is doing the reading. It has to be something beyond the body and mind. What is beyond body and mind? Whatever it is, it has the reading or knowing quality. It knows the experience of reading this page. This knowing is simply called Knowing Presence or Awareness because of its nature of possessing "knowing "or "awareness" quality. So we discover that it is not the body or the mind that is the knower of the experience of reading the page, it is the Awareness. Gurbani states that God is this very Awareness (Bibek). Gurbani addresses God in the following shabad that, O Lord, you are the Creator, the Doer, and you are One and many. You are Almighty, Omnipresent and the Awareness (ਬਿਬੇਕ). This shabad lets us conclude that this Awareness is God Himself or Herself.

ਤੂੰ ਕਰਤਾ ਤੂੰ ਕਰਣਹਾਰੁ ਤੂਹੈ ਏਕੁ ਅਨੇਕ ਜੀਉ ॥
ਤੂ ਸਮਰਥੁ ਤੂ ਸਰਬ ਮੈ ਤੂਹੇ ਬੁਧਿ ਬਿਬੇਕ ਜੀਉ ॥ (Ang 761)
(*You are the Creator, You are the Doer, You are the One and the Many.*
*You are All-Powerful, You are present everywhere, You are the*

*Awareness.*)

ਆਪਿ ਬਿਬੇਕੁ ਆਪਿ ਸਭੁ ਬੇਤਾ ਆਪੇ ਗੁਰਮੁਖਿ ਭੰਜਨੁ ॥ (Ang 552)
(*God Himself is Awareness, and He Himself is the Knower of all; He Himself breaks the bonds of the Gurmukh.*)

So we discover that the Knower of our experience of reading this page is the Awareness, which is God Himself or Herself. We also state that I am reading this page. By putting the two statements together, we find that God and I are not two but one. In other words, to get an experience of God inside us, all we have to do is to get an experience of our own self "I" which is our Real Self. That is why Gurbani always instructs us to go inside and find Him inside ourselves. But we do not pay attention to this advice and constantly do the opposite. If we mend ourselves, we will meet our "I", our Real Self and we will attain happiness upon meeting ourselves.

ਆਪੁ ਸਵਾਰਹਿ ਮੈ ਮਿਲਹਿ ਮੈ ਮਿਲਿਆ ਸੁਖ ਹੋਇ ॥ (Ang 1382)
(*If one reforms oneself, he or she shall meet "I". Meeting "I" one will find happiness.*)

With the belief that Divinity is the only entity present in us, we will come to realize that everything is being done by Him in our life. He is the one who sees through us, speaks through us, listens through us, tastes through us, the list can go on and on. The fact is that Only He is, we are not.

ਹਮ ਕਿਛੁ ਨਾਹੀ ਏਕੈ ਓਹੀ ॥
ਆਗੈ ਪਾਛੈ ਏਕੋ ਸੋਈ ॥ (Ang 391)
(*I don't have any entity, He is the One and Only,
He is the only One everywhere.*)

**God Outside Us:**

As stated earlier Gurbani says that God is not only inside us but outside too. But we think that we can find the Lord outside like we find the other objects of the world. That is not possible because God is not an object. Finding Him or Her outside is possible only, if we upgrade our perception of the world. He is not an object, but all objects are in Him. He has become everything. We see Him all the time, everywhere, all around us but we do not look deep enough to see through the objects to find him hiding there in plane sight. Even though He or She has become all of our forms, He still has no form of His own that can be seen. He has no form so He is infinite. That is why He cannot be grasped. How can a finite grasp an infinite, that is a mathematical impossibility. Even though He cannot be grasped, it is still the purpose of our life to see Him in everything outside.

ਏ ਨੇਤ੍ਰਹੁ ਮੇਰਿਹੋ ਹਰਿ ਤੁਮ ਮਹਿ ਜੋਤਿ ਧਰੀ ਹਰਿ ਬਿਨੁ ਅਵਰੁ ਨ ਦੇਖਹੁ ਕੋਈ ॥
ਹਰਿ ਬਿਨੁ ਅਵਰੁ ਨ ਦੇਖਹੁ ਕੋਈ ਨਦਰੀ ਹਰਿ ਨਿਹਾਲਿਆ ॥
ਏਹੁ ਵਿਸੁ ਸੰਸਾਰੁ ਤੁਮ ਦੇਖਦੇ ਏਹੁ ਹਰਿ ਕਾ ਰੂਪੁ ਹੈ ਹਰਿ ਰੂਪੁ ਨਦਰੀ ਆਇਆ ॥ (Ang 922)

(*O my eyes, the Lord has infused Light into you, do not see anybody other than the Lord.*
*Do not see any other than the Lord, see only the Lord.*
*This vast universe you see is the image of the Lord and only the image of the Lord is being seen.*)

We can get an experiential feeling of the Divine outside by analyzing our daily experience. Normally, we don't see beyond the surface, but if we go a little deeper than the surface, we can get a glimpse of the Divine outside.

**Experiencing God Outside Us:**

Gurbani says that whatever we see outside is God Himself or Herself. There is nobody else. We think we see people, animals and objects of the world but that is just an appearance. In reality there is no objective world out there. It is all God and God alone that we see.

ਸਭੁ ਗੋਬਿੰਦੁ ਹੈ ਸਭੁ ਗੋਬਿੰਦੁ ਹੈ ਗੋਬਿੰਦ ਬਿਨੁ ਨਹੀ ਕੋਈ ॥ (Ang 485)
(*Everything is God, everything is God, there is nothing else that God.*)

ਜਹ ਜਹ ਦੇਖਉ ਤਹ ਤਹ ਸਾਚਾ ॥
ਬਿਨੁ ਬੂਝੇ ਝਗਰਤ ਜਗੁ ਕਾਚਾ ॥ (Ang 224)
(Wherever I look, there I find the True Lord,
Without understanding, the world argues in falsehood.)

So Gurbani declares unequivocally that what we see outside is
God and God alone. Why don't we see Him? Why do we see
only the world, people, animals and objects? This is because
God Himself has become all these. How has God become people,
animals and objects, can be explained with an analogy. When we
have a dream at night our mind creates a dream world and then
enters into its own dream as a dream subject. The dream world
is made of people, animals and all kinds of objects, but it is our
mind that has become everything. The world we live in is made
like that too. God is having His own dream and has created a
dream world of His own, where all of us, the animals, birds etc
are all the subjects of His dream world. So this world we live in
is like a dream, but it is made of nothing else other than God
Himself. To us the dream world looks completely real, because
we are part of the dream. A disciple asked his master "can you
show me God?" The master said, "just look around you, you see
nothing but God".

ਜਿਉ ਸੁਪਨਾ ਅਰੁ ਪੇਖਨਾ ਐਸੇ ਜਗ ਕਉ ਜਾਨਿ ॥
ਇਨ ਮੈ ਕਛੁ ਸਾਚੋ ਨਹੀ ਨਾਨਕ ਬਿਨੁ ਭਗਵਾਨ ॥ (Ang 1427)
(Know this world to be just like the dream we see at night,
There is nothing true in this world, other than God.)

There is another way to look at this too. We see the world instead
of God, because of the fact that our minds are hypnotized to see
it that way. When we see an object, we receive a signal from it.
The signal is analyzed and interpreted by our mind and then
qualities of the object are deposited by our mind. The signal
coming from the object is completely abstract and does not
contain any qualities of the object. Our hypnotized minds assign
qualities to the signal received and thus create the object. This

is how we create our world from the abstract signals coming to us from the surroundings. The abstract signal that we receive is made of God Himself or Herself. Even though the signal is made of God, our minds interpret it to be the world that we see. This approach has been discussed in detail in the article "World is a Grand Illusion". For those who want to read its details please refer to that article. The fact of the matter is that there is only one Infinite Reality in the universe and that is Ek Onkar (ੴ) or God. This Reality has become everything in the universe. So when we look at any worldly object, we are looking at Ek Onkar or God and no one else

By understanding that God is in everything and everybody outside we come to realize that we are looking at Him wherever we look. We see Him in everyone and everything. When this understanding sinks deeper in us, we will stop blaming anybody and all the hate and jealousy will disappear from our minds. We will deal with other people like we are dealing with ourselves. Cheating and lying will disappear from our life. I can speak from my personal experience that by adopting this attitude that God is in everyone, I don't get frustrated as much anymore when I see someone behaving unfairly. In fact, a compassionate feeling arises in me when I see someone doing that, because it is God who is making the person behave the way he is behaving.

**To sum it up the ultimate purpose our life is to recognize our True Nature and thereby regain Supreme Bliss (ਪਰਮਾਨੰਦ).** We are Supreme Bliss, but have lost it by believing ourselves to be limited human beings. All we have to do is to trace our way back to our True Nature. Our destination is at the center of ourselves, so any outside effort will take us away from us. We just have to come back Home and stay in touch with our Real Self all the time. That does not mean that we have to give up dealing with friends, relatives and loved ones or the world in general. Gurbani tells us we can lead a family life and still stay in touch with our True Nature. An example of a lotus flower in water has been used in Gurbani to make the point clear. Just like the lotus flower stays in water but does not drown in water, no matter how high the water rises, the same way the householder should stay in the world but should not drown in the world, meaning should not lose himself or herself in the world.

ਵਿਚੇ ਗ੍ਰਿਹ ਸਦਾ ਰਹੈ ਉਦਾਸੀ ਜਿਉ ਕਮਲੁ ਰਹੈ ਵਿਚਿ ਪਾਨੀ ਹੇ ॥ (Ang 1070)
(*Leading the life of a householder, one should remain unattached, like the lotus flower in water.*)

◆ ◆ ◆

# SELF REALIZATION 101

ਆਪੁ ਪਛਾਣਹਿ ਪ੍ਰੀਤਮੁ ਮਿਲੈ ਵੁਠਾ
ਛਹਬਰ ਲਾਇ॥ *(Ang 1420)*

*(Recognizing your own Self, you
meet the beloved Lord; then His
Grace will rain in torrents.)*

Self realization, as the name implies, is recognizing one's own Real Self. Our real essence is Divinity itself. We have forgotten our real identity because we have lost ourselves in the world's attractions. In this article we will discuss the basic steps to realize our forgotten identity. Gurbani puts a lot of emphasis on realizing our Divinity or our Real Self, as the main goal of our life. It pleads with us or simply asks us to recognize our Real Self. At times it tells us what are the benefits of recognizing ourselves. Other times it uses tough words and scolds us for not taking it too seriously. Our nature is such that we let this advice come through one ear and let it go out the other. We do not take this seriously. This is because of our conditioning that we have acquired over our lifetime and over past lives. Our parents, our teachers or the culture in general never told us about our Real Nature. Our educational system is geared to growing our brains and making us bean counters in this material world. Guru Ji, in the following shabads gives us some precious advice about our Real Nature. He asserts that

164

one who recognizes himself or herself is the only knowledgeable person. He further says those persons who do not recognize their own Real Selves, are foolish.

ਪੂਰਵਤਿ ਨਾਨਕ ਗਿਆਨੀ ਕੈਸਾ ਹੋਇ ॥
ਆਪੁ ਪਛਾਣੈ ਬੂਝੈ ਸੋਇ ॥ (Ang 25)
(*Nanak asks, who is really a knowledgeable person,*
*One who recognizes himself, he understands God.*

ਸੋ ਮੂਰਖੁ ਜੋ ਆਪੁ ਨ ਪਛਾਣਈ ਸਚਿ ਨ ਧਰੇ ਪਿਆਰ ॥ (Ang 492)
(*He is a fool, who does not recognize his own Self,*
*And who does not enshrine love of the Truth.*)

## Our Current Understanding:

To get started on the path of self realization, we will start with our current understanding concerning where we are. If we look at our current world model, we find that we believe ourselves to be a body. Most of our relationships with other people are based on the belief that we are bodies. We think ourselves to be the bodies, because that is the way we have been brought up right from our childhood. While most of us believe ourselves to be bodies, some of us believe ourselves to be a combination of body and mind. We further claim that this combination has its own awareness. Everyone thinks himself or herself to have a separate independent existence, having free will to do whatever they want to do. One thing of great importance needs to be mentioned here, is that in dealing with other people, we consider ourselves to be the subjects and the others as the objects. Being a subject is defined as being the doer of an action. This statement may not make much sense right now but it is important because we will talk about this later. So in summary, we all believe ourselves to be bodies or body-mind combinations having independent existences with individual awareness and with the agency of doership.

There are other characteristics of our day to day living that are worth mentioning too. One is that our mind is always going out. It is never steady. It is always thinking of one thing or the other. If we pay attention to our daily activities we find that our attention is always going out. This is an important point and needs to be stressed. There are two possible directions for our attention to go to. It can go outwards or it can go inwards, but for some reason it is always going outwards. From the time we get up in the morning to the time we go to bed at night we are busy attending to the outside business, almost to the point of addiction. If we are not attending to business we are paying attention to other mundane things like talking to people, watching television or reading our emails etc. These days phones have become the focus of attention for most of us. The point is that all day long our attention is going out. If there is nothing else to do, we may be lost in thinking or daydreaming. Guru Ji describes the state of our mind in the following shabads.

ਮਨੁ ਚੰਚਲੁ ਧਾਵਤੁ ਫੁਨਿ ਧਾਵੈ ॥ (Ang 222)
(*The fickle mind runs after fleeting things.*)

ਮਨੁ ਖਿਨੁ ਖਿਨੁ ਭਰਮਿ ਭਰਮਿ ਬਹੁ ਧਾਵੈ ਤਿਲੁ ਘਰਿ ਨਹੀ ਵਾਸਾ ਪਾਈਐ ॥
(Ang 1179)
(*Every moment, mind wanders all over the place. It does not stay in its own home, even for an instant.*)

If we don't have anything to do we feel bored. It looks like we have to keep ourselves busy to avoid our own company. I am reminded of a real story of a doctor friend, who was working for a medical clinic in town. He was working a regular job from morning to evening, but was very sincere and would many times work longer hours than his job required. He was very much involved with his work. One time he took a week of vacation which he had to use, otherwise would lose it. He did not go anywhere for vacation but stayed home. He did a few things around the house the first two or three days but then he started getting bored. By Wednesday of the week he was feeling out of himself. On Thursday he could not stay home. In the evening, he went to his office, after the office working hours, so no one would see him. He sat in his office for couple of hours, reading some mail and other papers, and then came home. He told me that after sitting in his office for a couple of hours, he felt very good.

This is the problem with most of us. We get so caught up and become addicted to our work or everyday chores that we never think about ourselves. We don't know how to live in our own company. In fact, we get bored if we have to do that, just like my friend. Gurbani states our condition in the following shabads:

ਬਹੁ ਚਿੰਤਾ ਚਿਤਵੈ ਆਪੁ ਨ ਪਛਾਨਾ ॥
ਧੰਧਾ ਕਰਤਿਆ ਅਨਦਿਨੁ ਵਿਹਾਨਾ ॥ (Ang 159)
(One thinks incessantly, but does not recognize oneself,
Occupied in business, everyday is passing away.)

ਧੰਧਾ ਧਾਵਤ ਦਿਨੁ ਗਇਆ ਰੈਨਿ ਗਵਾਈ ਸੋਇ ॥
ਕੂੜੁ ਬੋਲਿ ਬਿਖੁ ਖਾਇਆ ਮਨਮੁਖਿ ਚਲਿਆ ਰੋਇ ॥ (Ang 948)
(Chasing after worldly affairs, the day is wasted,
Night is lost in sleep,
Speaking untruth one is corrupted,
The manmukh departs crying.)

**So to summarize our current state of affairs, we believe ourselves to be a body-mind combination having our own independent existence and individual awareness with the agency of doership. We consider ourselves the subject and everything else as the object. Additionally, our attention is so focused on the external world that we never even think of looking inwards.**

**Realizing Our True Identity:**

The next step in our life is to improve on our current state, by working on our daily experience. There is one main Improvement needed. We said that in our current life we consider ourselves to be subject and the other things as objects. This belief, that we are the subject, is not accurate, so this mindset has to be changed or corrected. When we consider ourselves to be the subjects we claim to be the doer. Being a doer keeps our ego intact and it becomes a hindrance on our path to spiritual progress. We are Atman or Awareness but believe ourselves to be body minds. The real subject is Atman or Awareness and not the body minds. The body and mind are objects just like other things in the world, such as animals, birds and trees etc. As long as we believe ourselves to be the body and minds to be the subject, with the sense of doership, there cannot be any spiritual progress and we will continue in the cycle of reincarnation. As said earlier, being a subject means being a doer. Gurbani says that as long as we think  we can do something, we cannot find peace.

ਜਬ ਲਗੁ ਜਾਨੈ ਮੁਝ ਤੇ ਕਛੁ ਹੋਇ ॥
ਤਬ ਇਸ ਕਉ ਸੁਖੁ ਨਾਹੀ ਕੋਇ ॥
ਜਬ ਇਹ ਜਾਨੈ ਮੈ ਕਿਛੁ ਕਰਤਾ ॥
ਤਬ ਲਗੁ ਗਰਭ ਜੋਨਿ ਮਹਿ ਫਿਰਤਾ ॥ (Ang 278)
(As long as one thinks that he or she is the doer,
He or She shall have no peace,
As long as one thinks he or she is one who does things,
He or she wanders in the cycle of reincarnation.)

So it is imperative that we improve our belief from being subject as body mind, to being subject as Atman or Awareness. Why is it important to understand body-mind combination is not the subject? It is because that is the truth. We will prove this fact from our experience later in this article. The understanding of this truth will take us a step higher than where we currently are. With this understanding we step back or step higher and become subjects of not only the world, but the body, mind and the world. We essentially start operating from a higher level of being Atman or Awareness or Real Self, rather than body minds. From there we can watch our own little self consisting of the body mind entity, struggling in the world and yet not be bothered by it. By stepping back we become our own Real Self.

We start to  put distance between our Real Self, that we are and our little self, that is body and mind combination. Gurbani uses an analogy of gold and its ornaments and water and water waves to make it clear. Gurbani says that we, the Divine Being have become the body minds. This is like gold becomes ornaments such as bracelets and rings etc. By upgrading our mindset and believing ourselves to be Atman or Awareness as the subject we are essentially, separating our Real Self from the body minds. This is similar to separating gold from an ornament.

ਤੋਹੀ ਮੋਹੀ ਮੋਹੀ ਤੋਹੀ ਅੰਤਰੁ ਕੈਸਾ ॥
ਕਨਕ ਕਟਿਕ ਜਲ ਤਰੰਗ ਜੈਸਾ ॥  (Ang 93)
(*What is the difference between You and me,*
*Just as between gold and its bracelets or water and its waves.*)

Gurbani uses another analogy to tell us how to stay in the world but not drown in it. It tells us that those who follow this understanding remain immaculately pure from the world turmoil. Gurbani uses an analogy of a kamal (lotus) flower to demonstrate how to stay above the world noise. Kamal flower grows in murky waters and dirty soil. Even though it comes out of the swampy soil, the flower is pure and beautiful. The flower stays unblemished by the murky water and the dirty soil. If the water level goes higher, the flower goes higher and stays above water. It never drowns in water. Gurbani wants us to live like that kamal flower in the world, by stepping higher to stay above the world drama. This does not mean that one should leave the world and become a renunciate. It is just changing the mindset. Do whatever you were doing earlier, just work from the new platform of being Atman or Awareness, our Real Self, rather than being a body mind.

ਬ੍ਰਹਮ ਗਿਆਨੀ ਸਦਾ ਨਿਰਲੇਪ ॥
ਜੈਸੇ ਜਲ ਮਹਿ ਕਮਲ ਅਲੇਪ ॥  (Ang 272)
(*God Conscious Being is always unattached,*

*As the lotus in the water remains detached.)*

ਗੁਰਮੁਖਿ ਨਿਰਮਲ ਰਹਹਿ ਪਿਆਰੇ ॥
ਜਿਉ ਜਲ ਅੰਤ ਉਪਰਿ ਕਮਲ ਨਿਰਾਰੇ ॥ (Ang 353)
*(The beloved Gurmukhs remain immaculately pure,*
*Like the lotus in the water, which remains above the water*
*untouched.)*

As already pointed out, our Real Self or Awareness is the subject and the body mind is the object. We will now prove it from our own everyday experience, if that statement is true. This topic of who we are has been discussed in detail in one of the articles in this book "Know Yourself and Meet the Lord" but we will go through it one more time very briefly.

Just analyze the current experience that you are having. You may be looking at an object, sitting in a room. If we take an overview of your experience it can be said that you as a "perceiver" on one end are a subject and whatever you are looking at is the object on the other end. Let us say you are looking at the fireplace in your family room. When you are looking at the fireplace, you as the perceiver are the subject, and the fireplace is the object. We can state that you as the subject are separate and different from the object. Next move your view closer to you, where you are looking at the table in the room. Here you as a perceiver are the subject, and the table is the object; and you are separate and different from the table. Keep moving your view closer and closer until you get real close. Let us say you are looking at your body, now you as the perceiver is the subject, and the body is the object. Also you are separate and different from the body.

Move your view closer yet and go inside the body to look at the mind. The mind is inside the body and consists of the two main categories, thoughts, and feelings. Look at a thought, any thought. Observe closely that you as a "perceiver" can perceive the thought. You can see the thought rise, stay for a few seconds and then disappear. You as a perceiver are separate and different from the thought. The same can be said of the other component of the mind, the feelings. In summation, it can be said that you as a perceiver are separate and different from thoughts and feelings. **This proves that you as a "perceiver" are the subject and body mind which is perceived is the object.** The "perceiver" here is something beyond the body and mind. We will try to find what this perceiver is.

We have now established from our experience that the body mind is not the subject. Our belief that body mind is the subject, is a misunderstanding and has to be gotten rid off. This misunderstanding results in the formation of our ego. In fact, believing our body mind to be the subject; and believing it to be an independent entity is called "ego". Until and unless we get rid of this misunderstanding we cannot make real progress in our spiritual journey. This is the most important and probably the most difficult step. This misunderstanding has become very deep and has become a part and parcel of our life. We have been brought up with this belief that we are body minds and have rehearsed this all our life.

Next we will try to understand what this "perceiver" is. The first characteristic of the perceiver that we have discovered is that this perceiver is the Knowing Presence by which everything is known or recognized. It is something like the light with which everything becomes visible. But knowing is even of greater importance than the light. If we don't have the cognitive faculty we will not be able to recognize anything, no matter how much light is shining. Gurbani calls this Knowing Presence as the Guru, and says that without the Guru it will be pitch dark even if there were thousands of suns illuminating.

ਜੇ ਸਉ ਚੰਦਾ ਉਗਵਹਿ ਸੂਰਜ ਚੜਹਿ ਹਜਾਰ ॥
ਏਤੇ ਚਾਨਣ ਹੋਦਿਆਂ ਗੁਰ ਬਿਨ ਘੋਰ ਅੰਧਾਰ ॥ (Ang 463)
(*If hundred moons and a thousand suns were to arise,*
*Even with so much light, it will be pitch dark without the Guru,*

*meaning the Knowing Presence.*)

Another characteristic of this "perceiver" is that It has no form. If you try to observe inside yourself to feel or get a sense of the perceiver, you will not find anything objective. You may come across thoughts, feelings, sensations etc. but these are not the perceiver as we have proven earlier. In fact, the perceiver has no objective qualities and cannot be identified like an object. That means that the perceiver has no form or shape or color by which it can be visualized. So it cannot be grasped by the mind and the senses. Since the perceiver has no form or shape, it is without limits. Anything without limits is infinite. So we have established that the "perceiver" is unlimited and all knowing. These are the same qualities that belong to Atman or Awareness, our Real Self. The "perceiver" in us is really Atman or Awareness. This conclusion has been arrived at through our experiential understanding.

Once we have discovered that we are not body and mind but are Atman or Awareness, we have to make adjustments in our everyday life to live in accordance with this new understanding. Basic change would be to believe in our new identity of being the Atman or Awareness rather than body minds. Our original belief of being a body mind has been proven to be false. We have to drop the old identity in favor of the new one of being Atman or Awareness.

Gurbani asks us over and over again to recognize our Essence. There are hundreds of shabads in Siri Guru Granth Sahib relating to recognition of our own self. Sometimes Guru Ji asks us lovingly and other times he is very blunt. Here is a shabad scolding us to recognize our true identity.

ਸੋ ਬਉਰਾ ਜੋ ਆਪੁ ਨ ਪਛਾਨੈ ॥
ਆਪੁ ਪਛਾਨੈ ਤ ਏਕੈ ਜਾਨੈ ॥  (Ang 855)
(*One is insane who does not recognize oneself,
Only recognizing oneself, one comes to know the One.*)

Guru ji says clearly in the following shabad that unless one recognizes his own identity there is no hope of one dispelling the fog of doubt.

ਜਨ ਨਾਨਕ ਬਿਨੁ ਆਪਾ ਚੀਨੈ ਮਿਟੈ ਨ ਭਰਮ ਕੀ ਕਾਈ ॥ (Ang 684)
(*O servant Nanak, without knowing one's own self, the moss of doubt is not removed.*)

**Staying With Our Real Self:**

Once we clearly understand our true identity, we need to stay with it. We need to make it our new home and work from home, so to speak. Bhagat Kabir Ji talks about this home as our heart. He says that God lives in our heart so we need to make that place as our Real Home. Since God lives there, we will practically be in good company when we stay there.

ਦਿਲ ਮਹਿ ਖੋਜਿ ਦਿਲੈ ਦਿਲਿ ਖੋਜਹੁ ਏਹੀ ਠਉਰ ਮੁਕਾਮਾ ॥ (Ang 1349)
(*Search in your heart, deep down, this is the home and place where God lives.*)

Gurbani gives great importance to staying in our home. It makes so many claims of reaping big benefits by staying Home. Gurbani says that if we come back Home our suffering will end, all our problems will be solved. We will live in peace and all your wishes will be fulfilled. The messenger of death will not be able to touch us. We will find Amrit in our Real Home and above all we will meet the Lord there. There are many more claims made by Gurbani about staying Home. Sometimes our little minds cannot believe all those claims and think that Guru Ji is over-promising. The difficulty is that we do not spend time in our Real Home. We may be talking about spending time there but in reality, some of us do not even go there once in our lifetime. Of course, if we don't go there, how can we experience those benefits? Following shabads speak of some of the benefits of staying Home.

ਤੁਮ ਘਰਿ ਆਵਹੁ ਮੇਰੇ ਮੀਤ ॥
ਤੁਮਰੇ ਦੋਖੀ ਹਰਿ ਆਪਿ ਨਿਵਾਰੇ ਅਪਦਾ ਭਈ ਬਿਤੀਤ ॥ (Ang 678)
(*Come Home my Friend, Lord will end your suffering and eliminate
your misfortune.*)

ਆਪਣੈ ਘਰਿ ਤੂ ਸੁਖਿ ਵਸਹਿ ਪੋਹਿ ਨ ਸਕੈ ਜਮਕਾਲੁ ਜੀਉ ॥ (Ang 569)
(*Dwell in peace and comfort in your Real Home, and the messenger
of death will not touch you.*)

ਮੇਰੇ ਮਨ ਪਰਦੇਸੀ ਵੇ ਪਿਆਰੇ ਆਉ ਘਰੇ ॥
ਹਰਿ ਗੁਰੁ ਮਿਲਾਵਹੁ ਮੇਰੇ ਪਿਆਰੇ ਘਰਿ ਵਸੈ ਹਰੇ ॥ (Ang 451)
(*O my beloved stranger mind, please come Home.
Meet the Lord-Guru, my dear, the Lord lives there.*)

Guru ji asks our foolish and ignorant mind to stay Home and
rather than wandering outside, turn inwards. contemplate the
Lord deep in yourself and leave the greed and temptation. This is
the way to achieve true Liberation.

ਘਰਿ ਰਹੁ ਰੇ ਮਨ ਮੁਗਧ ਇਆਨੇ ॥
ਰਾਮ ਜਪਹੁ ਅੰਤਰਗਤਿ ਧਿਆਨੇ ॥
ਲਾਲਚ ਛੋਡਿ ਰਚਹੁ ਅਪਰੰਪਰਿ ਇਉ ਪਾਵਹੁ ਮੁਕਤਿ ਦੁਆਰਾ ਹੇ ॥ (Ang 1030)
(*Remain in your own Home, O my foolish mind,
Meditate on the Lord by concentrating deep within,
Renounce greed, and merge with the infinite Lord.
In this way, you will find the door of liberation.*)

So this is the next step towards self realization. Once we
discover that we are Atman or Awareness and not body and
mind combination, we should remember this all the time. We
should abide in Atman or Awareness and stay there as much
as we can. Initially we will not be able to stay there all the
time. We have lived with the false identity all our life and may
be many past lives too. So it is not going to be easy because
any distraction will pull us away from staying with our new
identity. But unless we try we will never get anywhere. This is
where meditation comes in. Staying absorbed in ourselves for

some specified periods of time every day will be very helpful. Gurbani calls this meditation Naam Simran which is immersing ourselves in the Love of the Lord. Since the Lord lives in our heart we need to immerse in ourselves, deep into our own hearts, and be one with ourselves. So meditation is not an arduous task but is a very simple process. Just turn inwards into our own self and stay there. In other words, we have to spend time in our own company without going out.

Gurbani preaches us to do Simran or meditation as the first thing in the morning as we get up.

ਗੁਰ ਸਤਿਗੁਰ ਕਾ ਜੋ ਸਿਖੁ ਅਖਾਏ ਸੁ ਭਲਕੇ ਉਠਿ ਹਰਿ ਨਾਮੁ ਧਿਆਵੈ ॥
(Ang 305)
(*One who calls himself Guru's sikh, shall rise early in the morning and meditate on the Lord's Name.*)

One other point made in Gurbani is that one does not have to do anything else. Just by anchoring ourselves in our home, we can reap the benefits. There are many shabads asking us to be steadily anchored in our Real Self. In the following shabad Guru ji asks us to stay Home and asks us to be steady in doing so; and Satguru will take care of all our affairs. God will strike down all your enemies and preserve your honor. It is hard to believe that just by staying steady in ourselves, we can achieve all these benefits.

ਥਿਰੁ ਘਰਿ ਬੈਸਹੁ ਹਰਿ ਜਨ ਪਿਆਰੇ ॥
ਸਤਿਗੁਰਿ ਤੁਮਰੇ ਕਾਜ ਸਵਾਰੇ ॥
ਦੁਸਟ ਦੂਤ ਪਰਮੇਸਰਿ ਮਾਰੇ ॥
ਜਨ ਕੀ ਪੈਜ ਰਖੀ ਕਰਤਾਰੇ ॥ (Ang 201)

(Stay *steady in your own Real Self, O Lord's servant,*
*The True Guru will resolve all your affairs,*
*The Lord will kill all the wicked and evil and preserve the honor of*
*His servant.*)

Gurumaa, a contemporary Saint in Punjab also emphasizes

staying steady at home to realize oneself. She says that one does not have to do anything else. All one has to do is to stay home. There is a quote by her in one of her books and it goes like this:

"Forget everything thing else,
Just stay stilled in yourself all the time,
Remember you are Chetna, the Consciousness."

The Saint Gurumaa says that one does not need to do anything, just keep your attention focused on yourself. When the attention is not going out but focused inside, we are one with the Guru, the Atman or Awareness. Like the old saying "a man is known by the company he keeps" if we stay in the company of the Guru, it will transform us like the Philosopher's Stone transforms iron into gold. In the company of the Guru our identity becomes blissfully Divine.

ਗੁਰ ਪਾਰਸ ਹਮ ਲੋਹ ਮਿਲਿ ਕੰਚਨੁ ਹੋਇਆ ਰਾਮ ॥
ਜੋਤੀ ਜੋਤਿ ਮਿਲਾਇ ਕਾਇਆ ਗੜੁ ਸੋਹਿਆ ਰਾਮ ॥ (Ang 1114)
(*The Guru is the Philosopher's Stone, we are iron and we are transformed into gold by Guru company,*
*My body fortress becomes beautiful when it merges into the Divine Light.*)

**Aligning With The World:**

We have to abide in our heart regularly until our new identity becomes our first nature, not the second nature as normally believed. Once it has become our first nature we move to the next step of realization. The next stage of realization consists of going outwards in the world and trying to live our life in the world in accordance with our new understanding about our identity. The second step was to come inwards to discover who we really are. After discovering our true identity we need to go back into the world and relate with the world keeping our new identity in the forefront. This new understanding does not stop us from going out and relating with the world. In fact, mixing with the outside world and keeping in mind our real identity at the same time, firms up our anchoring in our new identity. It tests our commitment to stay connected with ourselves under all circumstances that we come across; and affords us an opportunity for practice.

Sikh religion encourages its followers to go out in the world and live a loving and friendly social life. It prohibits us from becoming a recluse unlike some other religions. It advocates mixing with people of other castes and even to serve humanity irrespective of their caste or religion. Feeding the poor, and humanity in general, is one of the three main pillars of sikh religion. The three pillars of sikh religion are to work and make an honest living, Naam Simran; and sharing food with other people (ਕਿਰਤ ਕਰਨਾ, ਨਾਮ ਜਪਨਾ ਤੇ ਵੰਡ ਛਕਣਾ). In sikh religion there is no inequality whatsoever. No one is better than the other, everyone is a child of the one God and hence equal.

ਏਕ ਨੂਰ ਤੇ ਸਭੁ ਜਗੁ ਉਪਜਿਆ ਕਉਨ ਭਲੇ ਕੋ ਮੰਦੇ ॥ (Ang 1349)
(*From One Divine Light the whole world is created, then who is good and who is bad.*)

So we should go out into the world to relate with it, but we have to keep in mind our true identity while doing so. With our new understanding we have discovered that we are not body minds and do not have individual entities. There is only one entity in the universe and that is Atman or Awareness that pervades through all of us. Gurbani calls this Reality Ek Onkar (ੴ). So we are all just one Being. We may think that we are all different from one another but that is a false belief and we have to eradicate that belief. We have arrived at this understanding through exploration of our own experience, that we are all one; and as such need to relate with each other with that understanding. The world we see out there is really God Herself or Himself. Gurbani says that there is only one reality called Ek Onkar. The shabads below emphasize that point. One thing to note in these shabads is that these shabads are not only talking about

177

the living creatures, like humans, animals or birds etc. but they include all the non-living things too, implying God has become everything bar none.

ਸਭ ਮਹਿ ਜੋਤਿ ਜੋਤਿ ਹੈ ਸੋਇ ॥
ਤਿਸਦੈ ਚਾਨਣਿ ਸਭ ਮਹਿ ਚਾਨਣੁ ਹੋਇ ॥ (Ang 663)
(*The Divine Light is present within everyone,*
*And that Light shines inside all.*)

ਆਪੇ ਪਟੀ ਕਲਮ ਆਪਿ ਉਪਰਿ ਲੇਖੁ ਭਿ ਤੂੰ ॥
ਏਕੋ ਕਹੀਐ ਨਾਨਕਾ ਦੂਜਾ ਕਾਹੇ ਕੁ ॥   (Ang 1291)
(*He Himself is the writing tablet, and He Himself is the pen. He Himself is the writing.*
*O Nanak, speak of only One Lord, there is no other.*)

So we need to approach the other with love and respect like they are our own self. This would lead to the disappearance of all the hatred and animosity from our lives. If everyone started living with this understanding, all the fighting and wars in the world would end. The world would be like Guru ji describes in this shabad.

ਨਾ ਕੋ ਮੇਰਾ ਦੁਸਮਨੁ ਰਹਿਆ ਨਾ ਹਮ ਕਿਸ ਕੇ ਬੈਰਾਈ ॥
ਬ੍ਰਹਮੁ ਪਸਾਰੁ ਪਸਾਰਿਓ ਭੀਤਰਿ ਸਤਿਗੁਰ ਤੇ ਸੋਝੀ ਪਾਈ ॥ (Ang 671)
(*No one is my enemy and I am no one's enemy.*
*God, who has expanded His expanse, is within all;*
*I learned that from the True Guru.*)

One thing that is worth mentioning here is that if you don't like a person because he or she may have done something wrong to us. Just reflect on what we have just learned. The person who has wronged us really cannot be blamed because the person has no independent entity of his or her own, and as such has no free will to act. It is only the Atman or Awareness which is working through the person. Body and mind does not have control over its actions. So blaming the person does not make sense. Best way to deal with such a person is to really believe that you are dealing with a person who has no control over his or her actions. It is the Divine working through each body. So it is the Divine that is responsible for what has happened. This does not mean that one should not respond to the situation appropriately, one definitely should but not with the spirit of revenge. The spirit of revenge will drag us down to the body and mind level. We just learnt that we are not body and mind but we are Divine. So we should respond from the Divine level without revenge or any kind of anger. Just respond like you normally would but with awareness and without anger. When you do that, the Reality will respond in kind. The relationship between you and the person will, in time, improve by itself.

This can be explained by an analogy. Imagine you are enjoying boating in a small boat in a lake. While boating you see another larger boat coming towards you. You watch this larger boat for a while and still see it is coming at you. You begin to feel worried that it may hit your boat if this continues. As the larger boat gets closer to you, you start blaming the boatman and start getting mad and angry at him or her. As the boat gets closer to you, you get out of the way to let the boat pass by you, but your anger at the boatman is still peaking. As the boat goes by you, you look for the boatman in the larger boat and find there is no boatman there. The boat had come loose from its anchor and was being pushed by the winds. All of a sudden your anger subsides, because there was no one to blame in that boat. You cannot blame the boat or the winds. Things in life happen like that. Lord Buddha once said "Things are happening, deeds are being done but there is no doer of them". So the best thing to do is to respond to the situation like avoiding the boat without being angry or mad.

There is one other important benefit, if we can call it a benefit, that comes as a result of the shift in understanding of our identity. By changing our identity we move into a higher sphere in life where we are not subject to the law of karma any more. The law of karma is applicable in the sphere, where we believe ourselves to be body minds. Once we rise above that sphere, the law of karma does not apply. Following shabad makes this clear.

ਸੋ ਹੰ ਸੋ ਜਾ ਕਉ ਹੈ ਜਾਪ ॥
ਜਾ ਕਉ ਲਿਪਤ ਨ ਹੋਇ ਪੁੰਨ ਅਰੁ ਪਾਪ ॥ (Ang 1162)
(*One who believes that "That I AM That", He is not affected by virtue or vice.*)

The statement "That I am That" is very commonly used in spiritual circles. It implies that I and the Lord are one. The shabad above is telling us that if we can change our identity, we will rise above karma.

This sums up the various steps of self realization. First we have to recognize the fact that we are not body minds. We have to let go of our false belief that we have been clinging to all our lives, and recognize that we are Atman or Awareness. So we have to break the conditioning we have been carrying with us in our lives. Once we understand our real identity of being Atman or Awareness, we have to abide in it as much as we can. Abiding does not mean we drop everything and lock ourselves in a room. It means we just keep our new identity in mind twenty four seven or as much as we can, while discharging our daily duties. We have to keep our new identity in mind so much that it becomes our very nature; and we are solidly established in it all the time. Next we start dealing with the world, and align all our activities in the world according to the new understanding. We have to treat everyone with love and respect. When we are dealing with other people we have to think that we are dealing with our own selves. We are all One Reality (ੴ) appearing in miraids of forms. With this mindset, God's Grace will definitely shower upon us and lead us to realization.

# WAKE UP MY MIND

ਜਾਗਿ ਲੇਹੁ ਰੇ ਮਨਾ ਜਾਗਿ ਲੇਹੁ ਕਹਾ
ਗਾਫਲ ਸੋਇਆ ॥ *(Ang 726)*

*(Wake up, O mind! Wake up! Why
are you sleeping unaware?)*

If a statement was made that ninety nine percent of people in the world are sleeping during the day, even while they are awake and working, it would not be wrong. It would not be surprising to find out that the percentage may really be even higher than ninety nine percent for the people who are asleep. What does all this mean that people are asleep while awake, and what does it mean to tell the mind to wake up? There are hundreds of shabads in Sri Guru Granth Sahib asking us to wake up. Gurbani tells us that we have been asleep not for one day or two days but for all our life and maybe even for many lives. Guru Ji asks us to wake up so we go through our remaining life wide awake and alert. Gurbani puts it very harshly and says that those people who are asleep are blind and foolish. What can be said to them? Their thinking is just upside down. They think that the person who is sleeping is awake; and a person who is awake is sleeping.

ਅੰਧੇ ਅਕਲੀ ਬਾਹਰੇ ਕਿਆ ਤਿਨ ਸਿਉ ਕਹੀਐ ॥

......................................

ਸੂਤੇ ਕਉ ਜਾਗਤੁ ਕਹੈ ਜਾਗਤ ਕਉ ਸੂਤਾ ॥
ਜੀਵਤ ਕਉ ਮੂਆ ਕਹੈ ਮੂਏ ਨਹੀ ਰੋਤਾ ॥ (Ang 229)

*(What can be said to them who are blind and lack wisdom,*

..........................................................................

*Those who are asleep, they call them awake, and those who are awake, they call them asleep.*
*Those who are awake to the Divine, they call them dead, those who are dead spiritually, they do not worry about.)*

Gurbani says that world culture has turned upside down. It has become acceptable to call a person awake who is really sleeping and vice versa. What is implied here is that the ones who are lost in the worldly attractions and have forgotten their own Real Self, are believed to be awake. Others who are spiritual minded and don't care about the worldly attractions are called asleep. Gurbani says that the truth is just the opposite. The truth is that those who are lost in the world are really sleeping even though they are awake. Being lost in the world means having one's attention fully absorbed in the experience of the world and not being aware of their own Self at all. These are the persons who are considered asleep. Then there are others who deal with the world while being aware of their own Self. These persons are considered to be awake. These are two ways to conduct business. One way is the way of a robot. The robot is not self aware when it is doing something. It is just obeying its programming. Then there is the other way where one does anything and everything with alertness and self awareness. Most of us are working like robots without being self-conscious. All our attention is taken up by the object of attention or the activity we are engaged in. That is why it is said most of us are asleep while going through our life.

If we look into our identity closely we find that there are two possible options. One is that we are a body mind combination and the second is that we are our Real Self, Atman or Awareness. This has been discussed in greater detail in the article "Know Yourselfand meet the Lord". Those who want to get a deeper understanding about this please refer to that article. It has been established in that article that we are not body minds but we are Atman or Awareness. So the two possible options are that we are body minds, which we believe ourselves to be, or we are our Real Self or Awareness. When we do something, believing that we are body minds we are considered to be asleep. This is because we are asleep to the fact that the body and mind is our apparent entity and not a real one. If we are doing things believing ourselves to be Atman or Awareness then we are considered to be awake.

We all remember in our school days in our classrooms when the teacher was trying to teach us something, our attention would wander away. As a result we would not understand the lesson being taught. This wandering away of our attention could be termed as the student being asleep as far as the lecture was concerned. Another example would be in everyday conversation if we are listening to someone talking to us and our attention does not stay focused on what is being said. As a result we do not understand what was being conveyed to us. We ask our friend to repeat what he or she said. This could be classified as us having gone to sleep too. But these types of distractions are normally termed as attention deficit or attention disorder, meaning that we are not attentive to the situation we are in. Gurbani talks about being asleep from a spiritual point of view, where we forget our own Real Self while conducting daily business in the world.

Being awake is similar to lucid dreaming. In lucid dreaming the dreamer is aware of himself or herself, and is also aware that he or she is watching a dream. The dreamer is not only aware of dreaming but, at times the dreamer can have some degree of control over what is going on in the dream. Our goal is to do the same in the waking state, which can be called lucid waking. If a person can stay aware of oneself in the waking state while conducting business then that person would be considered to be awake. He would not only be aware of himself but can also develop some control over what is happening during the waking state. So our goal would be to live the life like lucid dreaming and be constantly aware of ourselves and the experience simultaneously. Being awake is to be aware of our Real Self under all circumstances, when conducting our daily business in our life.

There is one particular situation that does reveal how unaware or asleep we are. This will be recognized especially by the grown up generation who have been doing Nitnem every morning. The author is reflecting a bit on his own experience when talking about this situation. Nitnem was mostly done by recital through memory in the not too distant past, but these days it is mostly done through listening from electronic devices. It is very common to notice the mind wandering away while listening to Paath. This happens more often when Paath is being recited from memory. When the mind returns, it cannot even remember where to restart. How many times have we experienced that? If the Paath (recital or listening of shabads) is being listened to from an electronic device, the mind would go away, and start solving some other problem while the Paath is going on in the background. At times the Paath would conclude while the mind is still solving other problems. One Gurbani preacher put it this way that doing the Nitnem, at least, gives us a measure of how awake we are. So by continuing to do the Nitnem daily, and using this feedback technique, we can improve upon our awareness. This kind of unawareness during the recital of Nitnem definitely indicates that we have a long way to go to be awake.

A simple analogy of what is considered to be awake would be to look at the role of an actor in a drama or a movie. The actor assuming a particular role in the play, while playing the assigned role, stays knowledgeable of the fact that he is just playing a role in the drama. He stays aware of his non-involvement or non-attachment with anything and everything that he comes in contact with in the play. He does not get lost in the play to the extent that he forgets his original identity. **This is exactly the problem with us. We forget our original identity when dealing with world. That is why it is said that we are asleep almost 100% of the time even when we are awake.** If the actor is playing the role of a rich man who handles large sums of money, he is constantly aware that the money does not belong to him, and it is just a role he is playing in the drama. When the play ends he does not put a claim to the money he possessed in the drama and does not walk away with all the money. Being awake or staying awake in life is similar to the actor's role. We have to lead our life like that. We have to be constantly aware of our real identity of being Atman or Awareness. Also we should not get lost in the attractions of the world to the point that we forget our identity.

**We are Atman or Awareness and we are playing the role of human beings in the drama of life. We need to keep this in mind all the time during our life as we deal with the world. We should not lose sight of our original identity. We can use all the objects, enjoy all the relationships and do anything, of course, within the law, but we should not forget that we are just playing a role. We should not get lost in our roles to the point that we completely forget our Real Identity. Staying aware and present in every situation in our lives is the basic requisite to be called awake.**

Gurbani gives us a definition of what is considered being awake in this shabad.

ਸੋ ਜਾਗੈ ਜਿਸੁ ਸਤਿਗੁਰੁ ਮਿਲੈ ॥
ਪੰਚ ਦੂਤ ਓਹੁ ਵਸਗਤਿ ਕਰੈ ॥
ਸੋ ਜਾਗੈ ਜੋ ਤਤੁ ਬੀਚਾਰੈ ॥
ਆਪਿ ਮਰੈ ਅਵਰਾ ਨਹ ਮਾਰੈ ॥
ਸੋ ਜਾਗੈ ਜੋ ਏਕੋ ਜਾਨੈ ॥
ਪਰਕਿਰਤਿ ਛੋਡੈ ਤਤੁ ਪਛਾਨੈ ॥

*(One is awake who has met the True Guru,*
*Such a person commands control over the five thieves.*
*One is awake who contemplates the Reality,*
*He kills his own ego and does not belittle others.*
*One is awake who knows that there only One Reality,*
*He abandons Maya, and realizes the Essence of Reality.)*

What is being implied in this Shabad is that one is considered awake if one stays in the company of the True Guru, his own Real Self and gets control over the temptations. One is awake if he or she recognizes his or her own Essence to be the One Reality; and as a result one gets rid of one's ego and respects everyone else. What Gurbani is saying here is that one is considered to be awake who knows that there is only One Reality and because of that he abandons his selfishness and becomes mindful and respectful of others. What has happened is that human beings have become so focused on the objective world that they have mostly forgotten about themselves. Our Real Self is a Conscious Being and it has become an Unconscious Being by attachment to the outside world. Divine Being has become a human being and as such, is considered to have gone to sleep. Gurbani says, metaphorically, in the following shabad that the Divine Being and the human being are laying in one bed, but the Divine Being is wide awake while the human being is sound asleep.

ਏਕਾ ਸੇਜ ਵਿਛੀ ਧਨ ਕੰਤਾ ॥
ਧਨ ਸੂਤੀ ਪਿਰੁ ਸਦ ਜਾਗੰਤਾ ॥ (Ang 737)
*(One bed is spread out for the bride and her husband Lord,*
*Bride is asleep, but the Husband Lord is always awake.)*

What is being said in this shabad is, that one is at the human level if one is asleep. But if one becomes aware and alert then the same person attains to Divine level. It is not that there is a human being and then there is Divine Being, there is only one Being. If one is sound asleep then he or she is a person, and if one is wide awake then he or she is a Divine Being. So being awake or being asleep is hugely important because it can convert a person into a Divine Being and vice versa. Gurbani says that one's who stay awake, realize God and they eradicate their ego.

ਜਾਗਤ ਰਹੇ ਤਿਨੀ ਪ੍ਰਭੁ ਪਾਇਆ ਸਬਦੇ ਹਉਮੈ ਮਾਰੀ ॥ (Ang 599)
(*Those who remain wakeful realize God,*
*And they eradicate their ego with the help of shabad.*)

**Causes Of Sleep:**

**Veil Of Maya:**

The biggest cause for this sleep is Maya, which is a sort of veil created by the Almighty to hide Himself or Herself from being visible to His or Her creation. We do see the Infinite Lord all the time everywhere but we have been fitted with the special glasses of the mind that make us think that we are seeing people, animals and worldly objects. This is the illusion of Maya. Maya is called the grand Illusion (ਭਰਮ) created by none other than the Almighty Himself. Gurbani defines Maya as an illusion that makes people forget the Lord and causes them to develop emotional attachment to the world and it's objects.

ਏਹ ਮਾਇਆ ਜਿਤੁ ਹਰਿ ਵਿਸਰੈ ਮੋਹੁ ਉਪਜੈ ਭਾਉ ਦੂਜਾ ਲਾਇਆ ॥ (Ang 921)
(*This is Maya, by which the Lord is forgotten; emotional attachment and love of the other wells up.*)

This veil of Maya that hides the Lord, is very enchanting. This veil is not like a curtain but It is like a magic show being played by the Lord Himself to entice us away from His own View. This magic show is what we call the world. This world has become an action packed movie for us, and this movie consumes all our attention. It is just like watching a movie on a TV screen. **We get so involved with the movie that we forget the light which has become the movie. No one thinks of the light while watching the movie even though the movie is made of light and nothing** else. Similarly, we get so involved with the world that we never think of God even though the world is made of God and nothing else. Fact of the matter is that God Himself is playing this world movie to keep our attention occupied so we cannot see Him. Even though the Lord is hiding right in there we do not care to see Him. We can say that God is visible in plain sight but we refuse to see Him. Even after knowing this fact that we see the Lord all around, we do not believe it and do not bring it into practice in our everyday life. Gurbani says that this Maya has intoxicated us all and has charmed us so much that we have become unaware and have gone to sleep, so to speak. Of course, this sleep is not the sleep we have at night, this sleep consists of us becoming unaware of the reality of the experiencer. We lose ourselves completely in the drama of the world. While we are sleeping or we are lost in the drama of the world, all the thieves are looting our homes right in front of our eyes. Thieves referred to here are the temptations of the world, named as anger, lust, greed, ego and attachment etc. Following shabads makes it very clear, what is asleep in us, and what are the consequences of that.

ਨੈਨਹੁ ਨੀਦ ਪਰ ਦ੍ਰਿਸਟਿ ਵਿਕਾਰ ॥ ਸ੍ਰਵਣ ਸੋਏ ਸੁਣਿ ਨਿੰਦ ਵੀਚਾਰ ॥
ਰਸਨਾ ਸੋਈ ਲੋਭਿ ਮੀਠੈ ਸਾਦਿ ॥   ਮਨੁ ਸੋਇਆ ਮਾਇਆ ਬਿਸਮਾਦਿ ॥
ਇਸੁ ਗ੍ਰਿਹ ਮਹਿ ਕੋਈ ਜਾਗਤੁ ਰਹੈ ॥ ਸਾਬਤੁ ਵਸਤੁ ਓਹੁ ਅਪਨੀ ਲਹੈ ॥
ਸਗਲ ਸਹੇਲੀ ਅਪਨੈ ਰਸ ਮਾਤੀ ॥   ਗ੍ਰਿਹ ਅਪੁਨੇ ਕੀ ਖਬਰਿ ਨ ਜਾਤੀ ॥
ਮੁਸਨਹਾਰ ਪੰਚ ਬਟਵਾਰੇ ॥         ਸੂਨੇ ਨਗਰਿ ਪਰੇ ਠਗਹਾਰੇ ॥   (Ang 182)
(*The eyes are asleep, in corrupt gazing the beauty of another,*
*The ears are asleep, listening to hateful stories about others,*
*The tongue is asleep, in its desire for sweet tastes,*
*The mind is asleep, fascinated by Maya.*
*Those who remain awake in this house are very rare,*
*But the one who stays awake, claims the whole prize.*
*All senses are intoxicated with their sensory pleasure,*
*They do not know how to guard their own home.*
*The five thug thieves, have attacked unguarded house.*)

ਸਭ ਮਦ ਮਾਤੇ ਕੋਊ ਨ ਜਾਗ ॥

ਸੰਗ ਹੀ ਚੋਰ ਘਰੁ ਮੁਸਨ ਲਾਗ ॥  (Ang 1193)
(*Everyone is intoxicated with Maya, no one is awake ,*
*The thieves are looting their homes, right in their presence.*)

Guru ji points out that all our main senses are asleep in their
respective temptations. The eyes are asleep in corrupt seeing,
the ears are asleep in hearing hateful discussions. The tongue
is asleep in tasting delicious meals and the mind is asleep in
the fascination with Maya. With all our senses, and especially
the mind are asleep,  there is no one guarding the house. As
a result, the five thieves are robbing our houses in plain sight,
without anybody stopping them. The five thieves referred here
are lust, anger, greed, attachment and arrogance (ਕਾਮ,ਕਰੋਧ, ਲੋਭ,
ਮੋਹ, ਹੰਕਾਰ). We all know from our own daily experience that we
are all lost in sight seeing, in listening to the shortcomings of
the other people; and are never satisfied eating delicious meals,
etc. Gurbani in another shabad says that the mouth is never
done speaking, ears are never done hearing, eyes are never done
seeing. Every organ is lost in its own sensory function.

ਆਖਣੁ ਆਖਿ ਨ ਰਜਿਆ ਸੁਨਣਿ ਨ ਰਜੇ ਕੰਨ ॥
ਅਖੀ ਦੇਖਿ ਨ ਰਜੀਆ ਗੁਣ ਗਾਹਕ ਇਕ ਵੰਨ ॥  (Ang 147)
(*The mouth is not satisfied speaking, and ears are not satisfied*
*hearing. The eyes are not satisfied  seeing. Each organ is hankering*
*after its own activity.*)

So Guru Ji asks us to wake up and be aware and alert all the time
in all circumstances. Guru ji assures us that if one stays awake in
life, he or she will get the ultimate prize (ਵਸਤੁ). The ultimate prize
is very precious and is defined by Gurbani as follows:

ਵਸਤੁ ਅਨੂਪ ਅਤਿ ਅਗਮ ਅਗੋਚਰ ਗੁਰੁ ਪੂਰਾ ਅਲਖੁ ਲਖਾਏ ॥  (Ang 607)
(*This prize is very beautiful, unapproachable, unfathomable.*
*Through the Perfect Guru the Unknowable is known.*)

Gurbani is hinting that the ultimate prize (ਵਸਤੁ) is God Himself
or Herself. So if one is awake he or she will meet the Lord.

We can get a feel of the effect of Maya by close analysis of our perceptions of the world. As stated earlier that the objects we see outside are not real, but illusory. We all know that the perception of an object is based on the signal that we receive from the object. The signal we receive is made of reflected sunlight from the object and it consists of a bunch of frequencies in the visible range. If we are looking at a tree, the signal coming from the tree is a mixture of frequencies. What is it in the tree that is reflecting these frequencies? Science tells us that the tree is made of atoms which are further made of protons, neutrons and electrons. Frequencies of the reflected sunlight depend upon the arrangement of atoms and its components. From the reflected light we make determination of the object. So the objects we see are just made of atoms in many permutations and combinations. Not only the tree is made of atoms, everything in the world is made of them. This essentially, is Maya. Simply stated, the whole world is just made of atoms arranged in different combinations. Take the example of graphite and diamond. These two minerals are identical chemically, but are completely different physically. Both minerals are composed of carbon atoms. It is hard to believe that they are identical chemically, for they are so different physically. Graphite is opaque and metallic earthly looking, while the diamond is transparent and brilliant. One is black and the other is shiny. The difference between graphite and carbon is only due to the arrangement of atoms. Overall, if we look at all the metals, they are made out of different arrangements of atoms. One day science will discover that the atoms, protons, neutrons and electrons are all made of only one entity, Ek Onkar (ੴ), which will confirm what Sri Guru Granth Sahib declared five centuries ago.

**Forgetting Our True Nature:**

Another cause of our sleep is due to our forgetting who we

really are. We think ourselves to be body minds, which we are not. We adopt big egos by believing we are the body minds. Let us explore this mode of our sleep in some detail. Gurbani tells us that we are Divine Being called Atman or Awareness; but we have contracted ourselves into a limited being called human being. Our original nature as Atman or Awareness is called Sat Chit Anand. These are three characteristics of our Divine Being. Sat means, it is True Being and not just a concept, Chit means it is Conscious and Anand means it is Bliss. So our original nature is Truth, Consciousness and Bliss. By contracting into a body the Divine Being that we are, has voluntarily made its residence in the body and has assumed all the limitations of the body. It has forgotten its original nature of Sat, Chit and Anand and has assumed the characteristics of the body, which are mainly desire and fear. Thinking itself to be a body, it imagines itself to be a small fragment and as such it wants to acquire things from outside through desire to complete itself. Also thinking itself to be a fragment, it has fear of being destroyed and as such wants to protect itself from the other. That is why each one of us has two main objectives in life: acquisition of objects, activities or relationships to fulfill ourselves; and protection of ourselves against the outer danger or the other. Our whole life is wrapped up in these two objectives. In spite of our contraction into the body, our essence of being Divine does not change. We are still that Sat Chit Anand even though we have forgotten that we are Sat Chit Anand. This forgetting of our True Nature is termed as us having gone to sleep. Gurbani is asking us to wake up from this sleep. Gurbani calls us kings and asks us in a friendly way to wake up from our sleep.

ਰਾਜਨ ਕਿਉ ਸੋਇਆ ਤੂ ਨੀਦ ਭਰੇ ਜਾਗਤ ਕਤ ਨਾਹੀ ਰਾਮ ॥
ਮਾਇਆ ਝੂਠੁ ਰੁਦਨੁ ਕੇਤੇ ਬਿਲਲਾਹੀ ਰਾਮ ॥ (Ang 548)
(O King, why are you sound sleep, why don't you wake up? Many have run after false Maya, and have cried to no use.)

**How To Stay Awake:**

**Live Consciously:**

Gurbani attaches great importance to being awake. There are many shabads in Sri Guru Granth Sahib about the need for us to wake up. Gurbani asserts that we need to stay awake all the time and as a result we will attain our Divine Kingdom. Gurbani asks us not to be misled by the false temptations of the world, which are based on false appearances of Maya and are not real. We are being urged to wake up. Guru Ji is being very kind, and is encouraging us here, by stating that there is nothing lost yet and it is still not too late.

ਕਹਾ ਭੁਲਿਓ ਰੇ ਝੂਠੇ ਲੋਭ ਲਾਗ ॥
ਕਛੁ ਬਿਗਰਿਓ ਨਾਹਿਨ ਅਜਹੁ ਜਾਗ ॥     (Ang 1187)
*(Why are being mislead by the false temptations,*
*Nothing is lost yet, there is still time to wake up.)*

To be awake and stay awake is to keep our True Nature in mind all the time and to live a conscious life. We should be conscious of our Essence every moment in life. In every experience in life, we should be fully aware of not only the experience, but also of ourselves, the experiencer. For example, when we are involved in doing something, there are two ways of doing that. First possibility is that we are doing it unconsciously, meaning we are not conscious of our own selves during the action. We are essentially, working like a machine, someone who acts and responds in a mechanical way. We are completely lost in the actions that we are involved in, unaware of ourselves. This situation is called working while being asleep. Nearly all of us are working like that, and are going through life sound asleep. We are so engrossed in the outside world that we are completely unaware of ourselves.

ਮੇਰਾ ਮੇਰਾ ਕਰਿ ਕਰਿ ਵਿਗੁਤਾ ॥
ਆਤਮੁ ਨ ਚੀਨੈ ਭਰਮੈ ਵਿਚਿ ਸੂਤਾ ॥ (Ang 362)
*(They cry this is mine, this is mine, and are ruined,*

*They do not recognize their Atman, and are sleeping in misunderstanding.*)

Second possibility of doing something is while we are involved in an activity, we are not only doing the activity but we are conscious of our own selves too. We are essentially present while we are experiencing the object, activity or a relationship. If we are conscious of our own selves when we are involved in any kind of activity, then we are considered to be awake.

In our normal life we are not conscious of ourselves while dealing with the world around us. We may be walking on a street and see many objects, people, and activities around us. We are conscious of the objects, people and the activities, but one thing we are not conscious of is ourselves. This is termed as a non-conscious experience. If we examine our everyday experience we will find almost 100% of our experience is non-conscious. Just do some introspection of yourself at the end of the day. At the end of the day before going to bed, just review how long you have been conscious of yourself during various activities throughout the day. I am sure you will be shocked to find that there was almost no time when you were conscious. This is how our whole life goes by, and is essentially wasted away. Gurbani say that we are sleeping while awake and are losing our life. And all the wealth that we have accumulated, which has been the cause of our sleep, will pass on to someone else when we go.

ਜਾਗਤੁ ਸੋਇਆ ਜਨਮੁ ਗਵਾਇਆ ॥
ਮਾਲੁ ਧਨੁ ਜੋਰਿਆ ਭਇਆ ਪਰਾਇਆ ॥ (Ang 792)
(*A person is asleep while awake, and thus losing his life,*
*The property and wealth he or she has accumulated, eventually becomes someone else's property.*)

Guru Ji is implying from this shabad that we are so busy making money in this world that we are completely asleep concerning our spiritual life. The money we accumulate is not going to go with us. So in the end we will have wasted our life because of our greed for the money that was the cause of our sleep.

**Naam Simran:**

The most effective way to wake up according to Gurbani, is doing Simran, which means remembering. Guru Ji says that just remember your Guru all the time and thus awaken your mind.

ਸਿਮਰਿ ਸਿਮਰਿ ਸਿਮਰਿ ਗੁਰੁ ਅਪੁਨਾ ਸੋਇਆ ਮਨੁ ਜਾਗਾਈ ॥ (Ang 758)
(*Remembering the Guru constantly, I awaken my sleeping mind.*)

We will analyze this shabad to understand how remembering the Guru will wake up our mind. Remembering is the basic process of bringing our forgotten memories to the forefront. If we lose something like our phone etc. we try to use the faculty of remembering to figure out where and when I had it last and where I could have put it. We go through that over and over and eventually the memory does pop up more often than not, and reveals where we put the item. The Alzheimer patients are asked to remember their past, so their memories can be brought to life again. They are shown pictures of their past life to help. That is what Guru Ji is saying that we need to do, remember constantly, notice shabad says remember, remember, remember three times, because repeated remembering will awaken the memory of our True Nature. Why is it being said that we remember the Guru? This is because Guru is our True Essence and resides inside us. When we remember our Guru we have to go where our Guru is, that is inside our own Self.

ਸੋ ਸਤਿਗੁਰੁ ਪਿਆਰਾ ਮੇਰੈ ਨਾਲਿ ਹੈ ਜਿਥੈ ਕਿਥੈ ਮੈਨੋ ਲਏ ਛਡਾਈ ॥ (Ang 588)
(*That Beloved True Guru is always with me, wherever I may be, He saves me.*)

When we take our attention inside us and keep it there, we are in the company of the Guru or we are one with the Guru. If we continue doing that, it will, one day, lead to our awakening or recognition of our True Identity. As pointed out earlier, those who meet the True Guru, are the awakened ones.

ਗੁਰ ਪੂਰੇ ਕੀ ਚਰਨੀ ਲਾਗੁ ॥
ਜਨਮ ਜਨਮ ਕਾ ਸੋਇਆ ਜਾਗੁ ॥  (Ang 891)
(*Reside at the feet of the True Guru,*
*And wake up after being asleep for many incarnations.*)

This can be made clear with an analogy. We all dream at night where we create a world and enter into the dream world as a subject in the dream. The subject in the dream does not know that he or she is a subject in a dream. He thinks that he is real and the world around him is real too. If he is told that he or she is a subject in the dream, and that he or she should try to wake up from the dream. Initially the subject in the dream will deny that he or she is in a dream. But if it does agree, what would be the best way for the subject in the dream to wake up from the dream? The best way would be for him or her to go inwards and try to get in touch with the one who is dreaming, his or her own self. Our situation is very much like that of the subject in the dream. In this analogy, our Atman or Awareness is dreaming the world that we see around us. We all are subjects in that dream like the subjects in our dream at night, but we do not know that we are subjects in the dream. What is the best way for us to wake up from this dream? Just like the subject in the dream, the best way for us is to go inwards and try to remember our own Real Self. This is because the self of the dream subjects, which are all of us, and the Self of the Dreamer which is Atman or Awareness, is one and the same. That is why there is so much emphasis in Gurbani about repeated rememberance (Simran). By repeated remembrance of our own Real Self, which is the same as Guru, Satguru, Atman, Awareness, Parmatma etc, we will one day wake up to our True Nature.

Those who may not like the analogy of a dream, Gurbani says that one truth we should firmly plant in our mind is that this world is like a dream. Our night dream is a micro sample of our waking life. So it offers a very valid comparison to the waking state.

ਰੇ ਨਰ ਇਹ ਸਾਚੀ ਜੀਅ ਧਾਰਿ ॥
ਸਗਲ ਜਗਤੁ ਹੈ ਜੈਸੇ ਸੁਪਨਾ ਬਿਨਸਤ ਲਗਤ ਨ ਬਾਰ ॥ (Ang 633)
(*O man, grasp this truth firmly in your mind,
The world is just like a dream. It can pass away in no time.*)

Bhagat Kabir Ji and Guru Tegh Bahadur Ji have stern messages
for the people who are asleep and continue to live like that. They
use similar language and say that people will wake up only when
the messenger of death hits them on their head.

ਕਹੁ ਕਬੀਰ ਤਬ ਹੀ ਨਰੁ ਜਾਗੈ ॥
ਜਮ ਕਾ ਡੰਡੁ ਮੂੰਡ ਮਹਿ ਲਾਗੈ ॥ (Ang 870)
(*Says Kabir, the man wakes up only, when the Messenger of Death
hits him over the head with his club.*)


ਜਮ ਕੋ ਡੰਡੁ ਪਰਿਓ ਸਿਰ ਉਪਰਿ ਤਬ ਸੋਵਤ ਤੈ ਜਾਗਿਓ ॥
ਕਹਾ ਹੋਤ ਅਬ ਕੈ ਪਛੁਤਾਏ ਛੂਟਤ ਨਾਹਿਨ ਭਾਗਿਓ ॥ (Ang 1008)
(*When the Messenger of Death's club falls on your head then you will
wake up from your sleep,
What good will it do then, you cannot escape by running.*)

There is a great truth in these shabads that nobody really wakes
up either until death hits him or her, or some other calamity
comes upon us. It is an unfortunate state for all of us that we are
passing our life in sleep and don't even know it. We have come to
love our dream so much that we keep falling into it deeper and
deeper rather than coming out of it.

There is a quantum mechanics scientific experiment that was
done in 1801, called "**Double Slit Experiment**" to find the nature
of a quantum particle. The purpose of the experiment was to
determine if it behaved as a particle or a wave. This experiment,
in my opinion, offers scientific proof of how an awake and alert
mind can keep the circumstances from turning unpleasant. in
other words, it shows how an awakened or alert mind helps us
stay  out of trouble. The results of the experiment have been

baffling scientists, and have been discussed all over the world. There is still no consensus on the results of the experiment. The test is simple and one can get its details on the internet. It will be described briefly here. In this experiment, quantum particles like electrons are shot at a board with two parallel slits. There is another board behind the board with the slits. Some electrons pass through the slits in the first board and make a pattern on the second board. The scientists expected a simple slit pattern on the second board, but they were surprised to see no slit pattern. They saw a wave pattern on the second board. This wave pattern is also called interference pattern. This wave pattern or the interference pattern on the second board was not expected, to say the least. So the scientists decided to observe the behavior of the electrons as they passed through the slits. They installed detectors to study the electron's behavior. When they did that, the electrons changed their behavior from wave to particle, and yielded a slit pattern on the second board. Why did the electrons change their behavior from wave to slit pattern upon observation? This is what is confusing the scientists and there is no agreeable theory that explains this phenomenon. This experiment has been repeated over and over again but the results are the same.

Why do electrons change their behavior when observed? There have been a lot of discussions on the topic. There have been innumerable theories to explain the phenomenon but none accepted universally. We won't go into the discussion as to why the electrons change their behavior but will focus on the fact that the electrons do change their behavior upon observation. Our mind is fine like the quantum particles, and may be even finer than that. When the mind is not observed and is given a free reign to run around, it exhibits an interference behavior. As a result, it creates more problems in life and hence the person loses peace and happiness. But when the mind is observed, it automatically changes its behavior like the electrons in the double slit experiment and behaves in a more controlled and predictable manner. That is why Gurbani tells us to keep a watch over our mind.

ਇਸੁ ਮਨ ਕਉ ਕੋਈ ਖੋਜਹੁ ਭਾਈ ॥ (Ang 1128)
(*O brother, keep a watch on this mind of yours*)

Watching the mind means keeping it alert and awake during our interactions with the world or when doing Naam Simran, so it does not wander away in its day dreaming. Doing Paath in the morning like Nitnem or any of the Gurbani from Nitnem is very helpful in waking the mind, if one pays attention to the Paath recital. In fact, it is strongly recommended that one should "listen" to Paath while it is being recited. Mind has to be awake and alert to be able to listen to Paath. As soon as awareness is lost, listening will be lost with it. In that situation the person would be considered to have gone to sleep. So doing daily Nitnem and listening to it with sincerity, will set up a feedback system and will awaken a person. It is not going to happen overnight. This process may take months, years or maybe even a lifetime. This statement is made not to discourage anyone, but being awake is one of the highest rungs of the spiritual ladder. Gurbani says that only a person who is awake, can meet the Lord. So being awake is one of the highest achievements.

ਜਾਗਤ ਰਹੇ ਤਿਨੀ ਪ੍ਰਭੁ ਪਾਇਆ ਸਬਦੇ ਹਉਮੈ ਮਾਰੀ ॥
ਗਿਰਹੀ ਮਹਿ ਸਦਾ ਹਰਿ ਜਨ ਉਦਾਸੀ ਗਿਆਨ ਤਤ ਬੀਚਾਰੀ ॥ (Ang 599)
(*Those who are awake, meet the Lord and conquer their ego.*
*While leading the family life, they ever remain detached*
*And reflect on the Essence of spiritual Wisdom.*)

◆ ◆ ◆

# WHAT IS MEDITATION

ਅਹਿਨਿਸਿ ਰਾਮ ਰਹਹੁ ਰੰਗਿ ਰਾਤੇ ਏਹੁ ਜਪੁ
ਤਪੁ ਸੰਜਮੁ ਸਾਰਾ ਹੇ ॥ *(Ang 1030)*

*(Day and night, remain immersed
in the Lord's Love. This is the
Essence of all the chanting,
meditation and self discipline.)*

**M**editation according to the dictionary means to take control of one's mind so it becomes more peaceful and focused. Our mind has been going out after the worldly attractions all our life. Meditation is the way to turn the mind around and bring it back home. Through meditation the meditator becomes more alert and aware. This may be attained through silence or with the aid of chanting. Meditation and its purpose has been defined in a number of ways. Some define the purpose of meditation to be focusing the mind to achieve a goal. Others define it as a way to achieve peace and relaxation in daily life. Still others define meditation to control the constantly running mind. Highest purpose of meditation is to go beyond the mind and achieve union with the Divine, and find peace and happiness.. All religions of the world advocate some form of meditation as a means to unite with the Divine. We will discuss meditation in general, and Gurbani's point of view on how to meditate, and find the peace and happiness in the process. It may be stated here that Gurbani advocates meditation for only one purpose and that is to attain union with the Lord.

There are basically two types of meditation, objective and subjective. Examples of objective or external meditations are repeating a mantra, doing breathing, focusing on a photo or a flame etc. There are other objective practices like doing pilgrimage by going from one religious place to the other, leaving home and living in forests and retiring from family life. These forms of objective meditations or practices are considered to purify the mind and stabilize it. These practices may help in making the mind a bit steady but cannot help in reaching the highest goal which is to attain union with the Divine. For the purpose of union with the Divine Self we need to follow subjective meditation. While there are a number of objective meditations, there is only one form of subjective meditation. It is primarily turning our attention inwards to the place where God resides.

We are too much attracted to the outside world and never think of going inwards. It is said that our mind went out from home many lifetimes ago and got lost. It has not come home since. Basic philosophy of meditation is to turn our mind around and bring it back to its home or its source and make it stay there. If we look at our overall experience, we can see that we are so engrossed in going outwards that we never think about looking inwards. Most of us go through our whole life without even getting a hint of going inwards. I am reminded of an incident that Sant Maskeen recited once during one of his katha sessions. He said he was traveling in a train to a remote location in India. There was a gentleman sitting across from him in a seat near the window. The journey was long and went on for the whole day. Sant ji had a disciplined mind so he kept seated calmly in his seat throughout the journey, but the gentleman in the seat across from him was feeling restless and bored. Sant Ji says that he noticed this man reading a newspaper, that he had brought with him. He read the paper one time and put it away. About an hour later, he picked up the same paper and started to read it again. After the second reading, he put the paper away again. After that, he still kept feeling bored, evident from his behavior. Sant ji kept watching his restlessness, and was amused to see that after a couple of hours, the gentleman picked up the same paper again and started reading it the third time. Sant ji said he could not contain himself anymore and said to the gentleman, "I have seen people do Akhand Paath of Sri Guru Granth Sahib, but never seen anyone do Akhand Paath of a newspaper." The gentleman responded, there is nothing else to do. Moreover, you do not respond if I ask you something. Sant ji asked him, why don't you spend time with yourself. The man said I don't know what you are talking about, I have never heard that before. This is the situation with most of us. We never spend time with ourselves. Like the gentleman, we don't even know what it means. That is where meditation comes in. It is essentially spending time with ourselves, which is our Real Self. That is the same as our Guru, Atman or Awareness. Our Real Self has been called by many other names such as Divine Being, Divine Presence, Paramatma, God and Source etc. To spend time with our Real Self, we have to first find the Real Self, recognize it and then live with it or more precisely, live in it. We will discuss a little later in the article how to connect with our Real Self. This process of locating our Real Self and then staying with it, is termed as meditation. Gurbani says that those persons who are attached to their Source, the Real Self, are the ones who find peace and happiness. Those who are attached to the branches meaning the worldly attractions waste their lives away.

ਇਕਿ ਮੂਲਿ ਲਗੇ ਓਨੀ ਸੁਖੁ ਪਾਇਆ ॥
ਡਾਲੀ ਲਾਗੇ ਤਿਨੀ ਜਨਮੁ ਗਵਾਇਆ ॥ (Ang 1051)
(*Those who are attached to their Source, they find peace and happiness.*
*But those who are attached to the branches, waste their lives away uselessly.*)

## General Discussion:

The objective forms of meditation have been condemned in Gurbani. There were numerous forms of objective meditations going on at the times of the Gurus. One of the more prominent was where people would leave their homes and would go to the forests and stay there. Once they retired from life they would stop dealings with the world. This was prevalent in the old days in India. Some would go out and would lock themselves up in a cave, so to speak, and make it their home, while others would make little huts in the forests and live there. They would go to the nearby villages to beg for food to fill their stomach. There were many other kinds of objective meditations followed in the old days too. In the following shabad from Sukhmani Sahib, are listed some of the objective meditation practices that were prevalent in those days. After listing various objective meditation practices, Gurbani says none of these rise to the level of Naam Simran, which is the subjective meditation. Guru ji says that people were practicing mantra meditation, yoga asanas, worshiping the devees and the devtas. Other practices they were following were fasting, making donations, cutting pieces of their body and offering to fire. These are only a few practices listed here from one Ashtapadi(ਅਸਟਪਦੀ) for the sake of brevity. There are more practices mentioned in the same Ashtapadi in Sukhmani Sahib.

ਜਾਪ ਤਾਪ ਗਿਆਨ ਸਭਿ ਧਿਆਨ ॥
ਖਟ ਸਾਸਤ੍ਰ ਸਿਮ੍ਰਿਤਿ ਵਖਿਆਨ ॥
ਜੋਗ ਅਭਿਆਸ ਕਰਮ ਧ੍ਰਮ ਕਿਰਿਆ ॥
ਸਗਲ ਤਿਆਗਿ ਬਨ ਮਧੇ ਫਿਰਿਆ ॥
ਅਨਿਕ ਪ੍ਰਕਾਰ ਕੀਏ ਬਹੁ ਜਤਨਾ ॥
ਪੁੰਨ ਦਾਨ ਹੋਮੇ ਬਹੁ ਰਤਨਾ ॥
ਸਰੀਰ ਕਟਾਇ ਹੋਮੈ ਕਰਿ ਰਾਤੀ ॥

ਵਰਤ ਨੇਮ ਕਰੈ ਬਹੁ ਭਾਤੀ ||
ਨਹੀ ਤੁਲਿ ਰਾਮ ਨਾਮ ਬੀਚਾਰ ||
ਨਾਨਕ ਗੁਰਮੁਖਿ ਨਾਮੁ ਜਪੀਐ ਇਕ ਬਾਰ || (Ang 265)

(*Chanting, intense discipline, spiritual wisdom and all sorts of concentration,*
*The six schools of philosophy and sermons on the scriptures,*
*The practice of Yoga and righteous conduct,*
*The renunciation of everything and wandering around in the forests,*
*Making all sorts of objective efforts,*
*Donations to charities and offering of ghee to fire,*
*Cutting the body into pieces and offering them to ceremonial fire,*
*Keeping fasts and making vows of all sorts,*
*None of these are equal to meditation on Name of the Lord,*
*O Nanak, even if it is chanted once by the Gurmukh.*

Gurbani emphasizes meditation called "Naam Simran". Naam Simran is subjective meditation. Gurbani states that the Naam Simran meditation is the highest form of meditation to unite us with the Lord.

ਵਡਾ ਸਾਹਿਬੁ ਊਚਾ ਥਾਉ || ਊਚੇ ਉਪਰਿ ਊਚਾ ਨਾਉ || (Ang 5)
(*Great is the Master, High is His Heavenly Abode. Highest of the High, above all is His Name.*)

Guru ji talks about Naam Simran over and over again and even says that life spent without Naam Simran is a wasted life. We make excuses all the time that we do not have time to do Naam Simran because we have too many things to do. Guru Ji calls the people foolish who do not remember the Lord and as such are wasting away their life. The people claim that they are too busy but Guru ji says that all other work done in our life is of no use.

ਮਨਮੁਖ ਮੁਗਧੁ ਹਰਿ ਨਾਮੁ ਨਾ ਚੇਤੈ ਬਿਰਥਾ ਜਨਮੁ ਗਵਾਇਆ || (Ang 600)
(*The foolish self willed people do not remember the Lord's Name, they waste away their life in vain.*

ਅਵਰਿ ਕਾਜ ਤੇਰੈ ਕਿਤੈ ਨ ਕਾਮ ॥
ਮਿਲੁ ਸਾਧਸੰਗਤਿ ਭਜੁ ਕੇਵਲ ਨਾਮ ॥  ( Ang 12)
(*Meditate on the Naam in the company of Sadh Sangat, any other
activity in life is not going to help you.*)

**Definition Of Meditation: (ਨਾਮ ਸਿਮਰਨ):**

Naam Simran is normally understood to be lovingly chanting
Waheguru, Waheguru with or without music early in the
morning. If the morning time is not possible it can be done other
times too. As pointed out earlier,Naam Simran is the highest
form of meditation. In this process, one gets fully absorbed in
the Love of the Lord. Gurbani defines meditation (ਨਾਮ ਸਿਮਰਨ) as
follows:

ਹਰਿ ਨਾਮਾ ਹਰਿ ਰੰਡੁ ਹੈ ਹਰਿ ਰੰਡੁ ਮਜੀਠੈ ਰੰਡੁ ॥
ਗੁਰਿ ਤੁਠੈ ਹਰਿ ਰੰਗੁ ਚਾੜਿਆ ਫਿਰਿ ਬਹੁੜਿ ਨਾ ਹੋਵੀ ਭੰਡੁ ॥  (Ang 731)
(*The Lord's Name is the Love of the Lord,
The Lord's Love is permanent color,
When the Guru blesses us, He colors us with His Love;
and then that color never fades away.*)

The message in this shabad is that meditation (ਨਾਮ ਸਿਮਰਨ)
consists of being soaked or colored in the Lord's or Guru's Love.
So when we do Naam Simran, it is of utmost importance that
we do it with extreme Love and respect. One thing else Gurbani
says in this shabad is that this Love of the Lord is of permanent
nature if we are blessed by our Guru. Gurbani also tells us that
our Guru is with us all the time taking care of us everywhere.

ਸੋ ਸਤਿਗੁਰੁ ਪਿਆਰਾ ਮੇਰੈ ਨਾਲਿ ਹੈ ਜਿਥੈ ਕਿਥੈ ਮੈਨੋ ਲਏ ਛਡਾਈ ॥  (Ang 588)
(*The Beloved True Guru is always with me,
Wherever I may be, He saves me*)

Guru is with us all the time and resides in our hearts. The
purpose of meditation is to bring the mind back home in our
hearts and make it bask in the company of the Guru. So the

real meditation is not focusing your mind on anything external but it is withdrawing the mind from outward attractions and bringing it back home. Gurbani tells us that the mind's essence is the Divine Light. So when we bring the mind back home and make it stay there, it's wandering stops, and it starts to abide in its Divine Essence.

ਮਨ ਤੂੰ ਜੋਤਿ ਸਰੂਪੁ ਹੈ ਅਪਨਾ ਮੂਲੁ ਪਛਾਣੁ ॥ ( Ang 441)
(*O my mind, you are the Embodiment of Divine Light, recognize your origin.*)

The mind has somehow forgotten its essence and believes itself to be a separate entity. It feels this wound of separation from its Source and feels unfulfilled and unhappy. To heal it's wound of unhappiness it goes out in the world looking for happiness in objects and relationships. It can't see its Source where real happiness resides, so it starts looking outwardly. It is said that the real reason the mind is wandering in the world is to find its Source and thereby regain its fulfillment and happiness. But it is under an illusion, and does not know where to look. It is misguided by the attractions of the world and thinks that its fulfillment lies in the attainment of worldly objects. When the mind gets a worldly object it has been longing for, its search comes to an end temporarily. It feels peaceful for a while. It feels peaceful because its search stops and it begins to rest in its own Divine Essence. After sometime the object becomes old, It does not bring the same happiness as it did in the beginning. So the search for a new object starts again. The person goes through this cycle all his or her life but never achieves lasting peace. Gurbani says that unless one gets the taste of his or her own Real Self, there is no permanent peace and happiness.

ਏ ਰਸਨਾ ਤੂ ਅਨ ਰਸਿ ਰਾਚਿ ਰਹੀ ਤੇਰੀ ਪਿਆਸ ਨ ਜਾਇ ॥
ਪਿਆਸ ਨ ਜਾਇ ਹੋਰਤੁ ਕਿਤੈ ਜਿਚਰੁ ਹਰਿ ਰਸੁ ਪਲੈ ਨ ਪਾਇ ॥  (Ang 921)
(*O my tongue, you are engrossed in other tastes,*
  *And your thirst is not being quenched.*
  *Your thirst cannot be quenched by any other means,*

*Until you attain the sublime taste of the Divine Essence.)*

ਮਨ ਮੇਰੇ ਹਰਿ ਰਸੁ ਚਾਖੁ ਤਿਖ ਜਾਇ ॥
ਜਿਨੀ ਗੁਰਮੁਖਿ ਚਾਖਿਆ ਸਹਜੇ ਰਹੇ ਸਮਾਇ ॥ (Ang 26)
*(O my mind, taste the Sublime Essence of the Lord,
and your thirst will be quenched.
Those Gurmukhs who have tasted it remain intuitively absorbed in
the Lord.)*

That is why it is important to stop the mind from going out after
worldly objects and reverse its direction inwards to rest in its
own Divine Essence.

**Meditation Techniques:**

**Passive Meditation:**

As stated earlier meditation is simply coming back home to
rest in oneself where our Guru or our Real Self resides. Once
we come back home then we just park there and live there.
When the mind lives there, it becomes quiet over time and stops
running around like nomads. Our old evil tendencies get cleaned
up in the company of the Guru. Gurbani compares Guru to
Philosopher's Stone, and us to iron. When iron comes in contact
with the Philosopher's Stone, the iron is transformed into gold.
Similarly when we abide in our heart in the company of the
Guru, we, the iron will be transformed into gold implying we
will be transformed into a Gurmukh.

ਮਨੂਰੈ ਤੇ ਕੰਚਨ ਭਏ ਭਾਈ ਗੁਰੁ ਪਾਰਸੁ ਮੇਲਿ ਮਿਲਾਇ ॥ (Ang 638)
*(One who is united with the Guru, the Philosopher's Stone,
Becomes transformed from rusty iron into gold.)*

How do we contact the Guru or Real Self? One of the easiest ways
is to listen to a continual low volume sound. This could be low
volume Waheguru simran or any other sound. The sound can be
recited by oneself or it can be an external sound. Only thing to

make sure is that the sound does not provoke thinking because we are trying to go beyond our mind or thinking. Close your eyes and just listen to the sound. But rather than focusing on the sound, follow the sound inwards to the one, who is listening to this sound, in you. Who is listening to the sound? It is neither the body nor the mind, but it is our Real Self. We have proven in the article "Come Home My Friend" that body and mind are not aware entities and hence cannot be the listeners of the sound. The intent of following the sound is to locate our Real Self who is the real listener; and is beyond both the body and mind. This may be hard for some people to do, because they have never tried to do this before. But with some practice it will become easy. Additionally, once this methodology is firmed up one may not even need any sound to reach our Real Self. Gurbani talks about this technique in the following shabad.

ਧੁਨਿ ਮਹਿ ਧਿਆਨੁ ਧਿਆਨ ਮਹਿ ਜਾਨਿਆ ਗੁਰਮੁਖਿ ਅਕਥ ਕਹਾਨੀ ॥ (Ang 878)
(*By focusing attention on a continual sound,*
*Gurmukh comes to know the Knowledge of the Unspeakable.*)

Gurbani says that by focusing our attention on the sound and following it, we will come to know our Real Self. Our attention, when listening to the sound, stops going out into the world and gets locked onto the sound. The attention then travels inwards with the sound to locate the listener. "Listening" is emphasized greatly in Gurbani. We are asked to attentively listen to Paath when doing Nitnem or reciting any Bani. Guru JI says in Jap Ji Sahib, that when reciting the Bani, listen to It and keep the Love of the Lord in mind. This way one will get rid of one's pain and achieve peace.

ਗਾਵੀਐ ਸੁਣੀਐ ਮਨਿ ਰਖੀਐ ਭਾਉ ॥
ਦੁਖੁ ਪਰਹਰਿ ਸੁਖੁ ਘਰਿ ਲੈ ਜਾਇ ॥ (Ang 2)
(*Sing, listen, and let your mind be filled with love.*
*You will be freed of pain and will achieve peace.*)

Let us explore how we listen to the sound to trace our way back to our Real Self. We may visualize sound being picked up by the ears, it travels through the auditory nerves to the brain. The sound still has not reached the listener. The listener is not the brain but our Real Self. It is, somehow, reading the sound signals in the brain to convert them into listening and understanding. How the Real Self is reading sound signals from the brain, is not understood by science yet. This is termed as the "Hard Problem of Consciousness". The sound is not heard by the brain but by the Real Self. Brain is only an instrument by which the sound signals are displayed. Only our Real Self is aware and that is the only entity that can know or hear anything. If one would pay very close attention to the location where the sound is being heard, one will realize that it is being heard at the navel level in a zone that can be labeled as a "field of Awareness". This is a very subtle point and needs full attention. To repeat, the sound is being heard in a zone near the navel. This shows that our Real Self is located near the navel. Sant Maskeen ji talks about this topic in one of his katha episodes. He points out that Real Self is located at the navel rather than at the heart. He says that the navel is the center of the body. Navel is called "dhunni" in the Punjabi language. Dhunni means the place from where a sound or dhun (ਧੁਨ) originates. Sant ji says that the navel is where the sound or the dhun originates in the human body. We have also established that the navel is the place, where sound is heard in the human body. In other words, both origination of the sound and listening of the sound, is happening at the same location in the body, at the navel, where the Real Self resides. Osho calls the navel as the seat of the soul. Osho says: "The journey of the meditator is downwards towards the roots. One has to descend from the brain to the heart, and from the heart to the navel. Only from the navel can anybody enter into the soul; before that, one can never enter it."

So when we are listening to the sound and then earnestly following the sound into ourselves, we end up at the navel where the Real Self or the Listener is located. Gurbani calls this technique of following sound back to its Source, "Surat Shabad Merger". In essence, when we listen to the sound and follow it to the navel location, we are uniting our attention (Surat) with the Sound (Shabad). Gurbani says when Surat and the Shabad unite in the heart, then one is bestowed with the drinking of Ambrosial Nectar.

ਸੁਰਤਿ ਸਬਦੁ ਰਿਦ ਅੰਤਰਿ ਜਾਗੀ ਅਮਿਉ ਝੋਲਿ ਝੋਲਿ ਪੀਜਾ ਹੇ ॥ (Ang 1074)
(*Awareness of Shabad has awakened within my heart. I drink Ambrosial Nectar with extreme joy.*)

ਸਬਦ ਸੁਰਤਿ ਸੁਖੁ ਉਪਜੈ ਪ੍ਰਭ ਰਾਤਉ ਸੁਖ ਸਾਰੁ ॥ (Ang 62)
(*Focusing our attention on the Shabad, happiness wells up. Attuned to God, most blissful peace is found.*)

So the passive meditation technique consists of coming back to our center, where our Real Self or the Guru resides, and meditating on it. Meditation, as stated earlier, is to come to our real home and stay there as long as we can. When we meditate on our Real Self, we are meditating on the Guru or God. Gurbani says that the Guru and God are one, there is no difference.

ਗੁਰੁ ਪਰਮੇਸਰੁ ਏਕੁ ਹੈ ਸਭ ਮਹਿ ਰਹਿਆ ਸਮਾਇ ॥ (Ang 53)
(*The Guru and the Lord are one and the same, pervading permeating amongst all.*)

That is the reason God's realization is often termed as Self Realization. With this understanding we find that God's realization is not something that is foreign to us but is extremely close to us. It is not even close to us, it is the realization of our own Real Self. Gurbani instructs us many times that we need to recognize ourselves and at times even scolds us for not doing so. Guru ji says that we do not recognize our Real Self and then claim that God is far away from us. We can't see Him that He is with us because He is not perceptible.

ਅਪਨਾ ਆਪੁ ਨ ਪਛਾਣਈ ਹਰਿ ਪ੍ਰਭੁ ਜਾਤਾ ਦੂਰਿ ॥ (Ang 854)
(*One does not care to recognize oneself,*

*And then he or she thinks the Lord is far away)*

ਹਉ ਢੂਢੇਦੀ ਸਜਣਾ ਸਜਣੁ ਮੈਡੇ ਨਾਲਿ ॥
ਜਨ ਨਾਨਕ ਅਲਖੁ ਨ ਲਖੀਐ ਗੁਰਮੁਖਿ ਦੇਹਿ ਦਿਖਾਲਿ ॥ (Ang 1318)
*(I was searching searching for my Friend, but my Friend is right here with me,*
*O servant Nanak, the Unseen cannot be seen, but He reveals Himself to the Gurmukh.*

There is a saying in Punjabi language "ਕੁਛੜ ਕੁੜੀ ਤੇ ਸਹਿਰ ਢੰਡੋਰਾ" which means that someone is carrying the child in his or her arms but has issued an amber alert in the city to find the child". These shabads above are essentially saying exactly the same thing that we are complaining that God is far away from us while He is right with us. We just do not recognize our own Real Self.

Baba Farid says that if we dig deep enough into ourselves we will meet our Real Self, which we call "I", and once we meet ourselves we will find peace and happiness.

ਆਪੁ ਸਵਾਰਹਿ ਮੈ ਮਿਲਹਿ ਮੈ ਮਿਲਿਆ ਸੁਖੁ ਹੋਇ ॥
*(If we reform ourselves we shall meet "I" and when we meet "I" we shall find peace and happiness.)*

In summary, passive meditation consists of locating our Real Self and meditating on it. Using the sound to access the Self will be helpful, especially in the early stages of practice. Listening to Paath or Kirtan sounds can be used for this purpose. Try to listen to Paath or Kirtan with your attention focused at the navel level. As the practice progresses the sound may not be needed. Eyes should be closed during passive meditation. Seeker is the sought. So we are trying to meet our own Real Self. We commonly call our Real Self as "I". We don't need to go anywhere to find "I". It is inside us. Just locate your "I" inside yourself and go there, that is our Real Self. We have covered this "I" with thousands of labels starting from our childhood. That is why we cannot find it. It like finding a needle in a heystack. We have called this "I" a child, a young boy, man, woman or an old person etc. in our life. With every stage in life we have added more labels to cover it further, like I am a teacher, engineer or a doctor, the list goes on. We identify with these labels, and at times feel proud of them. All our attention has been focused on these labels. This is similar to covering gold with all kinds of labels or names when it is converted into ornaments, even though the ornaments are still gold. One gold has been given many names. Similarly our Real Self "I" has been buried under all the labels. Meditation is to take our attention off these labels and focus it on the "I" which is hiding under these names and forms. So we have to locate our Real Self or "I" by cutting through all the labels. That is why Gurbani says we should die while living, meaning we should die to these labels and focus on our Real Self. Gurbani says that we cannot cross the world ocean without dying while living.

ਕਿਨ ਬਿਧਿ ਸਾਗਰੁ ਤਰੀਐ ॥
ਜੀਵਤਿਆ ਨਹ ਮਰੀਐ ॥ (Ang 877)
(*How can we cross over the world ocean?*
*Without dying while living.*)

Once our "I" or Real Self has been located, we need to try to feel it with deep love, respect and devotion. Just feel it. This is the Divine Presence in us. As stated earlier, our Real Self is in fact, our Guru, which is the same as God. We should feel it, abide in it, melt into it, and be one with it. This Real Self, is not body and mind, but is beyond them and is the Divine Light, our Real Essence. There is no other Reality there. Gurbani says there is only One Reality. We are that Reality. We have to become one with it. We believe ourselves to be separate from this Reality, which is a false belief. We are It or one with It. So searching our Real Self, is searching for God. Reaching our Real Self should not be that difficult. We don't have to go anywhere, no distance to cover. Just abide in ourselves. In fact, this is the easiest of the easiest tasks, if we can call it a task. No effort is needed.

All we have to do is " just be" what we are. We don't have to do anything or become anything. Just stay home and celebrate being our Real Self. Best time to do this meditation is early in the morning before or after taking shower. Morning time is very conducive because the mind is still calm and not yet involved in day to day issues. Meditation can be done by sitting up in the bed or sitting comfortably in a chair. No special preparation is needed. Gurbani asks us to do Naam Simran as soon as we get up in the morning. If the morning time is not feasible it can be done anytime during the day when time is available. If we do this meditation regularly we will definitely be blessed with peace and happiness in our life.

Swami Rama Tirtha, a Punjabi Saint writes in his book, "When you are fully established in your Real Self, you will develop powers to move the whole world. In other words, if you identify yourself with the unlimited Self, God, you will fill within yourself unlimited powers. Everything will be set in its proper place, if you are fully established on the Royal Throne of Godhood."

Guru Ji summarizes meditation in the following shabad, saying very simply that we need to take our attention away from the world and focus it on the One who made the world.

ਚਿਤਾ ਰਚਿਤ ਚਿਤੁ ਹੈ ਭਾਰੀ ॥
ਤਜਿ ਚਿਤੈ ਚੇਤਹੁ ਚਿਤਕਾਰੀ ॥
ਚਿਤੁ ਬਚਿਤੁ ਇਹੈ ਅਵਝੇਰਾ ॥
ਤਜਿ ਚਿਤੈ ਚਿਤੁ ਰਾਖਿ ਚਿਤੇਰਾ ॥   ( Ang 340)

(*The Lord has painted the great picture of the world,*
*Forget the picture and remember the Painter.*
*The picture is too beautiful, that is the only problem,*
*Leave the picture and focus your attention on the Painter.*)

**Non-Passive Meditation:**

We have discussed passive meditation where we sit down at one location, close our eyes and turn inwards to access our Real Self. But our everyday life is so busy that most of us do not have time to spare for passive meditation. In fact, that is the reason it is suggested to do the meditation early in the morning and before getting busy with never ending chores of the day. Keeping in mind the busy life, non-passive meditation presents itself as a viable alternative. The non-passive meditation is done while one is working or even when one is not working. This meditation technique consists of keeping our attention at one point at our center, the navel or the heart and continue doing our job. This meditation is also called dynamic meditation, since it is being done on the fly. Bhagat Nam Dev Ji talks about this meditation in the following shabad. Bhagat ji mentions five analogies in this shabad to make it perfectly clear, how to do this meditation.

ਆਨੀਲੇ ਕਾਗਦੁ ਕਾਟੀਲੇ ਗੂਡੀ ਆਕਾਸ ਮਧੇ ਭਰਮੀਅਲੇ ॥
ਪੰਚ ਜਨਾ ਸਿਉ ਬਾਤ ਬਤਊਆ ਚੀਤੁ ਸੁ ਡੋਰੀ ਰਾਖੀਅਲੇ ॥
ਮਨੁ ਰਾਮ ਨਾਮਾ ਬੇਧੀਅਲੇ ॥
ਜੈਸੇ ਕਨਿਕ ਕਲਾ ਚਿਤੁ ਮਾਂਡੀਅਲੇ ॥੧॥ (ਰਹਾਉ)
ਆਨੀਲੇ ਕੁੰਭ ਭਰਾਈਲੇ ਊਦਕ ਰਾਜਕੁਆਰਿ ਪੁਰੰਦਰੀਏ ॥
ਹਸਤ ਬਿਨੋਦ ਬੀਚਾਰ ਕਰਤੀ ਹੈ ਚੀਤੁ ਸੁ ਗਾਗਰਿ ਰਾਖੀਅਲੇ ॥
ਮੰਦਰੁ ਏਕੁ ਦੁਆਰ ਦਸ ਜਾ ਕੇ ਗਊ ਚਰਾਵਨ ਛਾਡੀਅਲੇ ॥
ਪਾਂਚ ਕੋਸ ਪਰ ਗਊ ਚਰਾਵਤ ਚੀਤੁ ਸੁ ਬਛਰਾ ਰਾਖੀਅਲੇ ॥
ਕਹਤ ਨਾਮਦੇਉ ਸੁਨਹੁ ਤਿਲੋਚਨ ਬਾਲਕੁ ਪਾਲਨ ਪਉਢੀਅਲੇ ॥
ਅੰਤਰਿ ਬਾਹਰਿ ਕਾਜ ਬਿਰੂਧੀ ਚੀਤੁ ਸੁ ਬਾਰਕ ਰਾਖੀਅਲੇ ॥ ( Ang 972)

(*The boy takes paper. Cuts it and makes a kite and flies it in the sky, He talks with his friends while flying the kite, but he keeps his attention on the kite string.*
*My mind has been pierced by the Name of the Lord, Like the goldsmith, whose attention is fixed in his work.*
*The young girl in the village takes a pitcher and fills it with water, She laughs and talks with her friends, but she keeps her attention focused on the pitcher on her head.*
*The cow is let loose, out of a structure which has ten gates, to graze in the field,*

*The cow grazes upto five miles away, but keeps its attention focused on its calf.*
*Says Naam Deo, listen, O Trilochan, mother puts the child in the cradle,*
*The mother works inside or outside the house, but she keeps her mind in the child.*

Bhagat ji says that a boy makes a kite and flies it in the sky. While flying the kite he talks to his friends, but he keeps his attention focused on the kite. He says in the next analogy, I keep the mind absorbed in God, just as the goldsmith keeps his attention focused on his work while making the ornaments. Next he talks about the village girl who goes to fetch water from the well outside the village. She puts the pitcher full of water on her head. While coming back home she chats with her friends but keeps her attention locked on to the pitcher on her head. Next Naam Deo Ji talks about cows going out far away from their calves to graze, but while grazing they keep their attention focused on their calves. The last analogy cited is of a mother who puts her child in the crib and then works around the house. However, while working around the house, the mother keeps her attention on the child. These analogies make it very clear how to do meditation while working. The mind has to be trained to do the work, while staying focused on our Real Self in the background. Naam Dev Ji in another shabad tells a contemporary Saint, Trilochan Ji, how to do this meditation. He says, O Trilochan, do all the work with your hands and feet, but stay consciously connected with the Lord.

ਨਾਮਾ ਕਹੈ ਤਿਰਲੋਚਨਾ ਮੁਖ ਤੇ ਰਾਮੁ ਸੰਮਾਲਿ ॥
ਹਾਥ ਪਾਉ ਕਰਿ ਕਾਮੁ ਸਭੁ ਚੀਤੁ ਨਿਰੰਜਨ ਨਾਲਿ ॥ (Ang 1375)
*(Naam Dev says, O Trilochan, chant the Lord's Name with your mouth,*
*Do all the work with your hands and feet, but stay consciously connected with the Lord.)*

This meditation requires us to do two things at the same time.

214

As they say, **walk and chew gum at the same time**. We will discuss in some detail what is meant by doing two things at the same time pertaining to meditation. Imagine looking at an object in front of us. If we look at the process closely, we can say that there are two things involved in the process of looking. There is the subject and the object, the subject paying attention to the object. We are the subject and the item we are looking at is the object. Normally, all our attention is taken up by the object when we are looking at the object. We never think about ourselves or the subject during the process. The purpose of this meditation is to pay attention to both the subject and the object simultaneously. So while keeping the attention on the object, we need to be aware of ourselves at the same time. However, when we try to do this, we run into a problem. When we bring our attention to ourselves we lose attention from the object. When we take our attention back to the object, we lose ourselves, the subject. So it is either the subject or the object. One may have to try many times to be aware of both the object and subject simultaneously. With some practice it is possible to do that. When you succeed in doing that, you can pat yourself on the back because you have taken a huge step in meditation. What is happening here is that, when we look at an object, we are the subject as a bodymind entity, looking at the object. To repeat, the subject bodymind is looking at the object. But when we become aware of both the subject and the object simultaneously, we rise above the subject and the object both. When we rise above the bodymind and the object both, we become our Real Self. The Real Self becomes aware of both the subject, which is the bodymind entity and the object. **Being aware of both, one has taken a huge step of going from being in the world to being a witness of the world.**

Osho calls this meditation, **"double arrow"** meditation. What he means by the double arrow is that when one looks at an object, he or she should look at it with the attention having a double arrow, meaning while the attention is going outwards to the object, it should also go inwards to the one who is looking at the object. Normally we have attention that has only one direction, and goes out to the object only. We need to change that habit and look at everything with double arrow attention. Osho says that whatever you do, do it with double arrow attention. This technique will bring Awareness in your life.

The purpose of being aware of both the subject and the object is to not get lost in the drama of the world, which is our normal way of life. We are being distracted by all the shiny objects around us. All our attention is taken up by our activities, so we completely forget ourselves. Forgetting ourselves means we become unaware or unconscious of ourselves. Those, who do Nitnem in the morning must have noticed that staying aware and conscious during the recital of the Paath is very important, but difficult at the same time. It is very easy to get lost during the recital, especially, if the Paath is being recited from memory. Doing Paath makes us aware of how unaware we are. Similarly our attention during the day is distracted all the time, and we are not even aware of it. It happens during our daily experiences, no matter what they are. It may be doing our daily chores, working in the office or anything else that we may be doing. If we are conscious of ourselves while doing our daily duties, we will not get lost in the drama of the world.

Gurbani says that we care more for the objects of the world which we are going to leave here, but we don't even think about the one who is always with us and is aware of these objects. What is implied in this shabad below, is that we spend all our attention on the things we are going to leave here, but we don't pay attention to our Real Self who is going to go with us.

ਛੋਡਿ ਜਿਾਇ ਤਿਸ ਕਾ ਸ੍ਰਮੁ ਕਰੈ ॥
ਸੰਗਿ ਸਹਾਈ ਤਿਸੁ ਪਰਹਰੈ ॥ (Ang 267)
(*They all struggle for what they must leave eventually,*
*but they turn away from the Lord, their help and support,*
*who is always with them.*)

216

We invest all our happiness in the objects of our attention and forget ourselves. When the object of our attention fails us, then it becomes the cause of our suffering. So the goal is to maintain self alertness all the time, so this exclusive attention in the objects does not lead to suffering. This is not going to be easy because we have lived as the bodymind for many years or even many lifetimes. It may take months or even years to get firmly anchored in Awareness, our Real Self. But the effort is worth the benefits. Gurbani says that those people who stay anchored in themselves will have their mind's desires fulfilled and will meet the Lord. This meditation is sometimes called awakened living or conscious living, where one is awake or conscious of one's Real Self, while dealing with everyday issues of his or her life.

ਮਨ ਚਿੰਦਿਆ ਫਲੁ ਪਾਇਸੀ ਅੰਤਰਿ ਬਿਬੇਕ ਬੀਚਾਰੁ ॥ (Ang 1422)
(*Those persons who are aware and alert, shall have their mind's desires fulfilled.*)

ਜਾਗਤ ਰਹੇ ਤਿਨੀ ਪ੍ਰਭੁ ਪਾਇਆ ਸਬਦੇ ਹਉਮੈ ਮਾਰੀ ॥ (Ang 599)
(*Those who remain wakeful meet God, and they conquer their ego through the word of the Shabad.*)

Maintaining contact with ourselves all the time is a matter of practice that should be done with serious intent. It can be started with simpler chores like walking, running, doing dishes or other stuff that does not engage the mind. Next we can move on to activities that require some mind engagement like watching TV, talking on the phone or any other conversation. These are the activities we spend a ton of time on, especially watching TV. This is particularly true of retired people like myself. However, this activity of watching TV offers a unique opportunity to practice this meditation. I am talking from personal experience, although it is difficult in the beginning but if one works on it diligently it does work out. While watching TV, bring your attention to the heart or the navel and anchor it there. This will establish you as Real Self or Awareness, and then start watching the TV while maintaining the anchoring of the attention at the navel. It will take time but it can be done. But when you are successful in doing it, then even watching TV becomes meditation. Doing dishes, walking etc. all become meditation. Any activity done while the attention is centered in yourself becomes meditation, because it takes us to our Real Self. Gurbani talks about our Real Home in the following shabad. Guru ji admonishes us for not even thinking about our Real Home where we have to live. We came here in the world to deal in gems and jewels but we are dealing with worthless things. We have got this precious life after wandering through 8.4 million incarnations, but like fools we are wasting it away by clinging to trivial pleasures.

ਲਖ ਚਉਰਾਸੀਹ ਭ੍ਰਮਤੇ ਭ੍ਰਮਤੇ ਦੁਲਭ ਜਨਮੁ ਅਬ ਪਾਇਓ ॥
ਰੇ ਮੂੜੇ ਤੂ ਹੋਛੇ ਰਸਿ ਲਪਟਾਇਓ ॥
ਅੰਮ੍ਰਿਤੁ ਸੰਗਿ ਬਸਤੁ ਹੈ ਤੇਰੈ ਬਿਖਿਆ ਸਿਉ ਉਰਝਾਇਓ ॥
ਰਤਨ ਜਵੇਹਰ ਬਨਜਨਿ ਆਇਓ ਕਾਲਰੁ ਲਾਦਿ ਚਲਾਇਓ ॥
ਜਿਹ ਘਰ ਮਹਿ ਤੁਧੁ ਰਹਨਾ ਬਸਨਾ ਸੋ ਘਰੁ ਚੀਤਿ ਨ ਆਇਓ ॥ (Ang 1017)

(*Wandering through 8.4 million incarnations, you have now got this precious life, You fool, you are clinging to such trivial pleasures. There is Ambrosial Nectar in you but you are engrossed in sin and corruption. You came here to trade in gems and jewels, but you have gathered only barren soil.*
**That Home within which you have to live permanently, you don't even think about that Home.**)

◆ ◆ ◆

# SCIENCE OF DOING NITNEM

ਮੇਰੇ ਮਨ ਨਾਮੁ ਨਿਤ ਨਿਤ ਲੇਹ ॥ ਜਲਤ ਨਾਹੀ ਅਗਨਿ ਸਾਗਰ ਸੂਖੁ ਮਨਿ ਤਨਿ ਦੇਹ ॥ *(Ang 1006)*

*(O my mind, continuously remember Naam, You shall not suffer from the insatiable worldly desires, and your mind and body shall be blessed with peace.)*

For those who are not familiar with Nitnem, it implies a daily practice of reciting and listening to a certain group of hymns from Sri Guru Granth Sahib, the Sikh Scripture. What is the purpose of doing Nitnem? Main purpose of doing Nitnem is to achieve union with the Divine or God. Union with God can happen through this process only if done sincerely and steadily. Mind has to be controlled to the point that it stops its wandering nature, and comes to rest in its Divine Nature. Sikh religion followers are asked to do Nitnem everyday. Nitnem, as the name goes, means daily practice of reciting or listening to Gurbani Hymns early in the morning, in the evening and at night before going to bed. There are a total of seven Banis, (a group of hymns), that are included in the Nitnem. There are five Banis, Jap Ji Sahib, Jaap Sāhib, Chaupai, Swayae and Anand Sahib to be recited and listened to, in the morning, Rehras Sahib in

219

the evening and Kirtan Sohilla at bedtime. Reciting and listening to these Banis is a "must" for the baptized sikhs, and should be done everyday without a miss. The practice is, however, recommended for all the followers of sikh religion, no matter whether they are baptized or not. In this article we will discuss the purpose of doing Nitnem in some detail and will explore the various stages of spiritual progress one goes through, as one continues to do the daily practice.

There are three ways to do the daily practice of Nitnem. The Banis can be recited from memory, read from a Gutka (small book) or by listening from an electronic device.

It is recommended to take a shower early in the morning before doing the first five Banis. If taking a shower is not feasible, one should still do the Nitnem. Gurbani does not emphasize taking shower because in the old days taking bath had become a ritual. Gurbani asks us to take a shower to generally keep the body clean, but not as a daily sacred ritual. There are three stages of doing the daily practice of Nitnem:

Stage 1: Mind Level
Stage 2: Heart Level
Stage 3: Beyond Heart Level

We will discuss the three stages in some detail to see what is involved in each stage.

**Stage 1: Mind Level:**

First thing we need to do when we start the practice of Nitnem, is to learn to read and recite the Banis correctly. There are special classes and camps held all over the world to teach young children the correct pronunciation and recital of the Banis. Also the recitation is done on a regular basis in almost all the Sikh Temples or Gurudwaras around the world; and some of the Gurdwaras broadcast it live. One can learn by attending the Gurudwara or listening to these broadcasts. Most of the older folks started reading from Gutka, a small book that was very popular until the new electronic devices came into use. Of course, these days every Bani is recorded in the electronic devices and one can use these devices to read and recite or just listen from there. Once one listens to Banis over and over again one can memorize them too. Then one does not even need the help of an electronic device to recite.

Once the correct pronunciation and recital has been learnt then one can pay attention to the meanings of the Paath. Gurbani is a very deep storehouse of Spiritual Wisdom, and also the wisdom that we can apply in our daily living. One should make an effort to understand the meanings of all the Banis in Sri Guru Granth Sahib, but especially, the Banis one is reciting everyday. Gurbani's meanings are very deep and sometimes mysterious but once understood they can change the lives of those who recite them everyday. Sant Maskeen Ji used to say in his katha that one should do the Nitnem anyway, no matter one knows the meanings of the Banis or not. He uses an analogy to explain his viewpoint. He says Gurbani recital and listening is like preparing and taking in food. He says one does not have to know what nourishments the food is offering to enjoy the benefits of the food. Food will give energy to the body irrespective of one's understanding of the food. So Maskeen Ji says that no matter whether one knows the meanings of Gurbani, it will affect the person's mind all the same. That is why he says one should do the Nitnem without any hesitation and do it regularly. Of course, doing the practice of Nitnem with the underlying message in mind invokes devotion and sincerity in the practitioner's mind. Gurbani says that one should try to understand the underlying meaning and then try to follow them. It says that one who follows and acts on what is being said in Gurbani, will attain salvation.

ਗੁਰੁ ਬਾਣੀ ਕਹੈ ਸੇਵਕੁ ਜਨੁ ਮਾਨੈ ਪਰਤਖਿ ਗੁਰੂ ਨਿਸਤਾਰੇ ॥ (Ang 982)

*(Whatever Gurbani is saying, if the follower believes, he or she will be emancipated.*

Next step is to use the practice of Nitnem to control the wandering of the mind. Gurbani says that wandering mind will stop automatically, if the practice of Nitnem is continued regularly in one's daily life. Wandering mind is one of the most difficult problems to tackle. Gurbani says that the mind can be controlled by the sound of the shabad. When the sound is listened to, the mind gets locked onto the sound, and as a result stops running around. The sound of the shabad acts like a support for the wandering mind. The mind finds something to hang on to, to stabilize itself. Gurbani says that as a pillar supports the building, the same way the sound of the shabad supports the mind.

ਜਿਉ ਮੰਦਰ ਕਉ ਥਾਮੈ ਥੰਮਨੁ ॥
ਤਿਉ ਗੁਰ ਕਾ ਸਬਦੁ ਮਨਹਿ ਅਸਥੰਮਨੁ ॥ (Ang 282)
*(As a building is supported by the pillars,*
*So does the Guru's shabad support the mind.)*

Control of the mind is very important in carrying out the practice of Nitnem. If the mind is not steady how can it understand the message of the Banis. We all know that control is necessary even in everyday affairs. Guru Ji states that one who can control the mind, can control the world.

ਮਨੁ ਜੀਤੇ ਜਗੁ ਜੀਤਿਆ ਜਾਂ ਤੇ ਬਿਖਿਆ ਤੇ ਹੋਇ ਉਦਾਸੁ ॥ (Ang 1103)
*(Those who have conquered their mind, have conquered the world.*
*Conquering the mind is the only way to end evil tendencies.)*

Controlling the mind in the context of doing Nitnem is in the form of keeping the mind engaged in the recitation and listening of the Paath (ਪਾਠ). Paath is a vocal recitation of Banis. I am sure some readers must have experienced that when they are doing Paath or listening to it, that their mind gets disconnected from the recitation or the Listening of Paath and takes off on its own on some tangent. The attention or mind goes away and gets busy solving some other problems, while the Paath is still going on. Once it is realized that a disconnect has happened, one has to trace one's way back to find out where the disconnect happened, so it can be reset to that point. This wandering of mind is exacerbated by the fact that many of the sikhs do the Nitnem while doing other chores. Best way to do the Paath recital is by sitting down at one place, and without doing other chores at that time. Anyway, stopping the wandering of mind is one of the goals of doing Nitnem. Doing the Nitnem regularly will, overtime, calm the mind down and make it more stable. One thing that helps in the process is the feedback system. When we do Paath and then we get lost, a sort of awareness comes into play by which we come to know of the distraction. So this awareness becomes a feedback system to sharpen our alertness, so distraction happens less and less. If we continue doing the practice, the mind will stop wandering over time. This is termed as the awakening of mind. Gurbani says that by remembering or doing recitals over and over again, the sleeping mind is awakened.

ਸਿਮਰਿ ਸਿਮਰਿ ਸਿਮਰਿ ਗੁਰੁ ਅਪੁਨਾ ਸੋਇਆ ਮਨੁ ਜਾਗਾਈ ॥ (Ang 758)
(*Repeatedly remember your Guru, the sleeping mind is awakened this way.*)

## Stage 2: Heart Level:

After the Nitnem becomes regular and the mind becomes steady during the recital or listening of the Paath, we then move down to the heart level. We start doing the Nitnem from our core or the center. As said earlier, the purpose of doing a Nitnem is to unite with the Divine. Gurbani has asserted many times that God lives in our heart and that is where we have to search for him. So moving to the heart and continuing to do the Nitnem regularly is the next step in our journey. Gurbani says that search for God in your own heart where He resides.

ਦਿਲ ਮਹਿ ਖੋਜਿ ਦਿਲੈ ਦਿਲਿ ਖੋਜਹੁ ਏਹੀ ਠਉਰ ਮੁਕਾਮਾ ॥ (Ang 1349)
(*Search in your heart, look deep in it, this is where God lives.*)

So our attention has to move down to our hearts so we can be close to Guru or God. Moreover, the heart is the location where love and emotional feelings are located. Gurbani says that unless we do Paath with feelings and emotion, there cannot be any transformation of the mind. It is like unless a piece of iron is brought in touch with the Philosopher's stone, the iron cannot be converted into gold.

ਪੜੀਐ ਗੁਨੀਐ ਨਾਮੁ ਸਭੁ ਸੁਨੀਐ ਅਨਭਉ ਭਾਉ ਨ ਦਰਸੈ ॥
ਲੋਹਾ ਕੰਚਨੁ ਹਿਰਨ ਹੋਇ ਕੈਸੇ ਜਉ ਪਾਰਸਹਿ ਨ ਪਰਸੈ ॥ (Ang 973)
(*One may read, listen and reflect on the Paath, but does not do it with the feeling of love,*
*How can the iron be transformed into gold, unless iron touches the Philosopher's Stone.*)

Maskeen Ji points out in his katha that if one is eating food; and after putting the food in one's mouth he or she does not take it down or does not swallow it, then it is not going to bring any nutrition to the body. Similarly, Maskeen Ji says that unless the recital of the Nitnem goes down to the heart level, or is done with the loving feelings from one's heart, it is not going to bear fruit. So it is imperative for our attention to move down from head to heart, and practice our daily Nitnem from the heart center.

Gurbani talks about this in another way that our attention needs to come back and sink to the heart level. It is called the merging of our surat (attention) into the Shabad (Real Self). This is a technique for bringing our mind, which is essentially called "attention", back home. Our attention runs around from object to object and does not find rest anywhere. So if we can reign in our attention and make it stay home, we have essentially brought our mind back home. This technique has been discussed in other parts of the book. We will go through it here very briefly in context with this article. The philosophy of "Surat Shabad merger" is based on the fact that whatever is pervading in the universe is Shabad or the Word.

ਏਕੋ ਸਬਦੁ ਏਕੋ ਪ੍ਰਭੁ ਵਰਤੈ ਸਭ ਏਕਸੁ ਤੇ ਉਤਪਤਿ ਚਲੈ ॥ (Ang 1334)
(*The One Shabad, One God, is pervading everywhere, All the Creation came from the One God.*)

Shabad is another Name of God. Shabad or God has two main attributes. Presence and Awareness meaning It is Present and it is Aware. Gurbani says that we are the image of God or Divine Light, so our Real Self also has the same two basic attributes of being Present and Aware.

ਮਨ ਤੂੰ ਜੋਤਿ ਸਰੂਪੁ ਹੈ ਆਪਣਾ ਮੂਲੁ ਪਛਾਣੁ ॥ (Ang 441)
(*O my mind, you are embodiment of the Divine Light,*
*recognize your own origin.*)

So our Real Self which is God or Shabad is Present and Aware. It can be said that our Real Self divides Itself into two, Presence and Awareness. The Presence of the Real Self is felt in our hearts. Even though God or our Real Self is present everywhere, Its Presence is felt only in our hearts. Just as the internet is present everywhere in the internet sphere but its presence is detected by an electronic device only. Awareness, on the other hand, is the same as our everyday attention, with which we know or are aware of the world around us. Make a note that Awareness which is Divine in its nature, willingly forgets its Divinity, and becomes attention (surat). As attention (surat), it has gotten lost in the attractions of the world. This very attention is called the "mind". The goal of the "Surat Shabad merger" is to turn the direction of attention (surat) from the material world and to bring it back to its Source, the Shabad or the Real Self. In other words, it is simply bringing our mind or attention back to its Source and merging into it. When done sincerely, our surat or our mind gets absorbed into the shabad, and our union is achieved. The attention or mind (surat) has now been united with the Divine

Presence. There is no more mind left to wander in the world; and as a result, we as Real Self enjoy our inherent peace. Gurbani says that those who kill their mind, their wandering comes to an end. Without killing the mind, how can one meet the Lord? Killing the mind here implies controlling or subduing the mind.

ਮਨੁ ਮਾਰੇ ਧਾਤੁ ਮਰਿ ਜਾਇ ॥ ਬਿਨੁ ਮੂਏ ਕੈਸੇ ਹਰਿ ਪਾਇ ॥ (Ang 159)
(*When someone kills and subdues his own mind, his wandering nature is subdued too,*
*Without such a death of the mind how can one find the Lord?*)

So "Surat Shabad merger" in context of practice of Nitnem consists of paying attention to the sound that is being listened to. The attention locks on to the sound and then travels inwards to its Source. Gurbani says that paying attention to the sound of the Shabad will reveal the Truth and we will come to know the Unspeakable mystery.

ਧੁਨਿ ਮਹਿ ਧਿਆਨੁ ਧਿਆਨ ਮਹਿ ਜਾਨਿਆ ਗੁਰਮੁਖਿ ਅਕਥ ਕਹਾਨੀ ॥ (Ang 879)
(*By keeping one's attention focused on the sound of the word, One comes to know the Unspeakable mystery.*)

When we lock our attention on the sound and let our attention follow the sound to its Source. The source of the sound of Nitnem is Shabad. In fact, that is the purpose of doing Nitnem anyway. By repetition, we progressively move towards ths Shabad or God, and eventually become one with It. Becoming one with It, our independent entity or our ego dissolves. Happiness wells up and we find ultimate peace.

ਸਬਦ ਸੁਰਤਿ ਸੁਖੁ ਊਪਜੈ ਪ੍ਰਭ ਰਾਤਉ ਸੁਖ ਸਾਰੁ ॥ (Ang 62)
(*Focusing one's attention on the Shabad, happiness springs up, and attuned to God, ultimate peace is found.*)

,

**Stage 3: Beyond Heart Level:**

This stage explains in more detail how we merge with our Real Self when we follow the sound. This is a very subtle stage, so full attention is warranted. To sum up where we are now, two things are going on in the process of doing Nitnem:

**Recital of the Paath**: The recital is going on either from memory or from the electronic device. We can say that the sound of the recital is coming from outside. Even if it is being recited by oneself, the sound created by the body is going out and then coming back through our ears.

**Listening of the Paath**: The process of listening to Paath is going on. This process of listening can be summarized as the sound hitting our ears drums and is then being fed to the brain through our auditory nerves. Then it is recognized by us as the sound.

In this stage we go beyond the mind and the heart. Some of the statements that are going to be made, may not make much sense to the reader in the beginning, but when he or she goes through the complete explanation, the reader will get a better understanding of what is being said here. I am sure this discussion is going to provoke some new thinking in the reader's mind. I would request the reader to read the full explanation before drawing any conclusions. The discussions coming up are subtle in nature so it would need full attention.

When we are listening to Paath there are two beliefs that are in play. Our first belief is that the sound is coming from an electronic device outside of us, and the second belief is that our body minds are listening to the sound of the recital. Next statement that is going to be made will surprise or even shock some reader. If we analyze these two beliefs it will be found that they are not completely true. This statement may throw the reader off, but patience is requested. **The truth of the matter** is that the sound of the recital is not coming from outside of us, even when we are listening to recital from an electronic device, and listening of the sound of Paath, is not being done by our body minds. What is really happening is that the sound of the recital is being generated by our Inner Self, and the listening of the sound is being done by our Inner Self too. Whole process of doing Nitnem is being done by our Inner Self, and not by us as body minds. Our Inner Self is synonymous to our Real Self, Guru, Sat Guru, Source, Atman, God and Awareness etc. We will discuss these assertions in detail and will try to understand these from our personal experience.

**Real Reciter Of Paath:**

If we are listening to Paath being played by an electronic device, we can logically say that the sound is being generated by the device outside of us. When we are reciting the Paath ourselves, we still hear the sound going out from our mouth and then coming back through our ears. In both cases we believe the sound is coming from outside. We will investigate if this statement is really true.

Use of an analogy will help us understand it clearly. We all dream at night where we create a dream world and then get into the dream world as a dream subject. Let us assume that one night you have a dream in which you are listening to Nitnem Paath from an electronic device in the dream. Just to repeat, you are a dream subject in your own dream; and are listening to Paath coming from the electronic device in your dream. This setup is exactly the same as you would normally have in your waking state. Now investigate your dream to find out where the Paath's sound is coming from, in the dream. While you are in the dream, you would say that the sound is coming from the device in the dream. But when you wake up you find that in reality, there was no device in the dream where the sound could come from. In fact, everything in the dream was an imagination of your mind and nothing was real. But you were experiencing the sound of Paath in the dream anyway. There was no device in the dream but still there was the experience of the sound of Paath in the dream. So where was the sound coming from? It had to be coming from you, the dreamer. There is no other source of sound in the dream.

Now carry this observation to your waking state. Gurbani says that the waking state is a dream too. This fact has been stated in Sri Guru Granth Sahib about fifty times. Our waking life is the dream of our own Real Self, Atman or Awareness. We all are the dream subjects in His or Her dream. Imagine a situation in this waking state dream, where you are listening to the Paath coming from the electronic device. Apply the facts we found from the dream analogy to the waking state dream. We found there was no electronic device in the night dream, which could produce sound. Similarly in our current waking state dream, there can be no real electronic device, which can produce sound. The device in our waking state dream is just an imagination of our mind like the device in the night dream. If there is no real device producing the sound in the waking state dream, where is the sound coming from? As in the night dream, the sound was coming from the dreamer which was you, similarly, the sound in the waking state dream is coming from the dreamer too, which is our Real Self. In fact, everything in your night dream was done by you, the dreamer, and everything in our waking state dream is done by our Real Self, the dreamer of the waking state. To summarize, we are finding that in our waking state the sound is coming from our own Real Self and not from the device. The device is our mind's imagination or a make believe device. There is no physical device in the waking state dream either, just like in your night dream. What we are finding is very significant. It is our Real Self or God Himself or Herself that is generating the sound. It is like He is calling us, so to speak, to come back home through the sound of the Paath. Gurbani says that God is speaking through everybody and everything, no matter if it is an animate or inanimate object. There is no one except God who can speak.

ਸਤੈ ਘਟ ਰਾਮੁ ਬੋਲੈ ਰਾਮਾ ਬੋਲੈ ॥ ਰਾਮ ਬਿਨਾ ਕੋ ਬੋਲੈ ਰੇ ॥  (Ang 988)
(*Within all hearts, the Lord speaks, the Lord speaks,*
*Who else can speak other than the Lord.*)

ਕਹਤਾ ਬਕਤਾ ਆਪਿ ਅਗੋਚਰੁ ਆਪੇ ਅਲਖੁ ਲਖਾਇਦਾ ॥ (Ang. 1036)
(*The unfathomable Lord Himself is the speaker and the preacher,*
*He Himself is unseen and then becomes the seen.*)

This is like our dream at night, our mind takes the form of many people. Some of these people may be talking with each other about different things in the dream. In the dream it looks like each person is speaking on his or her own. But when we wake up we find there was no individual person speaking, it was only the dreamer speaking in each one of them. If there was a radio playing in the dream, even its sound would be coming from the dreamer too. Similarly, God, our Real Self that has become all of us in His dream, is speaking through all of us.

One thing very significant comes out of this observation, that the Nitnem recital is coming from our Real Self or a God Himself. This is proof of His grace that is being showered on all of us, without us even being aware of it. The Lord is reciting the Nitnem for us but we don't even take the trouble of listening to it. While the Paath recital is going on, our attention goes wandering out somewhere else. Gurbani says that the Lord comes and pours Nectar in our hands but we do not take hold of it and let the Nectar fall to the ground.

ਕਰ ਮਹਿ ਅੰਮ੍ਰਿਤੁ ਆਣਿ ਨਿਸਾਰਿਓ ॥
ਖਿਸਰਿ ਗਇਓ ਭੂਮ ਪਰਿ ਡਾਰਿਓ ॥ (Ang 389)
(*The Lord came and poured the Nectar in our hands,*
*But it slipped through our hands and fell to the ground.*)

Gurbani further asserts that the sacred Nectar is located inside us, but we do not know it and are searching for it outside of us. Our condition is like that of the deer who detects kasturi fragrance around himself, which is coming from his own navel, but does not know it. So it runs all around the bushes looking for its source.

ਘਰਿ ਹੀ ਮਹਿ ਅੰਮ੍ਰਿਤ ਭਰਪੂਰੁ ਹੈ ਮਨਮੁਖਾ ਸਾਦੁ ਨ ਪਾਇਆ ॥
ਜਿਉ ਕਸਤੂਰੀ ਮਿਰਗੁ ਨ ਜਾਨੈ ਭ੍ਰਮਦਾ ਭਰਮਿ ਭੁਲਾਇਆ ॥
ਅੰਮ੍ਰਿਤੁ ਤਜਿ ਬਿਖੁ ਸੰਗ੍ਰਹੈ ਕਰਤੈ ਆਪਿ ਖੁਆਇਆ ॥
ਗੁਰਮੁਖਿ ਵਿਰਲੇ ਸੋਝੀ ਪਈ ਤਿਨਾ ਅੰਦਰਿ ਬ੍ਰਹਮੁ ਦਿਖਾਇਆ ॥ (Ang 644)
(*The Home within is filled with the Nectar, but the self willed manmukhs do not get to taste it,*
*They are like the deer, who does not recognize its own musk scent, but wanders around looking for it.*
*The manmukhs forsake the Nectar, instead gather poison, the Creator Himself has fooled them,*
*How rare are the Gurmukhs, who understand and behold the Lord within themselves.*)

**So next time you are listening to Paath from a device or from your own recital, take a pause and think where the Paath recital is coming from. Be aware of the fact that it is coming from God residing in your heart and not from outside. We may think that we are doing the Paath but that is not true. It is the Lord reciting it for us to guide us back to Him. He or she is trying to pull us towards Himself or Herself with His or Her Grace.**

ਆਪੇ ਗਾਵੈ ਆਪਿ ਸੁਣਾਵੈ ਇਸੁ ਮਨ ਅੰਧੇ ਕਉ ਮਾਰਗਿ ਪਾਏ ॥ (Ang 506)
(*Lord Himself sings, He Himself recites,*
*He puts this blind mind on the right path.*)

### Real Listener Of Paath:

This topic has been discussed in the book at other places, in reference to the other articles. Here will go through the discussions briefly in context of this article. Imagine yourself listening to Paath in a comfortable position sitting at home or anywhere else. Paath could be either being played from an electronic device or being recited by yourself. Just do some introspection on the process of listening. Try to identify who is really listening to Paath in you. Turn your attention on yourself and see if it is your body or your mind doing the listening. Apply a simple test to identify the listener. For anything to be the listener, it has to be satient, or conscious or has to have a knowing quality. There are three possible listeners, they can be our body, our mind or our Real Self. So we will apply this test to the body, mind and our Real Self to find out which is the listener in us.

Let us investigate if the body is doing the listening. We probably all agree that the body is not the listener. To put it simply the body is just made out of clay. Gurbani has called the body a puppet of clay. How can clay be the listener? The body is not satient so it can't be the listener. So we are going to count the body out right away and say it is not the listener. Let us look at the mind next. The mind is a mixture of thoughts, feelings and perceptions. None of these are satient either. None of these have a Knowing quality. However, they are known by us. We know a thought when it shows up and know it when it is gone. Same way we know our feelings and perceptions when they arise or when they leave. Since they are known they can't be the knowers or listeners. So the mind which comprises all these components, can't be the knower or the listener.

So we are finding that the body and the mind are not the listeners of the Paath. However, we are sure that something in us is listening. So something beyond body and mind is listening to Paath. This something beyond has to be our Real Self, which is an aware and sentient being. We can call it a Knowing Presence since it knows the listening experience. One thing particular about this Knowing Presence is that it has no objective qualities by which it can be visualized. If one tries to look for it, it cannot be grasped. It has no shape or form and hence is limitless. Being limitless it is infinite. Now there is only one Infinite Being, and that is our Real Self or God. **So it is God in us or our Real Self that is listening to Paath.** Gurbani says that in our body resides the Supreme Being which has no shape or form. This is the Listener in us that we are talking about.

ਸਰੀਰ ਸਰੋਵਰ ਭੀਤਰੇ ਆਛੈ ਕਮਲ ਅਨੂਪ ॥
ਪਰਮ ਜੋਤਿ ਪੁਰਖੋਤਮੋ ਜਾ ਕੈ ਰੇਖ ਨ ਰੂਪ ॥ (Ang 857)
(*Within the pool of the body, there is an incomparable beautiful lotus flower,*
*This is the Supreme Light, Supreme Soul, which has no shape or form.*)

Now we find that both the reciter and the listener of the Paath are one entity that is our Real Self or God. There is no person, no you, no me reciting and listening. So it is all the Almighty's own Activity, but we have been thinking it to be our activity. This observation is very significant because this knocks out our ego, the individual independent existence. Essentially, that is the purpose of doing Nitnem. We started doing Paath thinking we as individuals, are doing everything along the way. We thought we were getting up early in the morning and doing what Guru Ji asked us to do. Now we find we were not doing anything. It was our false belief that we were doing the Nitnem etc. We find that God is doing everything through us. Gurbani says that it is God Himself or Herself doing both, the reciting and listening.

ਆਪਿ ਕਥੈ ਆਪੁ ਸੁਨਨੈਹਾਰੁ ॥ (Ang 292)
(*He Himself is the speaker, and He Himself is the listener.*)

ਕਹਤਾ ਬਕਤਾ ਸੁਨਤਾ ਸੋਈ ਆਪੇ ਬਣਤ ਬਣਾਈ ਹੇ ॥ (Ang 1021)
(*He Himself is the speaker, orator and the listener,*
*He Himself has made the creation.*)

Once we realize it experientially, that both the reciter and the listener of the Paath is one entity, God Himself or Herself, we have essentially merged our surat (attention) into the Shabad (sound). Duality of shabad and surat has been eradicated. That is the goal of doing Nitnem and that goal has been achieved. Now for one who has realized this unity, there is only one entity in the universe and that is One God. Everything is happening in Him, everything is being done by Him and everything is known by Him.

ਆਪੇ ਜਾਣੈ ਕਰੇ ਆਪਿ ਆਪੇ ਆਣੈ ਰਾਸਿ ॥
ਤਿਸੈ ਅਗੈ ਨਾਨਕਾ ਖਲਿਹ ਕੀਚੈ ਅਰਦਾਸਿ ॥ (Ang 1093)
(*He Himself knows everything, He Himself does everything, He Himself sets everything right,*
*So stand before Him, O Nanak, offer your prayers.*)

One thing else that becomes clear from this understanding is that everything is happening inside us and not outside. When we say inside us it does mean inside the body and mind but inside our Real Self or Atman or Awareness. Everything is happening inside the One who is reciting the Paath as well as listening to the Paath. This is just like we discovered in our night dream that everything happens inside the one dreamer, there is nothing outside. Gurbani says that everything is happening inside us and one who knows this is happy everywhere.

ਸਭ ਕਿਛੁ ਘਰ ਮਹਿ ਬਾਹਰਿ ਨਾਹੀ ॥ ਬਾਹਰਿ ਟੋਲੈ ਸੋ ਭਰਮਿ ਭੁਲਾਹੀ ॥
ਗੁਰਪਰਸਾਦੀ ਜਿੰਨੀ ਅੰਤਰਿ ਪਾਇਆ ਸੋ ਅੰਤਰਿ ਬਾਹਰਿ ਸੁਹੇਲਾ ਜੀਉ ॥
(Ang 102)
(*Everything is within the home of the Self, there is nothing outside,*
*One who searches outside is deluded by doubt.*
*By Guru Grace, one who has found the Lord within is happy, everywhere.*)

From this point on, we need to listen to Paath with this new understanding in mind. When listening to Paath we should keep in mind that we are not listening to Paath or even Kirtan (singing of Gurbani) as body and mind but as Real Self. Our attention should be focused on our Real Self at the heart location, because everything is happening there. The Paath is being recited at that location and also being heard at that location. Once we focus our attention at that location more and more, we are spending more and more time with our Real Seal or with our Guru, because we are where our attention is. Over time our Guru will shower His Grace and let us in. Those who think that hearing is happening with the ears, Guru Ji has a special message for them in the following shabad. Guru Ji is instructing us in this shabad, not to see with eyes, not to hear with ears and not to talk with the tongue etc. Why Guru Ji is saying this is because that is not the reality of our experience. It is just an imagination of our mind. Things are really happening at the Real Self level. Just like in a night dream everything in the dream is happening in the mind of the dreamer. Gurbani wants us to upgrade our false beliefs.

ਅਖੀ ਬਾਝਹੁ ਵੇਖਣਾ ਵਿਣੁ ਕੰਨਾ ਸੁਨਣਾ ॥
ਪੈਰਾ ਬਾਝਹੁ ਚਲਣਾ ਵਿਣੁ ਹਥਾ ਕਰਣਾ ॥
ਜੀਭੈ ਬਾਝਹੁ ਬੋਲਣਾ ਇਉ ਜੀਵਤ ਮਰਣਾ ॥  (Ang 139)
(*See without the eyes, hear without the ears,*
*Walk without the feet, work without hands,*
*Talk without tongue, die like this while still alive.*)

So we should firm up our new understanding that it is our Real Self and not the body mind that is reciting and listening. This is like the unstuck sound (ਅਨਹਦ ਨਾਦ), which is being generated without any instrument. The sound of the recital is coming from inside us, is not being generated by any instrument. Gurbani says that the unstuck sound when realized, eradicates our ego.

ਅਨਹਦ ਬਾਣੀ ਪਾਈਐ ਤਹ ਹਉਮੈ ਹੋਇ ਬਿਨਾਸੁ ॥  (Ang 21)
(*Once the Unstruck Sound is realized then the egotism is eradicated.*)

When one gets to the level of hearing this Unstruck Sound, one comes to realize that there is no duality in life. It is all One Reality (ੴ) doing everything both reciting and listening. Gurbani talks about this type of listening in Jap Ji Sahib. Gurbani says that if one can listen to the Paath, not as body minds but from the Real Self level, they become Sidhs, Pirs, Naaths. They lose their sufferings and always stay blissful. There are many more benefits mentioned in Jap Ji Sahib than listed here.

ਸੁਣਿਐ ਸਿਧ ਪੀਰ ਸੁਰਿ ਨਾਥ ॥  ਸੁਣਿਐ ਧਰਤਿ ਧਵਲ ਆਕਾਸ ॥
ਸੁਣਿਐ ਦੀਪ ਲੋਅ ਪਾਤਾਲ ॥  ਸੁਣਿਐ ਪੋਹਿ ਨ ਸਕੈ ਕਾਲੁ ॥
ਨਾਨਕ ਭਗਤਾ ਸਦਾ ਵਿਗਾਸੁ ॥  ਸੁਣਿਐ ਦੂਖ ਪਾਪ ਕਾ ਨਾਸੁ ॥ (Ang 2)
(By proper listening, they become Sidhs, Pirs and warriors and masters,
By proper listening, they understand who supports earth and the sky,
By proper listening, they understand the oceans, the lands and the regions of the underworld,
By proper listening, death cannot even touch them.
O Nanak, the devotees are forever in bliss,
By proper listening, suffering and sin are eradicated.)

So when listening to Paath from the device or even reciting it yourself, try to envision that the sound is coming from inside you and is being heard by your Real Self inside you. Do not believe your thinking that listening is being done by the body mind. The sound of the Paath is being generated and heard inside you. That will take your attention where it should be, in one's own heart, Home of the Real Self. Keep your attention there as long as Nitnem is going on. If Nitnem is practiced everyday like suggested, the mind will slowly but surely become calm and more peaceful, and will eventually lead to our merger in the Almighty.

ਕੋਈ ਗਾਵੈ ਕੋ ਸੁਣੈ ਹਰਿ ਨਾਮਾ ਚਿਤੁ ਲਾਇ ॥
ਕਹੁ ਕਬੀਰ ਸੰਸਾ ਨਹੀ ਅੰਤਿ ਪਰਮਗਤਿ ਪਾਇ ॥ (Ang 335)
(Whosoever sings or listens to the Lord's Name with conscious Awareness or from Real Self level,
Says Kabir, without a doubt, will achieve the highest spiritual status.)

❖ ❖ ❖

# FINAL WORD

*I want to take this opportunity to thank everyone who has read this book in full or even portions of it. I just want to make sure that the reader has clearly grasped the main message in the book. Since you have read the book or portions of the book, I want to make sure that you understand who has read the book. Our normal belief would be that me as body mind, has read the book. I hope that after going through the book, your belief has changed and has been upgraded to the true reality of the experience. The true reality of the experience is that it is not the body mind that has read the book but it is your Real Self. Your Real Self is the only One Reality that can know anything or read anything. So please, take this one thing away with you, that you are not the body mind but you are the One Reality. Keep this truth in mind twenty four seven. You are Kings and Queens beyond compare, but have forgotten your real identity. Claim your real identity and be free.*

*The body mind that you believed yourself to be, is just like a vehicle given to you to navigate your way through the world. It is like an SUV, a very sophisticated SUV. This vehicle is by far, the best vehicle you will ever own, but it is still a vehicle. It is not you. You are the driver of this vehicle. You can use it as needed but don't become it. Gurbani calls the body, a horse. In old days a horse was like an SUV. Guru Ji says in the following shabad that we should ride the body horse through the world to reach the Supreme and Blissful Lord.*

ਚੜਿ ਦੇਹੜਿ ਘੋੜੀ ਬਿਖਮੁ ਲਘਾਏ ਮਿਲੁ ਗੁਰਮੁਖਿ ਪਰਮਾਨੰਦਾ ॥ *(Ang 575)*
(Riding the body horse, Gurmukh crosses the terrifying world ocean: and meets the Lord, Embodiment of Supreme Bliss.)

**Request to the reader:** If you enjoyed reading the book, please leave a review on Amazon.com, so other readers may be inspired to learn about their True Identity, and thereby claim their inherent peace and happiness.. Thanks.

◆ ◆ ◆

Made in the USA
Las Vegas, NV
29 June 2023